MEISTER ECKHART

Maurice O'Connell Walshe was born in London in 1911 and studied at University College, London, and the Universities of Berlin, Gottingen, Vienna and Freiburg. He taught medieval German language and literature at the Universities of Leeds, Nottingham and London and is the author of *Medieval German Literature: a Survey* and *A Middle High German Reader*. He retired in 1979 as Reader in German and Deputy Director of the Institute of Germanic Studies, University of London. He has had a keen interest in Buddhism for many years and has made translations from the Buddhist Scriptures.

IN MEMORIAM
JOSEF QUINT
1898–1976

MEISTER ECKHART

Sermons & Treatises

VOLUME I

Translated and Edited by
M.O'C. WALSHE

ELEMENT BOOKS

First published in Great Britain in 1979
by Watkins Publishing
This edition first published 1987 by
Element Books Limited
Longmead, Shaftesbury, Dorset
Second Impression 1989

Printed and bound in Great Britain by
Billings, Hylton Road, Worcester

Cover design by Humphrey Stone

British Library Cataloguing in Publication Data
Eckhart, *Meister*
[Meister Eckhart, die deutschen Werke.
English] Meister Eckhart.
Vol. 1: Sermons & treatises
I. [Meister Eckhart, die deutschen Werke.
English]   II. Title   III. Walshe, M. O'C.
193   B765.E32E5
ISBN 1-85230-005-1

CONTENTS

SERMONS

PREFACE

The figure of the greatest of German mystics, the Dominican Meister Eckhart, has been the object of so much speculation and controversy, often on the basis of unreliable translations or wrong attributions, that the publication of a new extended selection of his works in English translation calls for no excuse. What the translator has to do, however, in presenting such a selection, is to justify his choice and the textual basis from which he works. This is especially true in Eckhart's case, since the question of the very authenticity of many works ascribed to him has formed no small part of the general debate.

The present translation replaces that by the late Miss C. de B. Evans which appeared in two volumes in 1924 and 1931. Her work was conscientious and — though sometimes a little free — generally accurate. But its style, whimsically adorned with archaisms, is not always to the modern taste, and the translation was based (though far from uncritically) on the pioneer but now entirely outdated edition of Franz Pfeiffer (1857). At the time she wrote, this was inevitable. However, Eckhart scholarship has made immense progress since then, and my aim has been to incorporate the main results of the vast labours of German and other scholars in this new version. I have, however, not hesitated to retain Miss Evans renderings whenever, as often, I felt I could not better them. The basis of this translation has been what is now the only possible one, namely the monumental Kohlhammer edition, *Meister Eckhart, die deutschen Werke*, edited by

Josef Quint, of which the four principal volumes, namely those containing all the sermons and treatises considered by Professor Quint to be certainly authentic, have now appeared. These volumes represent an achievement — carried out virtually single-handed — which has few equals even in the illustrious annals of German scholarship. The parallel series of Latin works, also incomplete and no less impressive, is the production not of one man but of a team. The debt of all who are in any way seriously interested in Eckhart to all of these scholars is quite incalculable. I am grateful to the Kohlhammer Verlag, Stuttgart, for permission to use these editions.

Eckhart's vernacular language is the Middle High German of the early 14th century, which is perhaps slightly further removed from present-day German than is Chaucer's English from our own. His native dialect was that of Thuringia, but he must have considerably modified his linguistic forms during his extensive travels. In the 200-odd manuscripts painstakingly compared by Quint (Pfeiffer, a century previously, knew only 45), a wide variety of dialectal forms appear. These have been standardised by Quint except in a few cases where he is following a unique manuscript. The result, though artificial, is convenient, and eases the translator's task at times. As stated, the textual basis of this translation is, wherever possible, that of Quint in the Kohlhammer edition. In the case of a few German sermons not included in that edition, I have followed Pfeiffer's text as emended by Quint in his book *Die Uberlieferung der deutschen Predigten Meister Eckharts* (1932), or his modern German translation, *Meister Eckehart, Deutsche Predigten und Traktate* (1955), for kind permission to use which I am grateful to the Carl Hanser Verlag, Munich. In a few cases (indicated in the notes) I have ventured to differ from Quint's readings or interpretations.

Editions apart, there is a vast secondary literature on Eckhart, of very varying value, and — naturally — most of it in German. I have not thought it worth while to take up space by listing all these works, as probably the vast majority of readers of this translation will not know enough German to read them, and anyway would not have access to most of them. Some, indeed, have eluded me. However, in the bibliographical note I have mentioned the most important German works as well as those in English which seemed to me to be of value. With the aid of these, and in particular of Ernst Soudek's convenient little Metzler volume, further references can be looked up by those wishing to do so. Several other partial English translations exist, by far the best being that by the late Professor James Clark, whose work is extremely accurate. His introductions to the subject are most useful and informative, even if at times perhaps a shade pedestrian. The selection translated by Raymond Blakney is rather less reliable, but has some useful notes, and it also includes a nearly complete, though not entirely accurate, version of Eckhart's detailed reply to charges of unorthodoxy.

As regards the name of our author, I have followed established English practice in referring to him by the German designation Meister Eckhart, although there is perhaps no very good reason which we should not call him Master Eckhart in English. The name is also spelt Eckehart, and even Quint shows some hesitation (for reasons obscure to me) between these two forms. Occasionally, for some reason, one finds him referred to as Johannes Eckhart, but there is absolutely no warrant for this: his full name was in fact Eckhart von Hochheim.

Eckhart's works are in German and Latin. The German works now considered authentic consist of nearly a hundred sermons (with perhaps another fifty probably authentic), and three so-called treatises. Reference will be made in a special note to the question of the spurious and doubtful works. This volume contains the first part of the sermons. So as to maintain some continuity with Miss Evans translation, they follow as far as possible the same order, which is virtually that of the Pfeiffer edition. As regards their selection, I have included all those which seemed to me to be certainly or probably authentic, i.e., all those verified by Quint, together with a few others, some or all of which may yet appear in the Kohlhammer edition. Quint's principle of verification is based on the quotations in the trial documents (for which see Blakney); where these are lacking, he is guided by other criteria such as references back or parallels in the Latin works. In this way he has established an objective scale of decreasing certainty: thus Quint's Sermon No 1 (our No 6, as in Pfeiffer and Evans) occupies pride of place simply because on all such grounds it is the best attested, and so on. While this procedure was methodologically unimpeachable for the purpose of establishing a valid Eckhart 'canon', so far as that can be done, the order so arrived at has perhaps no particular merit for other purposes. In the almost total absence of reliable chronological indications,[1] then, it seemed justified to retain as far as possible Pfeiffer's order, which has a certain amount of manuscript support. In particular, it has seemed to me that the first few sermons in the order of Pfeiffer's edition provide an excellent general introduction to Eckhartian thought. And all but a handful of definitely authentic Eckhart sermons are included in Pfeiffer, even though sometimes in garbled form.

The sermons may be followed by the *Collations*, or *Talks of Instruction*, which can be dated before 1298, and then by the two treatises properly speaking, which are now recognised as genuine, namely the *Book of Divine Comfort* (1308?) with its appendix *The Nobleman*, and *On Detachment*. The remaining treatises ascribed by Pfeiffer to Eckhart have been convincingly shown by Adolf Spamer to be of other authorship. This is of some importance since, as Clark rather acidly remarks, 'British and American writers have an unfortunate predilection for the spurious works'.

With the translation I have supplied a basic minimum of notes to help the reader with technicalities, Biblical and patristic references, and so on. For these notes I have, naturally and gratefully, drawn heavily on Quint and the editors of the Latin works. As regards the style of this translation, I have made accuracy the first consideration without, I hope, sacrificing elegance. I have tried to avoid quaintness or unnecessary archaisms. I would draw attention to three particular points: The pronouns 'He' etc. when referring to God the Father (only), are capitalised for clarity, and this has on occasion proved a neat way of indicating my interpretation of a particular passage. Secondly, at the risk of preciosity, the feminine pronoun 'she' is also retained, for clarity's sake, when referring to the soul. Finally, Biblical references are translated direct from Eckhart's German and marked by *double* quotation marks, all other passages cited being in single quotes.

Institute of Germanic Studies, University of London. April 1978.

---

1. In many cases the day in the Church calendar, on which a particular sermon was preached, can be established, but not the year.

INTRODUCTION

There are many definitions of 'mysticism', some of which may seem more helpful than others. It is not my purpose here to propound views, whether my own or those of others, on the subject of mysticism in general or Eckhart's mysticism in particular. I seek only to allow him to speak for himself in an authentic translation, as far as this is possible, while providing such guidance by way of introductory matter and commentary as seems necessary and possible. Ideally this would, no doubt, involve an elaborate discussion of both mysticism and scholastic thought, together with a broad survey of the historical background. But for any full treatment of these matters the reader will have to turn elsewhere. Here, the barest minimum must suffice.

Mysticism, or something akin to it, is very ancient and is found in the religious traditions of the whole world. The specifically Christian mystical tradition can be traced back with some certainty to Alexandria. Its direct source was the Neoplatonism of Plotinus (ca. 204-270), who in his *Enneads* taught that all things emanate from the One, the return to which can be achieved by the contemplative path of detachment from all compounded things and a turning to 'pure simplicity'. Neoplatonism was incorporated into Christian thought by the anonymous writer who called himself Dionysius the Areopagite (ca. 500), who pretended to be St Paul's Athenian disciple (Acts 17:34), and by his Latin translator John Scotus Eriugena (ca. 810-880). It was brought into prominence by the German Hugo of St

Victor in Paris (d. 1142), who in turn influenced the famous St Bernard of Clairvaux (1090-1153), counsellor of kings and instigator of the Second Crusade.

In Germany, the so-called *St Trudperter Hohelied* (ca. 1140) is the first work to show true mystical tendencies. The influence of St Bernard is clearly visible in this prose paraphrase of the *Song of Solomon* which, written probably by a nun and certainly for nuns, combines theological learning with lyrical warmth. Whereas in earlier interpretations of the *Song* the bride is understood as being the Church, here the bride is interpreted as the Virgin Mary and, through her mediation, every individual soul. God can be found by turning away from the world, whereby the soul is purified and made ready for the divine embrace, the *unio mystica*, which may be glimpsed 'as in a dream'. Other mystical writings by nuns followed, of which we need only mention here the Latin *Scivias* ('Know the Ways') of the rather formidable abbess Hildegard of Bingen (1090-1179), which is adorned with gravely hieratic illustrations of her own visions, and above all the highly poetic *Flowing Light of the Godhead* of the Béguine Mechthild von Magdeburg (ca. 1250-65).

The other religious trend of the age, scholasticism, is often contrasted with mysticism, but the two are in fact, in medieval Christianity, complementary and indeed combined almost inextricably in the thought of Eckhart and others — who, by the way, never actually used the word 'mysticism'. The aim of scholasticism is, in brief, the philosophical clarification and justification of the Christian faith. Highly formalised, it developed a peculiar Latin style of its own. Its categories were originally those of Aristotle, but it was also enriched from Jewish and Arab sources. Of the two mendicant orders founded in the early 13th century, the Dominicans, to whom Eckhart belonged, were the more specifically 'learned' order, though the Franciscans also made a considerable contribution to scholastic thought. In 1300 these two orders were in a state of intense rivalry. One major point at issue between them was that the Franciscans regarded the will (and hence love) as the highest 'power' of the soul, while the Dominicans assigned priority to the intellect. In the great debate on the so-called 'universals' (i.e. the Platonic ideas as they came to be understood) they likewise took opposite sides. Is a general concept such as 'whiteness' something real, or merely a name? The Realists asserted the reality of such concepts, whereas their opponents, the Nominalists, declared 'whiteness', for example, to be a mere name or label. The Dominicans such as St Thomas Aquinas were moderate Realists, while an extreme form of Nominalism arose in Franciscan circles, being urged most strongly by Eckhart's brilliant English contemporary, William of Ockham (d. 1349), who comes briefly into the story of Eckhart's life. It has been said that the rise of Nominalism was a necessary precondition for the development of the modern scientific outlook. It is, in any case, a comment on changing views of 'reality' that the word Realism today suggests a viewpoint almost diametrically opposed to what was meant by the term in the Middle Ages.

Scholastic systematising reached its peak in the 13th century with the Dominicans Albert the Great (Albertus Magnus), Bishop of Regensburg (d. 1280), and his greater pupil St Thomas Aquinas (d. 1274), whose *Summa Theo-*

logica is its most impressive monument. One particular outcome of the scholastic method should be mentioned here: the *ars praedicandi* or 'how to construct a sermon'. Medieval sermons, including those of Eckhart, are usually built up according to a definite plan. They begin, as is still usual, with a scriptural text, and this is analysed and explained in a particular way. The most essential feature is the fourfold interpretation of Scripture. The first sense is the *literal* or historical. This is usually heavily subordinated to one or more of the other three, spiritual, senses: the *allegorical*, the *tropological* or moral, and the *anagogical*, which deals with eternal life. This scheme enabled a preacher to depart very far, sometimes, from what might seem the literal and obvious meaning of a text — a privilege of which Eckhart made the fullest use, sometimes even to the extent of reading into the text words which were not there at all!

While it would be altogether wrong — though it has been done — to attempt to explain the growth of mystical thought at this period entirely by reference to social conditions, there is little doubt that such conditions did to a certain extent provide a soil favourable to its development. The period round about 1300 was felt by many to be a terrible time. In fact, the 'Middle Ages' were passing away. The growth of big cities was creating entirely new socio-economic problems and conflicts. Old-established values were being called into question, and established institutions too — the Empire and the Papacy alike — were imperilled. The long Interregnum (1254-1273) in the Holy Roman Empire had brought with it times of anarchy and baronial rapacity which the strong rule of Rudolf von Habsburg (1273-1291) did much to mitigate but could not entirely overcome. At the same time the Papacy, owing to its conflict with the French crown which culminated in 1303 with the humiliating death of Boniface VIII at the hands of agents of the King of France, was at a low ebb; and during the greater part of the 14th century the Popes resided at Avignon as virtual pawns of the French king (the so-called Babylonian Captivity, 1309-77). In such times of weakened authority the search for spiritual consolation and security took on new and sometimes unorthodox forms. Despite brutal suppression, heresies of various kinds abounded. This was also partly due to the fact that, in the course of the struggles of the day, the normal sacraments and consolations of the church were often not available. Popes and bishops would place cities and regions under an interdict, sometimes for years. During this time the sacraments were not allowed to be dispensed. It was no wonder then that people turned in despair to such unofficial groups as the Beghards and the Brethren of the Free Spirit. 'Heresy' was often nothing more than a desperate form of self-help.

A particular feature of the times was, further, the growth of large numbers of nunneries, a fact which has been associated with the great loss of life among the knights in this troubled period. Many of the new nuns were certainly the widows and daughters of such knights, and often of aristocratic birth. As such they were frequently educated women whose spiritual needs rose above elementary levels. As we have seen, too, these had their predecessors, in Germany, from at least the 12th century. In the new sit-

uation it was of great significance that the instruction of
nuns was entrusted to the Dominicans — a task which the
latter did not always welcome. And one of those on whom
this particular burden fell was Meister Eckhart.

Concerning the details of Eckhart's life a considerable
amount of information has been gradually accumulated by
scholars. He was born, possibly of knightly stock, at
Hochheim near Gotha (or perhaps at another Hochheim
near Erfurt — at any rate in Thuringia), about the year
1260, and the date of his death can be fixed between
February 1327 and April 1328. The most important of the
established facts of his life (if we do not go into the details
of his journeyings) are soon told, and they can be enriched
with a few probabilities. He must have joined the
Dominican priory at Erfurt, which was near his home,
about 1275, and quite obviously he soon gained the recognition of his superiors for his outstanding gifts. He was
most probably sent to the famous Dominican *Studium
Generale* at Cologne, possibly just in time to hear the aged
Albert the Great, who had taught Aquinas. If so, this must
have been before 1280, when Albert died. In 1293 he was
taking part in disputations in Paris. Eckhart's earliest
datable German work is the *Collations*, or *Talks of Instruction*, which must have been delivered by him to the
novices in his charge not later than 1298, for the heading
given to these talks in the manuscripts describes him as being Prior of Erfurt and Vicar of Thuringia — two posts
which by a decision of that year were not allowed to be
combined in one hand. About 1300 he was again in Paris,
having been selected to study at the *Studium Generale* of

St Jacques — a great honour which clearly attests to the esteem in which he was held. During his stay in Paris he debated with the Spaniard Gonsalvus, a formidable opponent who later became General of the Franciscans. In Paris Eckhart gained the degree of Master of Theology after going through the prescribed course, which included lecturing on the 12th century *Sentences* of Peter Lombard, still regarded as the standard theological textbook at this time. This was in 1302, and he was henceforth always known as Meister Eckhart, an honourable designation which served effectually to distinguish him from the various other Eckharts (including members of his order) whom we hear of at this time.

When Germany was divided into the two Dominican Provinces of Saxony and Alemannia, Meister Eckhart was elected by the Erfurt Chapter in 1303 to be the first Provincial of Saxony (which covered most of North Germany and Holland), and in 1307 there was added to this a second, and certainly burdensome office, that of Vicar-General of Bohemia, with the special task of restoring order in the convents of that Province, where discipline was notoriously lax and 'heresy' rife. It is at least clear that at this time nobody can have thought Eckhart's views unorthodox, although, ironically, it was in all probability at this period, about 1308, that he composed the *Book of Divine Comfort* for the widowed Queen Agnes of Hungary — a work which his accusers were later to draw upon heavily. But even this appointment was not all, for in 1310 yet another onerous post was very nearly thrust on him, when he was chosen to be Provincial of the southern German Province of Alemannia. However, this election was not confirmed by the General Chapter of the Order, meeting at Naples, and instead, Eckhart was sent to Paris yet again, in order, it seems, to defend the interests of his order in the ever-sharpening conflict with the Franciscans. Precisely how long he stayed in Paris this time we do not know, but in 1314 we find him in Strassburg[1] in charge of the convent there. Strassburg was at this time a great centre of religious activity, and open to mystical ideas, and it is clear that Eckhart was extremely active here as a preacher and teacher. In fact his association with Strassburg was so close that at one time it was even thought to have been his birthplace. It seems probable, certainly, that many of his preserved German sermons were written down in Strassburg by nuns. But he also travelled widely in the course of his official duties, and we hear of his presence at various places in Alsace, in Switzerland, and elsewhere. It is however not true that he was at one time, as sometimes stated, Prior of Frankfurt, for the Eckhart who is recorded as holding that office was a somewhat disreputable character, whereas the records confirm that Meister Eckhart's personal life was, as we should expect, entirely above suspicion. Then, at some date unknown, but probably not earlier than 1322, Eckhart, who was by now a famous man, was called to the *Studium Generale* at Cologne to hold the chair once adorned by Albert the Great.

But this great honour proved Eckhart's undoing. The Archbishop of Cologne, the grim and aged Franciscan Heinrich von Virneburg, was bitterly hostile to anything smacking of 'mysticism', which he associated with the various semi-heretical sects then flourishing, and which he had long been attempting to put down by burnings and drownings. In 1326, the archbishop instituted proceedings against Eckhart before the Inquisition for spreading dangerous doctrines among the common people. Such a step, taken against so distinguished a teacher, was quite unprecedented. Eckhart declared that in accordance with the privileges of his order he was answerable only to the University of Paris or the Pope. Nevertheless, for the sake of his order's good name he was prepared to appear before the appointed inquisitors and defend himself. A manuscript in the municipal library at Soest (Westphalia) preserves a record of a large part of the proceedings. The story is rather complicated, and its presentation in some of the published literature does not necessarily help in clarifying it. One document (A)[2] contains 49 allegedly incriminatory articles: fifteen are from the *Book of Divine Comfort* along with six points from an otherwise unknown reply of Eckhart's concerning these; there are twelve articles from the Latin commentary on *Genesis* and other Latin sources, and, finally, sixteen passages taken from the German sermons. Another document (B) contains Eckhart's defence on all these points, and a further document (C) gives Eckhart's replies to a further list of 59 articles taken this time entirely from his German sermons. Thus 108 statements by Eckhart, or ascribed to him, are impugned, though this number must be somewhat reduced as there is some overlap between lists A and C. There is however evidence that at least one further list existed which has now been lost. Blakney's paperback volume contains a translation of these documents, not entirely accurate and made in ignorance of the modern German translation and commentary by Karrer and Piesch (1927). More recently, the subject has been investigated by Josef Koch (1960). The value to us of these documents is two-fold: they show Eckhart's replies to certain objections, and in addition they contain a series of actual extracts, in Latin translation or, in some cases, in Eckhart's own Latin, which confirm the genuineness of sermons and treatises attributed to him.

The names of three inquisitors appointed to deal with Eckhart's case are known. Two were Franciscans. One, Albert of Milan, was clearly an Italian and one, Dr Rainer, was a Frisian or a Dutchman, while the third, Petrus de Estate (Sommer), who was either the predecessor or the successor of Albert, was apparently a native of Cologne. Karrer identified the author of document A with Albert of Milan, drawing attention to his seemingly imperfect understanding of German. However this may be, it is clear that neither he nor the other censors had the necessary scholarly equipment for the task, as Eckhart, who had little difficulty in showing up their ignorance, gleefully noted. Many of the statements they objected to were certainly entirely orthodox.

At this point there is a gap in our documentation. It seems that heavier guns were now brought to bear on Eckhart. Cardinal Nicholas Cusanus (1401-64) knew of another list of incriminating passages, together with Eckhart's replies, taken this time from his commentary on St John's Gospel, and in fact several of the articles which were finally condemned by the Pope are taken from this commentary, and therefore probably figured in the third list.

At all events, the case soon took a complicated turn. Nicholas of Strassburg, who was Vicar-General of the Order and Visitor of the German Province, intervened in Eckhart's defence, but was overruled by the archbishop, who even took proceedings against him. As Koch points out, Nicholas's own position in the matter was a delicate one: as Lector in Cologne he was a subordinate of Eckhart's, but as Vicar and Visitor he was his superior. In any case he was, of course, an eminent man, and it is recorded that Albert of Milan behaved offensively towards him. We also know that many prominent members of Eckhart's order ostentatiously supported their beloved teacher, but eventually two Dominicans of notoriously bad repute, one of whom had actually been excommunicated, were found to testify against him. Finally Eckhart himself protested at the dilatory nature of the enquiry and appealed to the Pope, and on 13 February 1327 he made a solemn declaration in the Dominican church that he was not a heretic, though much that he had said had been (as he had also declared in replying to his accusers) distorted or misunderstood. If any error in faith or morals should be discovered in anything he had said or written, publicly or privately, this should be considered retracted and not said or written. The declaration was read out in Latin by Konrad of Halberstadt, who was probably Eckhart's *amanuensis*, and translated sentence by sentence by Eckhart himself, and the declaration itself then attested by a notary.

Eckhart's appeal to the Pope was disallowed by the archbishop. It seems, however, that the papal authorities had already begun to intervene. At any rate Eckhart made his way to Avignon, where a fresh hearing took place. Here the situation was very different. Pope John XXII appointed a commission of theologians to review the case, and they produced a new short-list of articles. Eckhart's principal judge here was the learned theologian Cardinal Jacques Fournier, who later became Pope Benedict XII. The Cardinal was also investigating the rather different case of the famous English Franciscan William of Ockham. Ockham, who shortly afterwards succeeded in making his escape from Avignon, shows exact knowledge of some of the charges against Eckhart, with whom, however, he had no sympathy — indeed he declared Eckhart's ideas to be mad! He was, however, at the time labouring under a sense of violent grievance at the real or alleged favoured treatment accorded by the Papacy to the Dominicans, and this may have coloured his judgement. Early in 1328 the Archbishop of Cologne wrote to the Pope urging a decision in Eckhart's case, and from the Pope's reply we learn that by 30 April of that year, Eckhart was dead.[3] Almost a year later, on 27 March 1329, the Pope issued a bull *In agro dominico* (the title is probably a play on the name of the Dominican order), in which 26 articles from Eckhart's Latin works were listed, of which the first fifteen were declared heretical and the remaining eleven termed 'dangerous and suspect of heresy', though just capable of an orthodox interpretation. A further two articles which Eckhart was said to have preached (in German) were also condemned. The bull ended with the statement that Eckhart had before his death revoked and denounced all statements of his which were heretical or might convey such an impression. This in fact he had already done in Cologne in 1327, and his Avignon statement was probably made in similar terms.

Incidentally, it is ironical that Eckhart should have been condemned, even posthumously, for heresy by John XXII, for that Pope was accused himself, and not only by Ockham and his supporters, of holding heretical views. As one of the chief architects of the Church's wealth, who left an enormous fortune behind him, he was understandably opposed to the belief of the 'spiritual Franciscans' that the Church should emulate the poverty of Christ. In this point he prevailed, and some unfortunate Franciscans suffered at the stake for their views. But when he put forward the doctrine that the Beatific Vision would not be vouchsafed to the souls of the just until the Day of Judgement he aroused so much opposition that he had to withdraw it, and this view was expressly condemned as heretical in 1336 by his successor.

The whole case has been the subject of much controversy among modern scholars. The 19th century Protestant scholar Wilhelm Preger and the Catholic scholar already mentioned, Otto Karrer, were both convinced that the entire proceedings had their roots in the rivalry between Franciscans and Dominicans. The Franciscans were certainly at loggerheads with the Pope at the time, and were bitterly aggrieved at the canonisation of Thomas Aquinas in 1323 — very shortly before the date of Eckhart's trial. Josef Koch on the other hand considered that the root of the matter did in actual fact lie in Eckhart's teachings, as was claimed. This is almost certainly true in one sense, but the whole matter was unquestionably inflamed and aggravated by the passions of inter-order rivalry, but for which proceedings might well never have been instituted in the first place. At best we can say that the case against the Franciscans for virtually 'framing' Eckhart is, as the wonderfully cautious Scottish verdict has it, not proven. We can also assume it as highly probable that no action would have been taken against Eckhart had he stayed in Strassburg instead of going to Cologne.

Archbishop Heinrich von Virneburg has sometimes been represented as a monster of iniquity. This is an exaggeration, though it is difficult for us to warm to him. He was a hard man who made full use of the harsh treatment then customary in dealing with heretics. He was also at this time an old man, set in his ways, and was genuinely worried at the spread of heretical ideas — and, it must be admitted, from his point of view, not without reason. He was also, incidentally, a Franciscan. Eckhart, as a distinguished preacher and scholar and a leading light of his order, was probably in little danger of the stake — which was generally reserved for humbler folk — but at least his accusers hoped to silence him and destroy his reputation. And in this they were, after all, not entirely unsuccessful. It is true his treatment at Avignon was different from that at Cologne. The two renegade Dominican witnesses against him were not even given a hearing, and all the impugned clauses were carefully reconsidered, most of them being rejected. Nevertheless, the verdict went against him. The final condemnation, about a year after Eckhart's death, was possibly deliberately delayed — doubtless to the archbishop's annoyance — until the heat had died down somewhat, and may have been meant by the Pope as a sop to the Franciscans. Eckhart himself, it has been suggested, may never even have known that his case had failed. In any case it is certainly not true as is sometimes stated, that Eckhart was formally excommunicated.

All the same, the condemnation of Eckhart's views as heretical had a fatal effect on his posthumous reputation. His two chief disciples, Suso and Tauler, kept his memory alive for a time, and the vast number of manuscripts (over 200) containing sermons and treatises attributed to him still attests his fame; but the dead hand of the Church was nevertheless able to prevent his influence from spreading as much as it might otherwise have done. In the 15th century the great Cardinal Nicholas Cusanus studied his writings with care and interest, though not endorsing them uncritically; and the 17th century mystic Johann Scheffler (Angelus Silesius) drew inspiration from him. Otherwise, he remained half-forgotten till the 19th century.

To what we know of Eckhart's life from the records we may add a comment and three more speculative items. The comment is this: one may be inclined to think of Eckhart as a gentle cloistered sage, devoting his life quietly to contemplation and instruction. But in fact he must have been intensely active and energetic, not only a great preacher but also a busy administrator, up to his neck in practical affairs whether he wished it or not. He must also have spent an enormous amount of his time on the roads, travelling on foot as was the custom of his order, from one place to another — to Cologne, Paris, Strassburg, Switzerland, throughout North Germany, Holland and Bohemia and, finally, when approaching seventy, to Avignon, facing all the dangers and discomforts of such travel on bad roads and through mountains and robber-infested forests. Life was not easy, comfortable or safe on such journeys which he undertook at frequent intervals, as a matter of course. His periods of solitary contemplation in a quiet cell must often have been severely rationed, and indeed he must have been a man of considerable stamina and physical endurance.

The three more speculative items which may perhaps be added to his biography are a poem, a possible vision of Eckhart's own, and a vision of his pupil Suso. A mystical poem of some merit has been preserved in several manuscripts to which the Latin title *Granum sinapis* ('The Grain of Mustard-Seed') was given, though the relevance of this title is not immediately obvious. A Latin commentary has also been found which shows that the poem was taken very seriously by somebody, and indeed it has great mystical depth. While there is absolutely no proof, some scholars have considered that this poem might possibly be by Eckhart himself. It certainly seems to be entirely in keeping with his thought. Though it would be rash to assume his authorship, it was in all probability at least composed under his influence, direct or indirect. Moreover, the dialect is his native Thuringian.[4] The following attempt at a metrical rendering therefore deserves a place at least in this introduction:

The Grain of Mustard-Seed

When all began
(beyond mind's span)

the Word aye *is*
Oh what bliss
When source at first gave birth to source!
Oh Father's heart
from which did start
that same Word:
yet 'tis averred,
the Word's still kept in womb perforce.

From both doth flow
a loving glow:
in double troth
known to both
comes forth from them the Holy Ghost,
of equal state
inseparate
The three are one:
who grasps it? None!
Itself it knows itself the most.

The threefold clasp
we cannot grasp,
the circle's span
no mind can scan:
for here's a mystery fathomless.
Check and mate,
time, form, estate!
The wondrous ring
holds everything,
its central point stands motionless.

The peak sublime
deedless climb
if thou art wise!
Thy way then lies
through desert very strange to see,
so deep, so wide,
no bound's descried.
This desert's bare
of *Then* or *There*
in modeless singularity.

This desert place
no foot did pace,
no creature mind
ingress can find.
It *is*, yet truly none knows what.
'Tis there, 'tis here,
'tis far, 'tis near,
'tis high, 'tis low,
yet all we know
is: *This* it's not and *That* it's not.

It's clear, it's bright,
it's dark as night;
no name or sign
can it define,
beginningless, of ceasing free.
Immobile, bare,
'tis flowing there.
Where it may dwell,

whoso can tell,
should teach us what its form may be.

As a child become,
both blind and dumb.
Thy own self's aught
must turn to naught.
Both aught and naught thou must reject,
without a trace
of image, time or space.
Go quite astray
the pathless way,
the desert thou mayst then detect.

My soul within,
come out, God in!
Sink all my aught
in God's own naught,
sink down in bottomless abyss.
Should I flee thee,
thou wilt come to me;
when self is done,
then Thou art won,
thou transcendental highest bliss!

The second item is this: Eckhart was emphatically not the type of mystic who was given to visions: he certainly never speaks of any. But in one sermon (No.19) he does tell us of an experience which seems to be autobiographical. He says: 'It seemed to a man as in a dream — it was a waking dream — that he became pregnant with Nothing, like a woman with child. And in the Nothing God was born: He was the fruit of Nothing.' This little story seems to have a peculiar significance. The impersonal mode of narration is probably due to modesty and also perhaps to the influence of St Paul, but in view of Eckhart's frequent references to the birth of the Son in the soul, we may well assume that he is here telling us of a personal experience. If this is so, it is especially precious to us precisely because of his general reticence about *how* he came to experience his mystical insights.

The third item is taken from the autobiography of his disciple Heinrich Suso, who *was* given to visions. Sometimes those who were passing away appeared to Suso at the time of their death, and he tells us that Eckhart so appeared to him. This is of course a well attested phenomenon, and we need not doubt its authenticity. Suso's very brief account of the incident is as follows:

'Among others there appeared to him the blessed master Eckhart and the saintly friar Johannes der Fuotrer of Strassburg. He was told by the master that he lived in transcendent glory in which his purified soul was deified in God. Then the servant (Suso) wanted to know two things of him; the first was, how those persons stand in God who strove to attain the highest truth by self-abandonment without any falsehood. Then it was shown to him that the absorption of these men into the formless abyss cannot be expressed in words by anyone. Then he asked further, what was the most profitable exercise for a man who would fain achieve this. The master replied: "He should sink away from himself, according to his selfhood, in profound abandonment (*gelassenheit*), and accept all things from God and not from creatures, and establish himself in quiet endurance in the face of all wolfish men'".[5] The last remark would seem to be an obvious reference to Eckhart's persecutors.

Only the briefest sketch of Eckhart's thought will be attempted here. In the first place, we should not be misled by references to Eckhart as a 'speculative mystic'. This does not mean, in its context, that his thought is the result of purely intellectual speculation, like that of most philosophers today, or even of his own time.[6] It is based on mystical *experience* whereby his ratiocinative processes are, as it were, illumined from above. He puts into intellectual terms as far as that is possible, that which he has seen and in a profounder sense experienced. 'Seeing' does not, of course, refer here to visions, for Eckhart unlike Suso was not the type of visionary mystic, which is why his kind of mysticism is, for want of a better word, termed 'speculative'. He would not have been particularly moved, except probably to mirth, by the suggestion of some modern philosophers that this kind of supra-rational seeing or experiencing had no validity. He would merely have pitied those who were unable to perceive what he could see so clearly. He was far more worried by the fact that some things he said were held to conflict with the orthodox assumptions of his day and his Church. Here we are faced with a real problem. Whether he was worried about this because he truly felt inwardly that the Church *had* to be right, or rather because he had to conform, is perhaps to a certain extent open to question. We might tentatively put it that Eckhart, being utterly convinced of the truth of what he was saying, *hoped* it was after all fundamentally orthodox or at least would pass for such, but felt he had to say it just the same. This is not a very satisfactory answer, and admittedly begs several questions. But since we can neither penetrate into the depths of Eckhart's insight nor see into his conscience, it is probably best to leave it at that.

In the so-called *Quaestiones Parisienses,* which date from his first stay in Paris, Eckhart discusses the question of whether Being and Knowing are identical in God, and he says (contrary to Aquinas), that God does not know because He *is,* but rather *is* because He knows: *est ipsum intelligere fundamentum ipsius esse.* Knowledge, understanding, wisdom, are for Eckhart always paramount. It is true that he later seems sometimes to shift his ground, and declares in his sermons that 'God is pure Being'. But this is not a real contradiction. God is pure Being in relation to *creatures,* who are in themselves nothing but only derive their being from God. In the Trinity, Eckhart maintains, the Father represents Knowledge, the Son Life, and the Holy Ghost, Being. But God is in reality a Unity (*Unum*) in which all these things are without distinction. He continually stresses that God is Unity, not one Person: *unum non unus.*

God, or the Godhead, is pure unity and pure being. Therefore there is no true being except in God, and all creatures are, strictly speaking, nothing. Creatures gain their being from God. This is one of the fundamental tenets of Eckhart's teaching. The subject is dealt with particularly by a Japanese scholar, Shizuteru Ueda.[7] Professor Ueda is one of the few Japanese scholars who know not only Middle High German well but are also well read in Medieval Latin scholastic texts. His 'confrontation' of Eckhart with Far Eastern thought (which he undertakes in a final chapter of his book) is based on a thorough acquaintance, such as few other scholars can lay claim to, with both fields. Other writers have of course tried to compare Eckhart's mysticism with aspects of Oriental thought, notably Rudolf Otto who compared it with Vedanta, and D.T.Suzuki who compared it with Zen Buddhism, as Ueda does. But as Ueda's very important book has not been translated into English, some account of it will be given here.

Ueda sees as the decisive point in Eckhart's doctrine of the Trinity its application to the relation between God and the individual human soul. Eckhart's regular formula for expressing this relation is: God begets His Son in the soul. Eckhart develops this theme further by asserting: 'God begets me as His Son and as the same Son'. In this way the soul is, as it were, drawn into the dynamic process of the Trinity, which is God's Being or Essence. At the same time, as we have seen, the unity of God is strongly stressed: *unum non unus.*

With the birth of the Son we come to Meister Eckhart's specific doctrine of the Incarnation, interpreted not historically but mystically (not, of course, that Eckhart in any way denied the historical Incarnation). Here especially we must bear in mind the thought of God as *unum*, the

One, pure simplicity. In his commentary on St John's Gospel, Eckhart says: 'God the Word (i.e. Christ) assumed the *nature*, not the *person* of a man'. Human nature is universal, and so is not the property of individual man. Christ therefore became *man*, not *a man*. There is therefore a real sense in which man can become Christ, or God.

This birth of Christ that Eckhart speaks of is not a historical event that occurred in Bethlehem on a particular date, once for all — it is in the Eternal Now.[8] God begets His Son in the soul continually and without interruption. It is possible for Christ to be born in any man's soul because human nature is one, and is therefore the same in Christ as in every man. Of course this birth of Christ does not in fact occur in every human soul, but the potentiality is there. It is only necessary to create the right conditions.

What, then, is the essential prerequisite for the birth of Christ in my soul? It is detachment, self-abandonment (*gelazenheit, abegescheidenheit*). 'The Eternal Word never put on a person. Therefore leave whatever is personal in you and whatever *you* are, and take just your bare *human nature*, then you will be to the Eternal Word just what his human nature is to him. For your human nature and his are *not different*: it is one nature, for what it is in Christ, that it is in you' (No.94).

It follows that there must be something in the soul wherein this mystical birth of the Son can take place. This is variously referred to as the peak of the soul, the castle (*bürgelin*), the spark (*vünkelin*), and so on. Occasionally the Greek term *synteresis* is used.[9] The idea of the 'spark in the soul' was not Eckhart's own invention. But he got into trouble for saying that there is in the soul something uncreated. This is the ground or essence of the soul, which Eckhart sharply distinguishes from its 'powers'. The powers of the soul work in the world, and as long as they are operative, their functioning excludes the operation of the divine birth in the soul. Thus Christ has to drive the merchants from the Temple (i.e. the soul) in order to be alone therein. But this 'castle' in the soul is so lofty that even God must shed all His attributes before He can enter into it. The pure oneness of the highest peak of the soul is reserved for God in His pure unity. If the soul is too distracted by outward things, all possibility of a return to God − of becoming the receptacle for God's birth in the soul − may be lost. That is the danger that threatens the soul with spiritual death.

One merit of Ueda's book, and one reason for citing it here, is its complete detachment from the various sectarian interpretations put forward by Western scholars. At the same time there is no attempt made to over-strain Eckhart's views in the direction of Eastern thought. The resemblances, in some respects, to Zen Buddhism, which have been noted by others, are admitted and given full weight, but the differences are not glossed over. If mysticism in the traditional Western sense implies communion with God, then there is a real sense in which Eckhart may be said to go beyond this, for according to him the soul has to proceed beyond 'God' to the nameless Oneness of the 'Godhead'. Nevertheless, the theistic 'sub-structure' remains an essential part of Eckhart's thought, and this, in Zen as in other schools of Buddhism, is wholly lacking.[10] Ueda illustrates the difference by quoting Eckhart's statement that 'God is nothing'. Since he still attributes 'substance' to the Godhead, he means that God is 'no thing' for man, or in terms that man can understand. But in Zen there might be a *mondo* (question-and-answer): 'What is God? — Nothing!', and in this the 'nothing' would not mean, as with Eckhart, 'God is nothing', but would rather be a total negation of the question itself, thus dissolving the dichotomy still present in Eckhart's statement.

The question of whether Eckhart's views were compatible with Catholic orthodoxy is probably of less general interest today than it was even quite recently. Ironically, the very Pope who condemned him was himself alleged to hold unorthodox views. What we can say is (despite certain voices which have declared the contrary), that Eckhart speaks with authority born of personal experience. But the 'object' of that experience is strictly indescribable and ineffable. It can be hinted at and to some extent defined by what it is *not.* This, of course, is the way of the so-called Negative (or Apophatic) Theology. At the same time Eckhart had necessarily to conform to acceptable dogmatic expressions. Yet he *has* to give utterance to what fills him, whether he is understood or not. As he says in one sermon (No.56): 'Whoever has understood this sermon, good luck to him. If no one had been here, I would have had to preach it to this offertory-box'.

Meister Eckhart remains a great, and for many a perplexing figure. Attempts at interpreting his thoughts are legion. The first task, however, is to try to present as clearly as possible what he *said,* not forgetting the context of his historical situation. Only when this has been done, can we hope to understand his message — if even then we are capable of doing so. The original texts have been and are being made available in Germany by the erudite and self-sacrificing editors of his works. Apart from one or two technical notes, the translator has nothing further to say, but simply and humbly to offer his version.

Notes

1. I use the German form Strassburg rather than Strasbourg, as this city was at the time, and for long afterwards, purely German.

2. A, B and C are not in this order in the manuscript, but this, as Karrer points out, is their logical order.

3. Presumably he died at Avignon. He was probably not actually imprisoned, but kept under some form of surveillance like that from which Ockham succeeded in escaping. Eckhart was in fact dead by the date of Ockham's escape, but Ockham clearly did not know this, and indeed never seems to have heard of the bull *In agro dominico*.

4. Edited by Kurt Ruh in *Festschrift für Josef Quint*, Bonn 1964, pp. 169-185. Cf. Maria Bindschedler, *Der lateinische Kommentar zum Granum Sinapis*, Basle 1949; A.M.Haas, 'Sermo mysticus. Bemerkungen zur Granum sinapis-Sequenz', *Verbum et Signum* II, Munich 1975, pp. 389-412. A version by Father John Gray is included in *The Oxford Book of English Mystical Verse*, Oxford 1917 etc., p. 574f., on the apparent assumption that it is a piece of original English verse. The ascription elsewhere of the original to one Konrad Immendorfer (1423) is incorrect: he was merely the scribe of one manuscript. The poem is about a century older.

5. Heinrich Seuse, *Deutsche Schriften*, ed. K.Bihlmeyer, 1907, pp. 22f. 'Seuse' is a rather unfortunate modernisation of the medieval *Süs* or *Süse*, latinised as *Suso*.

6. It might have seemed unnecessary to have to state categorically that Eckhart is a mystic — indeed one of the greatest of Christian mystics. But in 1960 Heribert Fischer (in *Meister Eckhart der Prediger*, ed. U.M.Nix & R.Öchslin) claimed that this designation was the invention of literary scholars, and Fischer's view is echoed by J.Margetts in *Die Satzstruktur bei Meister Eckhart*, 1969, p. 167.

A crushing rejoinder was given by the greatest of all Eckhart specialists, Josef Quint, 'Textverständnis und Textkritik in der Meister-Eckhart-Forschung', *Festschrift für Fritz Tschirch*, 1972, pp. 170-186. Cf. also Alois M.Haas, 'Das Verhältnis von Sprache und Erfahrung in der deutschen Mystik', *Deutsche Literatur des späten Mittelalters*, ed. W.Harms and L.P.Johnson, 1975, pp. 240-264.

7. See Bibliography, Ueda 1965.

8. Similarly with the question of whether the world had (historically) a beginning. Eckhart got into trouble for denying the creation in time. For him, time and all things temporal are seen from the standpoint of eternity, from which the question of whether the world had a beginning or not is of no consequence. Only when Eckhart was compelled to go into this question did he give the traditional answer. Joachim Kopper, *Die Metaphysik Meister Eckharts*, Saarbrücken 1955, pp. 71f.

9. See Note A: *Synteresis*.

10. See H. von Glasenapp, *Buddhism, a Non-Theistic Religion*, translated by Irmgard Schloegl, London 1970.

NOTE A: SYNTERESIS

The place in the soul where the mystical birth of the Son takes place is referred to by various names including, occasionally (as in No.32a and b), the Greek word *synteresis* (sometimes written, according to late Greek pronunciation, *synderesis* or even *sinderesis).*

Synteresis (synderesis) is used by St Thomas Aquinas for 'the habitual knowledge of the primary moral principles', or the light of conscience which never dies out, even in the damned, and the term goes back to St Jerome's commentary on Ezechiel. Some scholars consider that it is here a mere scribal error for *syneidesis,* which is the usual Greek word for 'conscience'. This is improbable. Warner Allen[1] suggests that it may be a parallel formation to *parateresis,* as in Luke 17:20, meaning 'observation' directed to external objects. He says: '*Synteresis* may have been formed antithetically to express the intuitive and inward observation which belongs to reflexive consciousness and which as we have shown discloses in the spiritual experience the immanent kingdom of God'. Eckhart himself ventures on two alternative, typically medieval etymologies: either 'without heresy' (*sine haeresi*) or *syn-* = Latin *con-* + *haereo,* thus 'co-herent', as being that which always adheres to the good (*LW* I, p. 672, *Liber parabolarum Genesis,* n. 199). Dom Justin McCann[2] quotes a commentator, Vercellensis,[3] on the *Mystical Theology* of 'Dionysius the Areopagite' who says: 'They (the pagan philosophers) thought that the highest cognitive faculty was the intellect, whereas there is another which as far excels the intellect as the intellect does the reason, or the reason the imagination; and this is the higher will (*principalis affectio*), and the same is the spark of conscience (*scintilla synderesis*) which alone may be united to the divine Spirit . . . In this exercise sense, imagination, reason, and intellect are suspended . . . and the point of the higher will (*apex affectionis principalis*) is united to the divine Spirit itself'. This comes close to Eckhart's teaching, though the assertion of the primacy of the will over the intellect is Franciscan.

Notes

1. Warner Allen, *The Uncurtained Throne*, London 1951, p. 112.
2. *The Cloud of Unknowing and Other Treatises*, 6th edition, London 1952, p. xiii; *ibid.*, p. 140.
3. Properly Thomas of St Victor, Abbot of Vercelli (d. 1246).

NOTE B: SPURIOUS AND DOUBTFUL WORKS

Pfeiffer's edition of 1857, on which Miss C. de B Evans's translation was mainly based, is divided into four parts: I. Sermons (*Predigten*), pp. 1-370, with an additional one on pp. 685-6; II. Treatises (*Traktate*), pp. 371-593; III. Sayings (*Sprüche*), pp. 595-627; and IV. the so-called *Liber Positionum*, pp. 629-684. The complex problems relating to the authenticity of all this material were discussed at length in the very important article by Adolf Spamer, 'Zur Überlieferung der Pfeiffer'schen Eckeharttexte' (1909: see Bibliography). Spamer's pioneer work on the problem of the Sermons (I) has been continued by Quint and others, and need not be further considered here. The following notes will serve to indicate the present view on the remaining material contained in Pfeiffer and translated by Miss Evans.

II. Treatises (*Traktate*). Of the 18 'Traktate' in Pfeiffer, only two were accepted by Spamer as genuine: *The Book of Divine Comfort* (V), and *The Talks of Instruction* (XVII), to which more recent scholars have added *On Detachment* (IX). Of the rest, many are curious 'mosaic' compilations of varied character, and though they do in places contain genuine Eckhartian thoughts or quotations, they can in any case quite certainly not be regarded as authentic works by him as they stand. Here, reference will only be made to three of these spurious 'treatises' (the term is, for some, a misnomer). The first is *Swester Katrei* or 'Sister Cathy' (VI), a work known to be spurious long before Spamer's article, but which, as Professor Clark has remarked, seems to be a favourite source of 'Eckhartian' quotations among British and American writers. It is, as Spamer points out, a conglomerate from various sources which has been attached to Eckhart's name. The fact that Eckhart himself appears as a figure in the narrative should alone suffice to show that he is not the author, even though some of his ideas are reflected in it. In fact it belongs to a well-known type of pious sub-mystical tale in which a young girl or an unlettered woman shows herself superior in wisdom and understanding to her confessor. Indeed, it is a fairly typical example of the often rather unorthodox lay piety of the times, as found among the Béguines,[1] the 'Friends of God',[2] and even in some convents. The name of the 'heroine', Katrei or Catherine, is possibly a reminiscence of the legend of St Catherine, who as a wise young virgin confounded the doctors of divinity. Though its true spiritual content has been overrated in some quarters, it is not without interest.

The case of No XII, entitled *Von dem Überschalle*, is also interesting. The title has been translated, misleadingly, by Miss Evans as 'The Drowning', and while it is difficult to render adequately, 'The Supernal Sound' would be more literal — meaning the transcendent harmony in which all that is creaturely is 'drowned'. The text as printed by Pfeiffer is in prose except for three lines of verse at the end, and as prose it is translated by Miss Evans. A simple inspection, however, borne out by reference to better MSS than Pfeiffer was able to use, shows the original to have been in verse. As poetry it is unpretending, but it is not without some mystical depth, and its thought is by no means alien to Eckhart's, which explains why it has attracted some attention. It has however been conclusively shown that this poem is based on Chapter 52 of Suso's mystical autobiography.[3] It was felt by somebody to be sufficiently important for it to be supplied with a 'gloss' or brief prose commentary, which follows it in Pfeiffer's edition.

Mention should be made further of No XVIII, *The Commentary on St John's Gospel.* This brief German treatise has in fact nothing to do with the elaborate Latin commentary which Eckhart did write on that gospel. As Spamer notes, Denifle had already pointed out that Pfeiffer's ascription of it to Eckhart was based on conjecture: where the Stuttgart MS has 'Wherefore Meister Eckhart affirms . . .', Pfeiffer's text reads (in Miss Evans's translation): 'Wherefore I, Meister Eckhart, do affirm . . .', and in fact the author is named in one MS as a certain Bruder Hans, or Johannes, who is also named in connection with another spurious treatise (No XI).

III. The so-called 'Sayings' (*Sprüche*), arranged by Pfeiffer under 70 numbers, are a very mixed collection of fragments, aphorisms, etc., ascribed in various sources to Eckhart. In many cases they are actually extracts from his German sermons or, as regards Nos 31-48, translated extracts from his Latin writings. The last five (66-70) are of a different character, being little tales of Eckhart which seem to have circulated in the convents, and which are not lacking in charm and a certain profundity.

IV. The title 'Liber Positionum' given by Pfeiffer to this whole section is completely unjustified, being based on an ill-founded guess. Pfeiffer did not know Eckhart's Latin works, which include an *Opus propositionum* (!), of which

Pfeiffer's title looks like a garbled version. But in fact there is no connection between this work and the collection of problems and sayings (some similar to those in III) here put together by Pfeiffer. The provenance of most of these passages is somewhat obscure, but they appear to contain little to connect them with Eckhart.

Notes

1. Béguines. Members of sisterhoods founded in the Netherlands in the 12th century. They led a semi-religious life but without vows. Later they were established in Paris, the Rhineland, and elsewhere.

2. The 'Friends of God' (*Gottesfreunde*), a group founded in Strassburg in the 14th century by Rulman Merswin, who invented a mysterious figure called 'Der Gottesfreund von Oberland', and produced much sub-mystical literature. See Clark, *Meister Eckhart*, pp.122-124.

3. Translated by J.M.Clark as *The Life of the Servant*, London 1952.

NOTE C: ARTICLES CONDEMNED IN THE BULL OF JOHN XXII

(IN AGRO DOMINICO), 27 MARCH 1329

1. On being asked why God did not create the world earlier, he answered then as now that God could not have created the world earlier because nothing can operate before it is. Therefore, as soon as God was, He created the world.

2. Likewise, it may be admitted that the world has existed from all eternity.

3. Likewise: At once, and as soon as God was, when He begot His co-eternal Son as God fully equal to Himself, He also created the world.

4. Likewise: In every act, even evil, in the evil of punishment just as much as in the evil of guilt, God's glory is equally revealed and shines forth.

5. Likewise: Whoever reviles anyone with abuse, he praises God through this very abuse, and the more he abuses and the worse he sins, the more he praises God.

6. Likewise: Even he who blasphemes against God praises God.

7. Likewise: Whoever prays for this or that, prays for something evil and in evil wise, for he prays for the denial of good and the denial of God, and he prays for God to

deny Himself to him.

8. Those who seek nothing, neither honour nor profit nor inwardness nor holiness nor reward nor heaven, but who have renounced all this, including what is their own — in such men God is glorified.

9. I recently wondered whether I should accept or desire anything from God. I will consider this very carefully, because if I received anything from God I would be beneath Him or below Him like a servant or slave, but He in giving would be like a master — and it should not be thus with us in eternal life.

10. We are fully transformed and converted into God; in the same way as in the sacrament the bread is converted into the body of Christ, so I am converted into Him, so that He converts me into His being as one, not as *like*. By the living God it is true that there is no difference.

11. All that God the Father gave His only-begotten Son in human nature He has given me: I except nothing, neither union nor holiness, He has given me everything as to him.

12. Everything that Holy Scripture says of Christ is entirely true of every good and holy man.

13. All that is proper to the divine nature is also proper to the just and godly man, therefore such a man performs everything that God performs, and he has created heaven

and earth together with God, and he is a begetter of the
eternal Word, and God could do nothing without such a
man.

14. The good man should so conform his will to the
divine will that he wills everything that God wills. And
since God in a certain sense wills that I should have sinned,
I should not wish to have committed no sins. And that is
true penitence.

15. If a man had committed a thousand mortal sins, and if
that man were in a proper state, he should not wish not to
have committed them.

16. God does not expressly command external works.

17. An external work is not really good and divine, and
God does not really perform and beget it.

18. Let us not offer up the fruits of external works, which
do not make us good, but those of internal works which
the Father dwelling within us does and performs.

19. God loves souls, not external works.

20. A good man is the only-begotten Son of God.

21. A noble man is that only-begotten Son of God whom
the Father begets from eternity.

22. The Father begets me as His Son and as the same Son.
Whatever God performs is one: therefore He begets me as
His Son without any distinction.

23. God is in every way and in every respect One, so that
in Him no multiplicity can be found, either in the intellect
or outside the intellect. For whoever sees duality or
distinction does not see God, since God is One outside all
number and above all number, and does not coincide with
anything. It therefore follows that in God no distinction
can exist or be discerned.

24. Every distinction is alien to God, both in His nature
and in the Persons. The proof: since His nature itself is one
(*una*) and this very One (*unum*), and each Person is one
and this same One as the nature.

25. When it says: "Simon, do you love me more than
these?" (John 21:15), the meaning is: more than you love
these, i.e. well, but not perfectly. For where there is first
and second, there is more and less, or rank and degree; but
in the One there is neither rank nor degree. Therefore he
who loves God more than these loves Him well, but not
perfectly.

26. All creatures are pure nothing. I do not say that they
are a little something, or anything at all, but that they are
pure nothing.

27. There is something in the soul that is uncreated and uncreatable. If the whole soul were of such a nature she would be uncreated and uncreatable. This is the intellect.

28. God is neither good nor better nor best. When I call God good I speak as falsely as if I were to call white black.

Of these articles (reduced from the 108 and more to which the Cologne inquisitors had objected), the first 15 were declared, both as to their literal sense and in context, to be erroneous or tainted with heresy. The same applied to the last two (Nos 27 and 28), which Eckhart was 'alleged to have preached'. The remaining 11 (Nos 16 to 26) were described as 'having a very bad sound and suspect of heresy, though capable, with many explanations and additions, of being interpreted in a Catholic sense.'

SELECT BIBLIOGRAPHY

Note: This is primarily intended for the English-speaking reader who knows little or no German. However, some German items have been included. These are either important textual sources or works which can be considered milestones in Eckhart research. The reader who seeks more can now be conveniently referred to Ernst Soudek, *Meister Eckhart* (Sammlung Metzler 120), Stuttgart 1973.

1845. F.Pfeiffer, *Deutsche Mystiker des 14. Jahrhunderts* I, Leipzig.

1857. F.Pfeiffer, *Deutsche Mystiker des 14. Jahrhunderts* II, *Meister Eckhart*, Leipzig (reprinted Aalen, 1962. The pioneer edition).

1875. A.Jundt, *Histoire du pantheisme populaire au moyen age*, Paris.

1885. H.S.Denifle, O.P., 'Actenstücke zu Meister Eckharts Process', *ZfdA* 29, 259-266.

1886. H.S.Denifle, O.P., 'Meister Eckharts lateinische Schriften und die Grundanschauung seiner Lehre', *ALKM* 2, 417-652 (contains trial documents).

1895. F.Jostes, *Meister Eckhart und seine Jünger. Ungedruckte Texte zur Geschichte der deutschen Mystik*, Fribourg. (82 sermons, etc., from a Nürnberg MS; 4 more in Appendix).

1900. H.Delacroix, *Essai sur le mysticisme spéculatif en Allemagne au 14e. siècle*, Paris.

1903. H.Büttner, *Meister Eckeharts Schriften und Predigten*, 2 vols., Jena (a very popular if free transaltion, frequently reprinted).

1909. A.Spamer, 'Zur Überlieferung der Pfeifferschen Eckharttexte', *PBB* 34, 307-420.

1911. Evelyn Underhill, *Mysticism*, London (reprinted 1960).

1912. A.Spamer, *Texte aus der deutschen Mystik des 14. und 15. Jahrhunderts*, Jena. (Latin and German texts from MSS in Berlin, Brussels, Cues, Oxford, &c.)

1919. Ph. Strauch, *Paradisus Anime Intelligentis* (*DTM* 30), Berlin. (From Oxford MS Laud Misc. 479).

1923. A.Daniels, 'Eine lateinische Rechtfertigungsschrift des Meister

Eckhart', *BBG*, Heft 5.

1924. C. de B.Evans, *Meister Eckhart by Franz Pfeiffer, Leipzig, 1857. Translation with some Omissions and Additions*, London, Watkins (=Evans I).

1926. Dom C.Butler, *Western Mysticism*, 2nd ed., London.

1926. G.Théry, 'Edition critique des pièces relevantes au procès d'Eckhart', *AHDL* 1, 129-168.

1927. O.Karrer & Herma Piesch, *Meister Eckeharts Rechtfertigungs-schrift von Jahre 1326. Einleitung, Übersetzung und Anmer-kungen*, Erfurt.

1931. C. de B.Evans, *The Works of Meister Eckhart*, vol. II, London, Watkins.

1932. Josef Quint, *Die Überlieferung der deutschen Predigten Meister Eckeharts*, Bonn. (A fundamental textual study of the sermons in Pfeiffer 1857, with numerous emendations.)

1934-6. *Magistri Eckhardi Opera Latina*, 3 parts, ed. G.Théry, R.Klibansky *et al.*, Leipzig (publication stopped for political reasons).

1936ff. *Meister Eckhart. Die deutschen und lateinischen Werke. Herausgegeben im Auftrage der deutschen Forschungsgemein-schaft*, Stuttgart, Kohlhammer. The German works (here referred to as *DW*) ed. Josef Quint, the Latin works (*LW*) by Ernst Benz *et al.* Both portions still in progress. The standard edition. (Note: the *LW* received official support at the ex-pense of the Théry-Klibansky edition, but there is no sign of political influence on the contents).

1941. R.B.Blakney, *Meister Eckhart. A Modern Translation*, New York & London.

1949. J.M.Clark, *The Great German Mystics: Eckhart, Tauler, Suso*, Oxford.

1953. F.C.Happold, *Mysticism. A Study and an Anthology* (Penguin), Harmondsworth.

1955. J.Quint, *Meister Eckehart, Deutsche Predigten und Traktate*, Munich. (A modern German translation. Contains some ser-mons not in *DW*).

SELECT BIBLIOGRAPHY

1957. D.T.Suzuki, *Mysticism, Christian and Buddhist*, London.

1957. J.M.Clark, *Meister Eckhart. An Introduction to the Study of his Works with an Anthology of his Sermons*, London.

1957. R.Otto, *Mysticism, East and West*, translated by B.L.Bracey & R.C.Payne, New York. (Compares Eckhart's mysticism and Vedanta) (from 1926 German edition).

1957. R.C.Zaehner, *Mysticism, Sacred and Profane*, Oxford.

1957. R.Petrie, ed., *Late Medieval Mysticism* (Library of Christian Classics 13), London. (A useful anthology with Introductions).

1958. J.M.Clark & J.V.Skinner, *Meister Eckhart, Selected Treatises and Sermons. Translated from German and Latin, with an introduction and Notes*, London.

1958. Jeanne Ancelet-Hustache, *Master Eckhart and the Rhineland Mystics*, translated by Hilda Graef, London.

1960. V.Lossky, *Théologie négative et connaissance de Dieu chez Maître Eckhart*, Paris.

1965. Shizuteru Ueda, *Die Gottesgeburt in der Seele und der Durchbruch zur Gottheit. Die mystische Anthropologie Meister Eckharts und ihre Konfrontation mit der Mystik des Zen-Buddhismus*, Gütersloh.

1966. Hilda Graef, *The Story of Mysticism*, London.

1967. I.Degenhardt, *Studien zum Wandel des Eckhartbildes*, Leiden.

1974. Heribert Fischer, *Meister Eckhart* (Kolleg Philosophie), Freiburg/München.

ABBREVIATIONS

AHDL

Archives d'histoire doctrinale et littéraire du moyen âge, Paris 1926ff.

ALKM

Archiv für die Litteratur und Kirchengeschichte des Mittelalters Berlin/Freiburg 1885ff.

BBG

Bäumkers *Beiträge zur Geschichte der Philosophie und Theologie des Mittelalters*, Münster 1891ff.

DTM

Deutsche Texte des Mittelalters.

DW

Deutsche Werke = Eckhart's German works in the Kohlhammer edition 1936ff.

Jostes

Jostes 1895.

Jundt

Jundt 1875.

LW

Lateinische Werke = Eckhart's Latin works in the Kohlhammer edition 1936ff.

MHG

Middle High German.

Par.an.

Strauch 1919.

PBB

Paul und Braunes *Beiträge zur Geschichte der deutschen Sprache und Literatur*, Halle 1874ff.

Pf

Germon sermons in Pfeiffer 1857.

Q

German sermons ed. Quint in *DW* (I, 1-24; II, 25-59; III, 60-86).

ABBREVIATIONS

QT
  German sermons translated by Quint 1955.

ZfdA
  Zeitschrift für deutsches Altertum, Berlin 1841ff.

DUM MEDIUM SILENTIUM TENERENT OMNIA ET NOX IN SUO
CURSU MEDIUM ITER HABERET, ETC.

(Sap. 18:14)

Here, in time,[2] we are celebrating the eternal birth which
God the Father bore and bears unceasingly in eternity,
because this same birth is now born in time, in human
nature. St Augustine[3] says: 'What does it avail me that
this birth is always happening, if it does not happen in
me? That it should happen in me is what matters.' We
shall therefore speak of this birth, of how it may take
place in us and be consummated in the virtuous soul,
whenever God the Father speaks His eternal Word in the
perfect soul. For what I say here is to be understood of
the good and perfected man who has walked and is still
walking in the ways of God; not of the natural, un-
disciplined man, for he is entirely remote from, and
totally ignorant of this birth. There is a saying of the wise
man: "When all things lay in the midst of silence, then
there descended down into me from on high, from the
royal throne, a secret word." This sermon is about that
Word.[4]

Three things[5] are to be noted here. The first is, *where*
in the soul God the Father speaks His Word, where this
birth takes place and where she[6] is receptive of this act,
for that can only be in the very purest, loftiest, subtlest
part that the soul is capable of. In very truth, if God the
Father in His omnipotence could endow the soul with

1

anything more noble, and if the soul could have received from Him anything nobler, then the Father would have had to delay the birth for the coming of this greater excellence. Therefore the soul in which this birth is to take place must keep absolutely pure and must live in noble fashion, quite collected and turned entirely inward; not running out through the five senses into the multiplicity of creatures, but all inturned and collected and in the purest part — there is His place, He disdains anything less.

The second part of this sermon has to do with man's conduct in relation to this act, to God's speaking of this Word within, to this birth: whether it is more profitable for man to co-operate with it, so that it may come to pass in him through his own exertion and merit — by a man's creating in himself a mental image in his thoughts and disciplining himself that way by reflecting that God is wise, omnipotent, eternal, or whatever else he can imagine about God — whether this is more profitable and conducive to this birth from the Father; or whether one should shun and free oneself from all thoughts, words and deeds and from all images created by the understanding, maintaining a wholly God-receptive attitude, such that one's own self is idle, letting God work within one. Which conduct conduces best to this birth? The third point is the profit, and how great it is, which accrues from this birth.

Note in the first place that in what I am about to say I shall make use of natural proofs, so that you yourselves can grasp that it is so, for though I put more faith in the scriptures than in myself, yet it is easier and better for you to learn by means of arguments that can be verified.

First we will take the words: 'In the midst of silence there was spoken within me a secret word'. — 'But sir,[7] where is the silence and where is the place where the word is spoken?' — As I said just now, it is in the purest thing that the soul is capable of, in the noblest part, the ground[8] — indeed, in the very essence of the soul which is the soul's most secret part. There is the silent 'middle', for no creature ever entered there and no image, nor has the soul there either activity or understanding, therefore she is not aware *there* of any image, whether of herself or of any other creature.

Whatever the soul effects, she effects with her powers.[9] What she understands, she understands with the intellect. What she remembers, she does with memory; if she would love, she does that with the will, and thus she works with her powers and not with her essence. Every external act is linked with some *means*. The power of sight works only through the eyes; otherwise it can neither employ nor bestow vision, and so it is with all the other senses. The soul's every external act is effected by some means. But in the soul's essence there is no activity, for the powers she works with emanate from the ground of being. Yet in that ground is the silent 'middle': here nothing but rest and celebration for this birth, this act, that God the Father may speak His word there, for *this* part is by nature receptive to nothing save only the divine essence, without mediation. Here God enters the soul with His all, not merely with a part. God enters here the ground of the soul. None can touch the ground of the soul but God alone. No creature can enter the soul's ground, but must stop outside, in the 'powers'. Within, the soul sees clearly the image

3

whereby the creature has been drawn in and taken lodging. For whenever the powers of the soul make contact with a creature, they set to work and make an image and likeness of the creature, which they absorb. That is how they know the creature. No creature can come closer to the soul than this, and the soul never approaches a creature without having first voluntarily taken an image of it into herself. Through this presented image, the soul approaches creatures — an image being something that the soul makes of (external) objects with her own powers. Whether it is a stone, a horse, a man or anything else that she wants to know, she gets out the image of it that she has already taken in, and is thus enabled to unite herself with it.

But for a man to receive an image in this way, it must of necessity enter from without through the senses. In consequence, there is nothing so unknown to the soul as herself. Accordingly, one master says that the soul can neither create nor obtain an image of herself. Therefore she has no way of knowing herself, for images all enter through the senses, and hence she can have no image of herself. And so she knows all other things, but not herself. Of nothing does she know so little as of herself, for want of mediation.

And you must know too that inwardly the soul is free and void of all means and all images — which is *why* God can freely unite with her without form or likeness. Whatever power you ascribe to any master, you cannot but ascribe that power to God without limit. The more skilled and powerful the master, the more immediately is his work effected, and the simpler it is. Man requires many means for his external works; much preparation of the material is

4

needed before he can produce them as he has imagined them. But the sun in its sovereign mastery performs its task (which is to give light) very swiftly: the instant its radiance is poured forth, the ends of the earth are full of light. More exalted is the angel, who needs still less means for his work and has fewer images. The highest Seraph has but a single image: *he* seizes as a unity all that his inferiors regard as manifold. But God needs *no* image and has no image: without any means, likeness or image God operates in the soul — right in the ground where no image ever got in, but only He Himself with His own being. This no creature can do.

'How does God the Father give birth to His Son in the soul — like creatures, in images and likenesses?'

No, by my faith, but just as He gives birth to him in eternity — no more, no less.

'Well, but how *does* He give birth to him then?'

Now see: God the Father has a perfect insight into Himself, profound and thorough knowledge of Himself by Himself, and not through any image. And thus God the Father gives birth to His Son in the true unity of the divine nature. See, it is like this and in no other way that God the Father gives birth to the Son in the ground and essence of the soul, and thus unites Himself with her. For if any image were present there would be no real union, and in that real union lies the soul's whole beatitude.

Now, you might say, there is by nature nothing in the soul but images. Not at all! If that were so, the soul could never become blessed, for God cannot make any creature from which you can receive perfect blessedness — otherwise God would not be the highest blessing and the final goal,

5

whereas it is His nature to be this, and it is His will to be the alpha and omega of all things. No creature can constitute your blessedness, nor can it be your perfection here on earth, for the perfection of *this* life — which is the sum of all the virtues — is followed by the perfection of the life to come. Therefore you have to be and dwell in the essence and in the ground, and *there* God will touch you with His simple essence without the intervention of any image. No image represents and signifies itself: it always aims and points to that of which it is the image. And, since you have no image but of what is outside yourself (which is drawn in through the senses and continually points to that of which it is the image), therefore it is impossible for you to be beatified by any image whatsoever. And *therefore* there must be a silence and a stillness, and the Father must speak in that, and give birth to His Son, and perform His works free from all images.

The second point is, what must a man contribute by his own actions, in order to procure and deserve the occurrence and the consummation of this birth in himself? Is it better to do something towards this, to imagine and think about God? — or should he keep still and silent in peace and quiet and let God speak and work in him, merely waiting for God to act? Now I say, as I said before, that these words and this act are only for the good and perfected people, who have so absorbed and assimilated the essence of all virtues that these virtues emanate from them naturally, without their seeking; and above all there must dwell in them the worthy life and lofty teachings of our Lord Jesus Christ. They must know that the very best and noblest attainment in this life is to be silent and

6

and let God work and speak within. When the powers have been completely withdrawn from all their works and images, *then* the Word is spoken. Therefore he said: 'In the midst of the silence the secret word was spoken unto me'. And so, the more completely you are able to draw in your powers to a unity and forget all those things and their images which you have absorbed, and the further you can get from creatures and their images, the nearer you are to this and the readier to receive it. If only you could suddenly be unaware of all things,[10] then you could pass into an oblivion of your own body as St Paul did, when he said: "Whether in the body I cannot tell, or out of the body I cannot tell; God knows it" (2 Cor. 12:2). In this case the spirit had so entirely absorbed the powers that it had forgotten the body: memory no longer functioned, nor understanding, nor the senses, nor the powers that should function so as to govern and grace the body, vital warmth and body-heat were suspended, so that the body did not waste during the three days when he neither ate nor drank. Thus too Moses fared, when he fasted for forty days on the mountain and was none the worse for it, for on the last day he was as strong as on the first. In this way a man should flee his senses, turn his powers inward and sink into an oblivion of all things and himself. Concerning this a master[11] addressed the soul thus: 'Withdraw from the unrest of external activities, then flee away and hide from the turmoil of inward thoughts, for they but create discord'. And so, if God is to speak His Word in the soul, she must be at rest and at peace, and *then* He will speak His Word, and Himself, in the soul — no image, but Himself!

7

Dionysius[12] says: 'God has no image or likeness of Himself, for He is intrinsically all goodness, truth and being'. God performs all His works, whether within Himself or outside of Himself, in a flash. Do not imagine that God, when He made heaven and earth and all things, made one thing one day and another the next. Moses describes it like that, but he really knew better: he did so for the sake of people who could not conceive or grasp it any other way. All God did was this: He willed, He spoke, and they *were*! God works without means and without images, and the freer you are from images, the more receptive you are for His inward working, and the more introverted and self-forgetful, the nearer you are to this.

Dionysius[13] exhorted his pupil Timothy in this sense saying: 'Dear son Timothy, do you with untroubled mind soar above yourself and all your powers, above ratiocination and reasoning, above works, above all modes and existence, into the secret still darkness, that you may come to the knowledge of the unknown super-divine God.' There must be a withdrawal from all things. God scorns to work through images.

Now you might say, 'What does God do without images in the ground and essence?'

That I cannot know, because my soul-powers receive only in images; they have to know and lay hold of each thing in its appropriate image. They cannot recognise a horse when presented with the image of a man; and since all things enter from without, that knowledge is hidden from my soul — which is to her great advantage. This *not-knowing* makes her wonder and leads her to eager pursuit, for she perceives clearly *that* it is, but does not

know *how* or *what* it is. Whenever a man knows the causes
of things, then he at once tires of them and seeks to know
something different. Always clamouring to know things,
is for ever inconstant. And so this unknown-knowing
keeps the soul constant and yet spurs her on to pursuit.

About this, the wise man said: "In the middle of the
night when all things were in a quiet silence, there was
spoken to me a hidden word. It came like a thief by
stealth" (Sap. 18:14,15). Why does he call it a word, when
it was hidden? The nature of a word is to reveal what is
hidden. It revealed itself to me and shone forth before me,
declaring something to me and making God known to me,
and therefore it is called a Word. Yet what it *was*, remained hidden from me. That was its stealthy coming in
a whispering stillness to reveal itself. See, just because it
is hidden one must and should always pursue it. It shone
forth and yet was hidden: we are meant to yearn and sigh
for it. St Paul exhorts us to pursue this until we espy it,
and not to stop until we grasp it. After he had been caught
up into the third heaven where God was made known to
him and he beheld all things, when he returned he had
forgotten nothing, but it was so deep down in his ground
that his intellect could not reach it; it was veiled from him.
He therefore had to pursue it and search for it in himself
and not outside. It is all within, not outside, but wholly
whithin. And knowing this full well, he said: 'For I am
persuaded that neither death nor any affliction can sepa-
rate me from what I find within me" (Rom. 8:38-39).

There is a fine saying of one pagan master[14] to another about this. He said: 'I am aware of something in me
which shines in my understanding; I can clearly perceive

9

that it is something, but what it may be I cannot grasp. Yet I think if I could only seize it I should know all truth'. To which the other master replied: 'Follow it boldly! for if you could seize it you would possess the sum-total of all good and have eternal life!' St Augustine[15] spoke in the same sense: 'I am aware of something within me that gleams and flashes before my soul; were this perfected and fully established in me, that would surely be eternal life!' It hides, yet shows itself; it comes, but like a thief with intent to take and steal all things from the soul. But by emerging and showing itself a little it aims to lure the soul and draw her towards itself, to rob her and deprive her of herself. About this, the prophet says: 'Lord, take from them their spirit and give them instead thy spirit' (Ps. 103: 29-30). This too was meant by the loving soul when she said: "My soul dissolved and melted away when Love spoke his word" (Cant. 5:6). When he entered, *I* had to fall away. And Christ meant this by his words: "Whoever abandons anything for my sake shall be repaid a hundred-fold, and whoever would possess me must deny himself and all things, and whoever will serve me must follow me and not go any more after his own" (Mk. 10.29 etc.).

But now you might say, 'But, good sir, you want to change the natural course of the soul and go against her nature! It is her nature to take things in through the senses in images. Would you upset this ordering?

No! But how do you know what nobility God has bestowed on human nature, not yet fully described, and still unrevealed? For those who have written of the soul's nobility have gone no further than their natural intelligence could carry them; they had never entered her ground, so that much remained obscure and unknown to them. So the prophet said: "I will sit in silence and hearken to what God speaks within me" (Ps. 84:9). Because it is so secret, this Word came in the night and in darkness. St John says: "The light shone in the darkness, it came into its own, and as many as received it became in authority sons of God; to them was given power to become God's sons" (John 1:5, 11-12).

Now observe the use and the fruit of this secret Word and this darkness. The Son of the heavenly Father is not born alone in this darkness, which is his own: you too can be born a child of the same heavenly Father and of none other, and to you too He will give power. Now observe how great the use is! For all the truth learnt by all the masters by their own intellect and understanding, or ever to be learnt till Doomsday, they never had the slightest inkling of this knowledge and this ground. Though it may be called a nescience, an unknowing, yet there is in it more than in all knowing and understanding without it, for this unknowing lures and attracts you from all understood things, and from yourself as well. This is what Christ meant when he said: "Whoever will not deny himself and will not leave his father and mother, and is not estranged from all these, is not worthy of me" (Matt. 10:37), as though he were to say : he who does not abandon creaturely externals can be neither conceived nor born in this divine birth. But divesting yourself of yourself and of everything external does truly give it to you. And in very truth I believe, nay I am sure, that the man who is established in this cannot in any way ever be separated from God. I say he can in no way lapse into

11

mortal sin. He would rather suffer the most shameful death, as the saints have done before him, than commit the least of mortal sins. I say such people cannot willingly commit or consent to even a venial sin in themselves or in others if they can stop it. So strongly are they lured and drawn and accustomed to *that*, that they can never turn to any other way; to this way are directed all their senses, all their powers.

May the God who has been born again as man assist us to this birth, eternally helping us, weak men, to be born in him again as God. Amen.

Notes

1. This sermon epitomises some of the most important aspects of the whole of Eckhart's teaching.

2. Christmas Day. But Eckhart is not interested in 'real' time, and goes straight on to speak of the Eternal Birth. See Introduction, n.8.

3. Quotation untraced, as often. Eckhart's quotation from authorities are often very free, obviously from memory, and therefore hard to verify. Where this has been done, usually by Quint, the source is given in these notes. See also note 15.

4. The Word for Eckhart is the *Logos* of St John's Gospel, i.e. the Son in the Trinity. The text, from the *Wisdom of Solomon*, is freely chosen by Eckhart to express his ideas, which are paralleled in his Latin commentary on this work. The preamble provides the link between the text and Eckhart's real theme, which is in fact, as Quint remarks, his sole theme: the birth of the Word in the soul.

5. These three points are in accordance with the fourfold principle of interpretation (see Introduction, p.xiii). The first or literal sense Eckhart omits: the first point here represents the allegorical interpretation of the text, the second is the moral, and the third is the anagogical, which deals with eternal life. These points are then developed in turn.

6. I call the soul 'she' for clarity in accordance with the preliminary note, but in the present context 'she' is particularly appropriate.

7. A fictitious question from the audience.

8. The 'ground of the soul', where the birth takes place, to which Eckhart constantly refers under a variety of names: the 'spark', the 'castle', and so on. It is sharply distinguished from the 'powers'.

9. The 'powers' of the soul are the agencies through which it operates. The higher powers are intellect, memory and will, and the lower powers are the (lower) intellect, anger and desire, as well as the senses. The 'higher intellect' is not the ratiocinative faculty, but the intuitive in the highest sense of that term.

10. A possible clue to the nature of Eckhart's own meditative experience.

11. Anselm of Canterbury.

12. The so-called Dionysius the Areopagite. Quotation untraced.

13. *De mystica theologia* 1 (MPG 3, 997). See the modern English rendering of the 14th century *Denis Hid Divinity*, in *The Cloud of Unknowing and other Treatises by a 14th century English Mystic*, revised, edited and introduced by Abbot Justin McCann, O.S.B., London, Burns Oates, 6th ed., 1952. It is remarkable that the introduction mentions Tauler, Suso, Ruysbroeck and St Catherine of Siena as 14th century contemplatives, but not Eckhart! There are of course many parallels to Eckhart's thought in *The Cloud of Unknowing*.

14. Untraced.

15. There may be something wrong in the text here, as the (untraced) Augustine quotation virtually duplicates the story told immediately above. Probably the listener who recorded the sermon muddled the quotations. This well illustrates the difficulty of establishing the exact wording of the sermons.

UBI EST QUI NATUS EST REX JUDAEORUM?

(Matt. 2:2)

"Where is he who is born King of the Jews?" Now observe, as regards this birth, *where* it takes place: "*Where* is he who is born?" Now I say as I have often said before, that this eternal birth occurs in the soul precisely as it does in eternity, no more and no less, for it is *one* birth, and this birth occurs in the essence and ground of the soul.

Now certain questions arise. First of all, since God is in all things as intelligence, and is more truly in them than they are in themselves, and more naturally, and since wherever God is there He must needs work, knowing Himself and speaking His Word — in what special respects, then, is the soul better fitted for this divine operation than are other rational creatures in which God also is? Pay attention to the explanation.

God is in all things as being, as activity, as power. But He is fecund in the soul alone, for though every creature is a vestige of God, the soul is the natural image of God. This image must be adorned and perfected in this birth. No creature but the soul alone is receptive to this act, this birth. Indeed, such perfection as enters the soul, whether it be divine undivided light, grace or bliss, must needs enter the soul through this birth, and in no other way. Just await this birth within you, and you shall experience all good and all comfort, all happiness, all being and all truth. If you miss it, you will miss all good and blessedness.

15

Whatever comes to you in that will bring you pure being and stability; but whatever you seek or cleave to apart from this will perish — take it how you will and where you will, all will perish. This alone gives being — all else perishes. But in this birth you will share in the divine influx and all its gifts. This cannot be received by creatures in which God's image is not found, for the soul's image appertains especially to this eternal birth, which happens truly and especially in the soul, being begotten of the Father in the soul's ground and innermost recesses, into which no image ever shone or (soul-)power[1] peeped.

The second question is: Since this work of birth occurs in the essence and ground of the soul, then it happens just as much in a sinner as in a saint, so what grace or good is there in it for me? For the ground of nature is the same in both — in fact even those in hell retain their nobility of nature eternally.

Now note the answer. It is a property of this birth that it always comes with fresh light. It always brings a great light to the soul, for it is the nature of good to diffuse itself wherever it is. In this birth God streams into the soul in such abundance of light, so flooding the essence and ground of the soul that it runs over and floods into the powers and into the outward man. Thus it befell Paul when on his journey God touched him with His light and spoke to him: a reflection of the light shone outwardly, so that his companions saw it surrounding Paul like the blessed (in heaven). The superfluity of light in the ground of the soul wells over into the body which is filled with radiance. No sinner can receive this light, nor is he worthy to, being full of sin and wickedness, which is called 'darkness'. Therefore it says: "The darkness shall neither receive nor comprehend the light" (John 1:5). That is because the paths by which the light would enter are choked and obstructed with guile and darkness: for light and darkness cannot co-exist, or God and creatures: if God shall enter, the creatures must simultaneously go out. A man is fully aware of this light. Directly he turns to God, a light begins to gleam and glow within him,[2] giving him to understand what to do and what to leave undone, with much true guidance in regard to things of which before he knew or understood nothing.

'Where do you know this from, and in what way?'

Just pay attention. Your heart is often moved and turned away from the world. How could that be but by this illumination? It is so charming and delightful that you become weary of all things that are not God or God's. It draws you to God and you become aware of many a prompting to do good, though ignorant of whence it comes. This inward inclination is in no way due to creatures or their bidding, for what creatures direct or effect always comes from without. But by this work it is only the ground (of the soul) that is stirred, and the freer you keep yourself the more light, truth and discernment you will find. Thus no man ever went astray for any other reason than that he first departed from *this*, and then sought too much to cling to outward things. St Augustine says there are many who sought light and truth, but only outside where it was not to be found. Finally they go out so far that they never get back home or find their way in again. Thus they have not found the truth, for truth is within, in the ground, and not without. So he who would

17

see light to discern all truth, let him watch and become aware of this birth within, in the ground. Then all his powers will be illuminated, and the outer man as well. For as soon as God inwardly stirs the ground with truth, its light darts into his powers, and that man knows at times more than anyone could teach him. As the prophet says: "I have gained greater understanding than all who ever taught me".[3] You see then, because this light cannot shine or lighten in sinners, that is why this birth cannot possibly occur in them. This birth cannot co-exist with the darkness of sin, even though it takes place, not in the powers, but in the essence and ground of the soul.

The question arises: Since God the Father gives birth only in the essence and ground of the soul and not in the powers, what concern is it of theirs? How do they help just by being idle and taking a rest? What is the use, since this birth does not take place in the powers? A good question. Listen well to the explanation.

Every creature works towards some end. The end is always the first in intention but the last in execution. Thus too, God in all His works has a most blessed end in view, namely Himself: to bring the soul and all her powers into that end — Himself. For this, all God's works are wrought, for this the Father bears His Son in the soul, so that all the powers of the soul shall come to this. He lies in wait for all that the soul contains, bidding all to this feast at His court. But the soul is scattered abroad among her powers and dissipated in the action of each: the power of sight in the eye, the power of hearing in the ear, the power of tasting in the tongue — thus her ability to work inwardly is enfeebled, for a scattered power is imperfect. So, for her inward work to be effective, she must call in all her powers and gather them together from the diversity of things to a single inward activity. St Augustine says the soul is rather where she loves than where she gives life to the body. For example, there was once a pagan master[4] who was devoted to an art, that of mathematics, to which he had devoted all his powers. He was sitting by the embers, making calculations and practising this art, when a man came along who drew a sword and, not knowing that it was the master, said: 'Quick, tell me your name or I'll kill you!' The master was too absorbed to see or hear the foe or to catch what he said: he was unable to utter a word, even to say, 'My name is so-and-so'. And so the enemy, having cried out several times and got no answer, cut off his head. And this was to acquire a mere natural science. How much more then should we withdraw from all things in order to concentrate all our powers on perceiving and knowing the one infinite, uncreated, eternal truth! To this end, then, assemble all your powers, all your senses, your entire mind and memory; direct them into the ground where your treasure lies buried. But if this is to happen, realise that you must drop all other works — you must come to an *unknowing*, if you would find it.

The question arises: would it not be more valuable for each power to keep to its own task, none hindering the others in their work, nor God in His? Might there not be in me a manner of creaturely knowing that is not a hindrance, just as God knows all things without hindrance, and so too the blessed in heaven?[5] That is a good question. Note the explanation.

19

The blessed see God in a single image, and in that image, they discern all things. God too sees Himself thus, perceiving all things in Himself. He need not turn from one thing to another, as we do. Suppose in this life we always had a mirror before us, in which we saw all things at a glance and recognised them in a single image, then neither action nor knowledge would be any hindrance to us. But we have to turn from one thing to another, and so we can only attend to one thing at the expense of another. For the soul is so firmly attached to the powers that she has to flow with them wherever they flow, because in every task they perform the soul must be present and attentive, or they could not work at all. If she is dissipated by attending to outward acts, this is bound to weaken her inward work. For at this birth God needs and must have a vacant free and unencumbered soul, containing nothing but Himself alone, and which looks to nothing and nobody but Him. As to this, Christ says: "Whoever loves anything but me, whoever loves father and mother or many other things is not worthy of me. I did not come upon earth to bring peace but a sword, to cut away all things, to part you from sister, brother, mother, child and friend that in truth are your foes." (Matt. 10:34-36) (cf.Matt. 19:28). For whatever is familiar to you is your foe. If your eye wanted to see all things, and your ear to hear all things and your heart to remember all things, then indeed your soul would be dissipated in all these things.

Accordingly a master says: 'To achieve an interior act, a man must collect all his powers as if into a corner of his soul where, hiding away from all images and forms, he can get to work.' Here, he must come to a forgetting and an unknowing. There must be a stillness and a silence for this Word to make itself heard. We cannot serve this Word better than in stillness and in silence: *there* we can hear it, and there too we will understand it aright — in the unknowing. To him who knows nothing it appears and reveals itself.

Another question arises. You might say: 'Sir, you place all our salvation in ignorance. That sounds like a lack. God made man to know, as the prophet says: "Lord, make them know!" (Tob. 13:4). Where there is ignorance there is a lack, something is missing, a man is brutish, an ape, a fool, and remains so long as he is ignorant.' Ah, but here we must come to a *transformed* knowledge, and this unknowing must not come from ignorance, but rather from *knowing* we must get to this unknowing.[6] Then we shall become knowing with divine knowing, and our unknowing will be ennobled and adorned with supernatural knowing. And through holding ourselves passive in this, we are more perfect than if we were active. That is why one master declares that the sense of hearing is nobler than that of sight, for we learn more wisdom by hearing than by seeing, and in it live the more wisely. We hear of a pagan master who lay dying. His disciples discussed in his presence some noble art, and, dying though he was, he lifted up his head to listen, saying: 'Oh let me learn this art now, that I may rejoice in it for ever!' Hearing draws in more, but seeing rather leads outwards — the very act of seeing does this. Therefore in eternal life we shall rejoice far more in our power of hearing than in that of sight. For the act of hearing the eternal Word is within me, but the act of seeing goes forth from me: in hearing, I am passive, but in

21

seeing I am active.

But our bliss lies not in our activity, but in being passive to God. For just as God is more excellent than creatures, by so much is God's work more excellent than mine. It was from His immeasurable love that God set our happiness in suffering,[7] for we undergo more than we act, and receive incomparably more than we give; and each gift that we receive prepares us to receive yet another gift, indeed a greater one, and every divine gift further increases our receptivity and the desire to receive something yet higher and greater. Therefore some teachers say that it is in *this* respect the soul is commensurate with God. For just as God is boundless in giving, so too the soul is boundless in receiving or conceiving. And just as God is omnipotent to act, so too the soul is no less profound to suffer, and thus she is transformed with God and in God.[8] God *must* act and the soul must suffer, He must know and love Himself in her, she must know with His knowledge and love with His love, and thus she is far more with what is His than with her own, and so too her bliss is more dependent on His action than on her own.

The pupils of St Dionysius asked him why Timothy surpassed them all in perfection. Dionysius replied: 'Timothy is a God-suffering man. Whoever is expert at this could outstrip all men.'

In this way your unknowing is not a lack but your chief perfection, and your suffering your highest activity. And so in this way you must cast aside all your deeds and silence your faculties, if you really wish to experience this birth in you. If you would find the newborn King, you must outstrip and abandon all else that you might find.

That we may outstrip and cast behind us all things un-pleasing to the newborn King, may He help us who became a human child in order that we might become the children of God. Amen.

Notes

1. Cf. 1, note 9.
2. Cf. 1, notes 14 and 15.
3. Cf. Eccles. 1:16 (Q).
4. Archimedes, who is said to have been killed by a Roman soldier while making geometrical drawings in the dust in his own garden at Syracuse (212 B.C.).
5. i.e. those in heaven, not the 'saints', as Miss Evans translates.
6. This is, as Quint points out, the same as the *Docta ignorantia* of Nicholas Cusanus (1401-1464).
7. MHG *lîden* means both 'suffering' and 'passivity'.
8. *In gote* (dative), not, as Miss Evans translates, 'into God'.

SERMON THREE[1]
(Pf 3)

IN HIS QUAE PATRIS MEI SUNT, OPORTET ME ESSE
(Luke 2:49)

"I must be about my Father's business". This text is most appropriate to what we have to say concerning the eternal birth which took place in time[2] and still happens daily in the innermost part of the soul, in her ground, remote from all adventitious events.[3] In order to become aware of this interior birth it is above all necessary for a man to be concerned with his Father's business.

What are the Father's attributes? Power is ascribed to Him more than to the other two Persons. And so, none assuredly can experience or approach this birth without a mighty effort. A man cannot attain to this birth except by withdrawing his senses from all things. And that requires a mighty effort to drive back the powers of the soul and inhibit their functioning. This must be done with force, without force it cannot be done.[4] As Christ said: "The kingdom of heaven suffers violence, and the violent take it by force" (Matt. 11:12).

A question arises about this birth of which we have spoken: Does it happen continuously, or at intervals, when a man applies himself to it and exerts himself with all his might to forget all things and be conscious in this alone? Now note the explanation. Man has an active intellect, a passive intellect and a potential intellect.[5] The *active* intellect is ever ready to act, whether it be in God or in creatures, for it exerts itself rationally in creatures in the

25

way of ordering the creatures, and bringing them back to their source, or in raising itself, to the honour and glory of God. All that is in its power and its domain, and hence its name *active*. But when God undertakes the work, the mind must remain *passive*. But potential intellect pays regard to both, to the activity of God *and* the passivity of the soul, so that this may be achieved as far as possible. In the one case there is activity, where the mind does the work itself; in the other case there is passivity, when God undertakes the work, and then the mind should, nay must, remain still and let God act. Now before this is begun by the mind and completed by God, the mind has a prevision of it, a potential knowledge that it can come to be thus. This is the meaning of 'potential intellect', though often it is neglected and never comes to fruition. But when the mind strives with all its might and with real sincerity, then God takes charge of the mind and its work, and then the mind sees and experiences[6] God. But since this enduring and vision of God places an intolerable strain on the mind while in this body, God accordingly withdraws at times from the mind, and that is why he said: "A little while you shall see me, and again a little while you shall not see me" (cf. John 16:16).

When our Lord took his three disciples with him up the mountain and had shown them privately the illumination of his body which he had through union with the Godhead, and which we too shall have at the resurrection of the body, St Peter at once, on seeing it, wished to remain there always. Indeed, when a man finds the good he cannot easily part from it in so far as it is good. Where this is recognised by knowledge, love must needs follow, and memory, and all the (powers of) the soul. And our Lord, well knowing this, is constrained to hide at times, for the soul is a simple form of the body, and wherever she turns, she turns as a whole. Were she always conscious of the good which is God, im-mediately and without interruption, she would never be able to leave it to influence the body.

Thus it befell Paul: if he had remained for a hundred years at the spot where he came to know the Good,[7] he would never have returned to the body, he would have forgotten it completely. And so, because that is not con-ducive to this life and alien to it, God in His mercy veils it when He will and reveals it when He will and when He knows, like a trustworthy physician, that it is most use-ful and helpful for you. This withdrawal is not yours, but His who does the work: He can do it or not as He will, well knowing when it avails you best. It is in His hands to reveal or conceal, according as He knows you can endure it. For God is not a destroyer of nature: rather He perfects it, and God does this ever more and more, the more you are fitted for it.

But you might say, 'Oh sir, if this requires a mind free of all images and all works (which lie in the powers by their very nature[8]), then how about those outward works we must do sometimes, works of charity which all take place without, such as teaching or comforting the needy? Should people be deprived of this? As our Lord's disciples were so much occupied with such things, as (according to St Augustine) St Paul was so burdened and preoccupied with people's cares as if he were their father — shall we then be deprived of this great good because we are engaged in works of charity?'

27

Now note the answer to such questions. The one thing is noblest, the other very profitable. Mary was praised for choosing the best; but Martha's life was of very great profit, for she served Christ and his disciples.[9] St Thomas says the active life is better than the contemplative, in so far as in action one pours out for love that which one has gained in contemplation. It is actually the same thing, for we take only from the same ground of contemplation and make it fruitful in works, and thus the object of contemplation is achieved. Though there is motion, yet it is all one; it comes from one end, which is God, and returns to the same, as if I were to go from one end of this house to the other; that would indeed be motion, but only of one in the same. Thus too, in this activity, we remain in a state of contemplation in God. The one rests in the other, and perfects the other. For God's purpose in the union of contemplation is fruitfulness in works: for in contemplation you serve yourself alone, but in works of charity you serve the many.

To this Christ admonishes us by his whole life and those of all his saints, every one of whom he drove forth into the world to teach the multitude. St Paul said to Timothy, "Beloved, preach the Word" (2 Tim. 4:2). Did he mean the outward word that beats the air? Surely not. He meant the inwardly born and yet hidden Word that lies secreted in the soul. That was what he bade him preach aloud, that it might be made known to and might nourish the (soul's) powers, so that a man might give himself out in all those aspects of external life in which his fellow-men had need of it — and that all this may be found in *you* to accomplish to the best of your ability. It must be within you in thought, in intellect, and in will, and it must shine forth, too, in your deeds. As Christ said, "Let your light shine forth before men" (Matt. 5:16). He had in mind those who care only for the contemplative life and neglect the practice of charity, which, they say, they have no further need for, having passed that stage. It was not these that Christ meant when he said: "The seed fell on good soil and yielded fruit a hundredfold" (Matt. 13:8). He meant *them* when he said: "The tree that bears no fruit shall be cut down" (Matt. 3:10, 7:19).

Now you might say, 'But sir, what of the silence you told us so much about? For *this* implies images galore. Every act must accord with its appropriate image, whether the act is internal or external, whether I am teaching one or comforting another, or arranging this or that, so what quiet can I get?[10] For if the mind sees and formulates, and the will wills and memory holds it fast, are not all these images?'

Now observe. We spoke just now of an active intellect and a passive intellect. The active intellect abstracts images from outward things, stripping them of matter and of accidents, and introduces them to the passive intellect, begetting their mental image therein. And the passive intellect, made pregnant by the active in this way, cherishes and knows these things with the aid of the active intellect. Even then, the passive intellect cannot keep on knowing these things unless the active intellect illumines them afresh. Now observe: what the active intellect does for the natural man, that and far more God does for one with detachment: He *takes away* the active intellect from him and, installing Himself in its stead, He Himself undertakes all that the active intellect ought to be doing.

Indeed, when a man is quite unpreoccupied, and the active intellect within him is silent, then God *must* take up the work and must be the master-workman who begets Himself in the passive intellect. See if it is not so. The active intellect cannot give what it has not got: and it cannot entertain two images together, it has first one and then the other. Though the air and light show many forms and colour all at once, you can only observe them one after the other. So too does the active intellect, which is similar. But when God acts in place of the active intellect, He engenders many images together in one point. For if God prompts you to a good deed, at once all your powers proffer themselves for all good things: your whole mind at once tends to good in general. Whatever good you can do takes shape and presents itself to you together in a flash, concentrated in a single point. Surely, this demonstrates and proves that it is not the intellect's work, for it has not the perfection or the resources for this: rather it is the work and the offspring of Him who has all images at once in Himself. As Paul says: "I can do all things in Him who strengthens me" (Phil. 4:13); in Him I can do not merely this or that but all things in undivided unity. You must know, then, that the images of these acts are not yours. Neither are they from nature: they belong to the author of nature, in which He has implanted act and image. So do not lay claim to it, for it is His, not yours. Though conceived by you in time, it is begotten and given by God beyond time, in eternity beyond all images.

You might ask, 'Since my intellect is divested of its natural activity and no longer has any image or action of its own, where is its support? For it must always find lodgement somewhere: the powers always seek to fasten on something and act on it, whether it be memory, intellect or will.'

Now note the explanation of this. Intellect's object and lodgement is essence, not accident,[11] but pure un-mixed being in itself. When the intellect discerns true being it descends on it, comes to rest on it, pronouncing its intellectual word about the object it has seized on. But, so long as the intellect does not find true being and does not penetrate to the ground, so as to be able to say, 'this is this, it is such and not otherwise', so long does it remain in a condition of questing and expectation, it does not settle down or rest, but labours on, seeking, expecting and rejecting. And though it may perhaps spend a year or more investigating a natural truth, to see what it is, it still has to work long again to strip off what it is *not*. All this time it has nothing to go by and makes no pronounce-ment at all, as long as it has not penetrated to the ground of truth with full realisation. Therefore, the intellect never rests in this life. However much God may reveal Himself in this life, yet it is still as nothing to what He really *is*. Though truth is there, in the ground, it is yet veiled and concealed from the intellect. All this while, the intellect has no support to rest on in the way of a changeless object. It still does not rest, but goes on ex-pecting and preparing for something yet to become known, but so far hidden. Thus there is no way man can know what God *is*. But one thing he does know: what God is *not*. And this a man of intellect will reject. Mean-time the intellect, finding no real object to support it, waits as matter awaits form. Just as matter will never rest until it is filled with all forms, so the intellect cannot rest except in the essential truth that embraces all things. Only the essence will satisfy it, and this God withdraws from it step by step, in order to arouse its zeal and lure it on to seek and grasp the true, groundless good, so that it may be content with nothing but ever clamour for the highest good of all.

Now you might say, 'Oh sir, you said so much about how all our faculties should be quiet, and now you go setting up a great clamour of yearning in this quietness. That would be a great moaning and outcry for something we haven't got, and that would be the end of this peace and quiet. Whether it were desire or purpose or praise or thanksgiving, or whatever else the mind might beget or imagine — it would not be perfect peace or absolute still-ness.'

Let me explain. When you have completely stripped yourself of your own self, and all things and every kind of attachment, and have transferred, made over and abandoned yourself to God in utter faith and perfect love, then *whatever* is born in you or touches you, within or without, joyful or sorrowful, sour or sweet, that is no longer yours, it is altogether your God's to whom you have abandoned yourself. Tell me, whom does the spoken word belong to? To the speaker or the hearer? Though it falls to the hearer, it really belongs to the speaker who gave it birth. Here is an example. The sun casts its light into the air, the air receives the light and gives it to the earth, thus enabling us to distinguish different colours. Now, though the light is *formally* in the air, *essentially* it is in the sun: the light actually comes from the sun, where it originates, and not in the air. It is received by the air which passes it on to anything that is receptive to light. It is just the same with the soul. God bears the Word in the soul, and the soul conceives it and passes it on to her powers in varied guise: now as desire, now as good intent, now as charity, now as gratitude, or however it may affect you. It is all His, and not yours at all. What God thus does, you must accept all that as His and not as your own, just as it is written: 'The Holy Ghost makes intercession with countless mighty sighs' (Rom. 8:26). He prays within us, not we ourselves. St Paul says: "No man can say 'Lord Jesus Christ' but in the Holy Ghost" (1 Cor. 12:13).

This above all else is needful: you must lay claim to nothing! Let go of yourself and let God act with you and in you as He will. This work is His, this Word is His, this birth is His, in fact every single thing that you are. For you have abandoned self and have gone out of your (soul's) powers and their activities, and your personal nature. Therefore God must enter into your being and powers, because you have bereft yourself of all possessions, and become as a desert, as it is written: "The voice of one crying in the wilderness" (Matt. 3:3). Let this eternal voice cry out in you as it listeth, and be as a desert in respect of yourself and all things.

Now you might say, 'But sir, what must a man do to be void as a desert in respect of himself and all things? Should a man wait all the time for God to work and do nothing himself, or should he do something in the meantime, like praying or reading or some other good occupation such as listening to sermons or studying scripture?

33

Since such a man is not supposed to take anything in from
without, but only from within, from his God, does he not
miss something by not doing these things?

Now listen. All outward works were established and
ordained to direct the outer man to God and to train him
to spiritual living and good deeds, that he might not stray
into ineptitudes: to act as a curb on his inclination to
escape from self to things outside; so that when God
would work in him He might find him ready and not have
to draw him back from things alien and gross. For the
greater the delight in outward things the harder it is to
leave them, the stronger the love the sharper the pain when
it comes to parting.

See then: All works and pious practices — praying,
reading, singing, vigils, fasting, penance, or whatever
discipline it may be — these were invented to catch a man
and restrain him from things alien and ungodly. Thus,
when a man realises that God's spirit is not working in him
and that the inner man is forsaken by God, it is very important for the outer man to practise these virtues, and
especially such as are most feasible, useful and necessary
for him; not however from selfish attachment, but so that,
respect for truth preserving him from being attracted and
led astray by what is gross, he may stay close to God, so
that God may find him near at hand when He chooses to
return and act in his soul, without having to seek far afield.
But if a man knows himself to be well trained in true inwardness, then let him boldly drop all outward disciplines,
even those he is bound to and from which neither pope
nor bishop can release him. From the vows a man has
made to God none can release him, but they can be

turned into something else: for every vow is a contract with God. But if a man has taken solemn vows of such things as prayer, fasting or pilgrimage, if he then enters some order, he is released from them, for in the order he is vowed to goodness as a whole, and to God Himself.

And so I say the same here: Whatever a man's vows to manifold things, by entering into true inwardness he is released from them. As long as this inwardness lasts, be it a week, a month, or a year, none of this time is lost by the monk or nun, for God, who has captured and imprisoned them, must answer for it. On returning to himself, a man should perform his vows for the time present; but as for what you may think you have neglected in the preceding time, you need not bother to make it up, for God Himself will make it up for the period during which He caused you to be idle. You should not wish to make it up by any act of creatures, for the least act of God outweighs all the works of creatures.

This is said to learned and illumined people, who have been taught and illumined by God and scripture. But how is it with a simple layman who knows and understands nothing but corporal discipline, and who has taken on some vow, whether of prayer or the like? To him I say this: If he finds it hampering and that he draws nearer to God without it, let him boldly give it up. For any work that brings you nearer to God and God's embrace is the best. That is what Paul meant when he said: "When wholeness comes, the partial vanishes" (1 Cor. 13:10). There is a big difference between a vow taken before a priest and vows taken in simplicity to God Himself. If a man vows anything to God it is with the laudable intention of binding himself thus to God, which at the time a man thinks to be for the best. But if he learns of a better way, then, knowing by experience that it is better, let him be quite free of the first, and content.

This is easy to prove, for one should consider the fruits and the inward truth rather than the outward act. As Paul says: "The letter (that is, all outward practices) kills, but the spirit gives life" (2 Cor. 3:6), that is, an inward realisation of truth. You should take good note of this and follow above all whatever befits you best for this. Your spirit should be elevated, not downcast, but rather ardent, and yet in a detached, quiet stillness. No need to tell God what you need or desire: He already knows. Christ said to his disciples: "When you pray, do not use many words in your prayers like the Pharisees, for they think to be heard with much speaking" (Matt. 6:7).

That we may here so seek this peace and inward silence, that the eternal Word may be spoken within us and understood, and that we may become one therewith, may the Father help us, and that Word, and the Spirit of both. Amen.

Notes

1. Quint (QT p. 525) doubts the authenticity of this sermon. But cf. *LW* IV, 102.
2. The historical birth of Jesus as distinct from the 'eternal birth'.
3. *zuoval*, i.e. 'accidentals' in the scholastic sense.
4. This stress on force (*gewalt*) seems rather un-Eckhartian.
5. Eckhart as a Dominican places the intellect above the will, as opposed to the Franciscans. He had debated this question in Paris with the Franciscan General Gonsalvus.
6. *lîdet*, lit. 'suffers': cf. 2, note 2.
7. On the road to Damascus.

8. i.e. the eye cannot help seeing, and so on.

9. In the commentary to St John's Gospel (*LW* III, 112), Eckhart places Mary above Martha, according to tradition (Clark). The contradiction is more apparent than real.

10. Eckhart the busy administrator must have been acutely aware of this problem.

11. See note 3.

SERMON FOUR

(Pf 4, QT 59)

ET CUM FACTUS ESSET JESUS ANNORUM DUODECIM ETC.

(Luke 2:42)

We read in the Gospel that when our Lord was twelve years old he went with Joseph and Mary to the Temple in Jerusalem, and when they left, Jesus stayed behind in the Temple without their knowing; when they reached home and missed him, they sought him among acquaintances, among their kindred and amidst the throng, and they could not find him. They had lost him in the crowd. And so they had to go back to where they had come from. And when they got back to their starting-point, the Temple, they found him.

And so in truth, if you would find this noble birth,[1] you must leave the crowd and return to the source and ground whence you came. All the powers of the soul, and all their works — these are the crowd. Memory, understanding and will, they all diversify you, and therefore you must leave them all: sense-perceptions, imagination, or whatever it may be that in which you find or seek to find yourself. After that, you *may* find this birth but not otherwise — believe me! He was never yet found among friends, nor among kindred or acquaintances: there, rather, one loses him altogether. Accordingly the question arises, whether a man can find this birth in any things which, though divine, are yet brought in from without through the senses, such as any ideas about God as being good, wise, compassionate, or anything the intellect can conceive

39

in itself that is in fact divine — whether a man can find this birth in all these. In fact, he cannot. For although all this is good and divine, it is all brought in from without through the senses. But all must well up from within, out of God, if this birth is to shine forth truly and clearly, and all your activity must cease, and all your powers must serve His ends, not your own. If this work is to be done, God alone must do it, and you must just suffer it to be. Where you truly go out from *your* will and *your* knowledge, God with His knowledge surely and willingly goes in and shines there clearly. Where God will thus know Himself, there *your* knowledge cannot subsist and is of no avail. Do not imagine that your reason can grow to the knowledge of God. If God is to shine divinely in you, your natural light cannot help towards this end. Instead, it must become pure nothing and go out of itself altogether, and *then* God can shine in with His light, and He will bring back in with Him all that you forsook and a thousand times more, together with a new form to contain it all. Of this we have a parable in the Gospel. When our Lord had spoken in such friendly fashion to the Gentile woman at the well, she left her pitcher and ran to the town announcing to the people that the true Messiah had come. The people, not believing her words, went out with her and saw for themselves. *Then* they said to her: "Now we believe, not because of your words: we believe rather because we have seen him ourselves" (John 4:42). So in truth, no creaturely skill, nor your own wisdom nor all your knowledge can enable you to know God divinely. For you to know God in God's way, your knowing must become a pure unknowing, and a forgetting of yourself

40

and all creatures.

Now you might say, 'Well sir, what use *is* my intellect then, if it is supposed to be empty and functionless? Is *that* the best thing for me to do — to raise my mind to an unknowing knowledge that can't really exist? For if I knew anything at all it would not be ignorance, and I should not be empty and bare. Am I supposed to be in total darkness?'

Certainly. You cannot do better than to place yourself in darkness and in unknowing.

'Oh sir, must everything go then, and is there no turning back?'

No indeed, by rights there is no returning.

'But what *is* this darkness? What do you call it? What is its name?'

The only name it has is 'potential receptivity', which certainly does not lack being nor is it deficient, but it is the *potential* of receptivity in which you will be perfected. That is why there is no turning back from it. But if you do turn back, that is not on account of any truth, but because of something else — the senses, the world or the devil. And if you give way to the impulse to turn back, you are bound to lapse into sin, and you may backslide so far as to fall eternally. Therefore there is no turning back, but only a pressing forward, so as to attain and achieve this possibility. It never rests until it is filled with all being. Just as matter never rests till it is filled with every possible form, so too intellect never rests till it is filled to its capacity.

On this point a pagan master says: 'Nature has nothing swifter than the heavens, for they surpass all else in

41

swiftness'. Yet surely the mind of man outstrips them by its speed! If only it were to retain its potentiality intact, remaining undefiled and unrent by base and gross things, it would outstrip the highest heaven, never ceasing till it reached the summit, there to be fed and cherished by the Greatest Good.

As for what it profits you to pursue this possibility, to keep yourself empty and bare, just following and tracking this darkness and unknowing without turning back — it contains the chance to gain Him who is all things. And the more barren you are of self and unwitting of all things, the nearer you are to Him. Of this barrenness it is said in Jeremiah: "I will lead my beloved into the wilderness and will speak to her in her heart".[2] The true word of eternity is spoken only in solitude, where a man is a desert and alien to himself and multiplicity. For this desolate self-estrangement the prophet longed, saying: "Who will give me the wings of a dove that I may fly away and be at rest?" (Ps. 55:6). Where does one find peace and rest? There, truly, where there is rejection, desolation and estrangement from all creatures. Therefore David says: "I would rather be rejected and spurned in the house of my God than dwell with great honour and wealth in the tavern of sinners" (Ps. 84:10).

Now you might say, 'Oh sir, is it really always necessary to be barren and estranged from everything, outward and inward: the powers and their work, must that all go? It is a grievous matter for God to leave a man without support, as the prophet says "Woe is me that my exile is prolonged" (Ps. 120:5), if God prolongs my exile here, without either enlightening or encouraging me or working within me, as your teaching implies. If a man is in such a state of pure nothingness, is it not better to do something to beguile the gloom and desolation, such as praying or listening to sermons or doing something else that is virtuous, so as to help himself?'

No, be sure of this. Absolute stillness for as long as possible is best of all for you. You cannot exchange this state for any other without harm. That is certain. You would like to partly prepare yourself and partly let God prepare you, but this cannot be. You cannot think or desire to prepare yourself more quickly than God can move in to prepare you. But even if it were shared, so that you did the preparing and God did the working or the infusion — which is impossible — then you should know that God *must* act and pour Himself into you the moment He finds you ready. Do not imagine that God is like a human carpenter, who works or not as he likes, who can do or leave undone as he wishes. It is different with God: as and when God finds you ready, He has to act, to overflow into you, just as when the air is clear and pure the sun has to burst forth and cannot refrain. It would surely be a grave defect in God if He performed no great works in you and did not pour great goodness into you whenever He found you thus empty and bare.

In the same sense the masters write that in the very instant the material substance of the child is ready in the mother's womb, God at once pours into the body its living spirit which is the soul, the body's form. It is one instant, the being ready and the pouring in. When nature reaches her highest point, God gives grace: the very instant the spirit is ready, God enters without hesitation or delay. In the Book of Secrets it says that our Lord declared to mankind: "I stand at the door knocking and waiting; whoever lets me in, with him I will sup" (Rev. 3.20). You need not seek Him here or there, He is no further than the door of your heart; there He stands patiently awaiting whoever is ready to open up and let Him in. No need to call to Him from afar: He can hardly wait for you to open up. He longs for you a thousand times more than you long for Him: the opening and the entering are a single act.

Now you might say, 'How can that be? I can't feel Him.' — Pay attention. Your being aware of Him is not in your power but in His. When it suits Him He shows Himself, and He can hide when He wishes. This is what Christ meant when he said to Nicodemus:"The spirit breathes where it will: you hear its voice but do not know where it comes from, or where it is going" (John 3:8). In so speaking he contradicted himself: "You hear, yet know not." By hearing we come to know. Christ meant that by hearing it is imbibed or absorbed, as if to say: you receive it, but unawares. You should know, God cannot leave anything void or unfilled, God and nature cannot endure that anything should be empty or void. And so, even if you think you can't feel Him and are wholly empty of Him, that is not the case. For if there were anything empty under heaven, whatever it might be, great or small, the heavens would either draw it up to themselves or else, bending down, would have to fill it with themselves. Therefore, stand still and do not waver from your emptiness; for at this time you can turn away, never to turn back again.

Now you might say: 'Well sir, since you are always

assuming that some day this birth will occur in me, that the Son will be born in me — now, can I have any sign by which to recognise that this *has* taken place?'

Yes indeed! There are three certain signs. I will tell you just one of them. I am often asked if a man can reach the point where he is no longer hindered by time, multiplicity, or matter. Assuredly! Once this birth has really occurred, no creatures can hinder you; instead, they will all direct you to God and this birth. Take lightning as an analogy. Whatever it strikes, whether tree, beast or man, it turns at once towards itself. A man with his back towards it is instantly turned round to face it. If a tree had a thousand leaves, they would all turn right side up towards the stroke. So it is with all in whom this birth occurs, they are promptly turned towards this birth with all they possess, be it never so earthy. In fact, what used to be a hindrance now helps you most. Your face is so fully turned towards this birth that, no matter what you see or hear, you can get nothing but this birth from all things. All things become simply God to you, for in all things you notice only God, just as a man who stares long at the sun sees the sun in whatever he afterwards looks at. If *this* is lacking, this looking for and seeking God in all and sundry, then you lack this birth.

Now you might ask, 'Ought anyone so placed to practise penance? Does he lose anything by dropping penitential exercises?'

Pay attention. Penitential exercises, among other things, were instituted for a particular purpose: whether it be fasting, watching, praying, kneeling, being disciplined,[3] wearing hair-shirts, lying hard or whatever it may be, the reason for all that is because body and flesh are always opposed to spirit. The body is often too strong for the spirit, and there is a real fight between them, an unceasing struggle. Here in the world the body is bold and strong, for it is at home, the world helps it, the earth is its father-land, it is helped by all its kin: food, drink, soft living — all is opposed to spirit. The spirit is an alien here, but in heaven are its kin, its whole race: *there* it has good friends, if it strives for there and makes its home there. And so, in order to succour the spirit in this alien realm, and to im-pede the flesh somewhat in this strife lest it should conquer the spirit, we put on it the bridle of penitential practices, thus curbing it so that the spirit can resist it. All this is done to bring it under control; but if you would capture and curb it in a thousand times better fashion, then put on it the bridle of love! With love you overcome it most surely, with love you load it most heavily. Therefore God lies in wait for us with nothing so much as with love. For love resembles the fisherman's hook. The fisherman cannot get the fish till it is caught on the hook. Once it takes the hook, he is sure of the fish; twist and turn as it may, this way or that, he is assured of his catch. And so I say of love: he who is caught by it has the strongest of bonds, and yet a pleasant burden. He who has taken up this sweet burden fares further and makes more progress than by all the harsh practices any men use. And, too, he can cheer-fully bear and endure all that befalls him, whatever God inflicts on him, and can also cheerfully forgive whatever evil is done to him. Nothing brings you closer to God or makes God so much your own as the sweet bond of love. A man who has found this way need seek no other. He who hangs on this hook is caught so fast that foot and hand, mouth, eyes and heart, and all that is man's, belongs only to God.

Therefore you cannot better prevail over this foe[4] and prevent him from harming you, than by love. Therefore it is written: "Love is as strong as death and as hard as hell" (Cant. 8:6). Death separates soul from body, but love separates all things from the soul — it will not tolerate what is not God or God's. Whoever is caught in this net, whoever walks in this way, whatever he does is all one: whether he does anything or nothing is of no account. And yet the least action or practice of such a man is more profitable and fruitful to himself and all men, and more pleasing to God, than all the works of others who, though free from mortal sin, are inferior to him in love. His rest is more useful than another's labour. Therefore, just watch for this hook, so as to be blessedly caught: for the more you are caught, the more you are free.

That we may be thus caught and freed, may He help us who is love itself. Amen.

Notes

1. The transition is a little abrupt: we are back with Eckhart's constant theme of the birth of the Word in the soul. cf. 1, note 4.
2. Actually Hosea 2:14.
3. i.e. scourged.
4. The body.

SERMON FIVE
(Pf 5, Q 65)

DEUS CHARITAS EST ET QUI MANET IN CHARITATE IN DEO

MANET ET DEUS IN EO

(1 John 4:16)

"God is love, and he who dwells in love dwells in God, and God in him". Let us take the first phrase: "God is love". That is so, because whatever can love and is capable of loving, that He compels with His love, to love Him. "God is love", secondly, because everything God ever created and that is capable of loving, that compels *Him* by its love to love *it*, whether He will or no. Thirdly, "God is love" because with His love He drives everything that is capable of loving out of all plurality. As far as God is lovable in plurality, the love that He is drives this out of all plurality into His own oneness. "God is love", fourthly, because with His love He gives all creatures their being and life, and maintains them with His love.

Should anyone ask what God is, this is what I should now say: that God is love, and in fact so loveable that all creatures seek to love His loveableness, whether they know it or not, or whether they wish to or not. So much is God love, and so loveable, that everything that *can* love *must* love Him, whether it will or no. There is no creature so worthless that it could love anything evil; for whatever one loves must either seem good or be good. Now if we gather up all the good that all creatures can do — that is pure badness compared with God. St Augustine says: 'Love what you can gain with love, and keep that which can satisfy your soul'.

"God is love". Now, my children, I beg you to mark my words. God loves my soul so much that His life and being depend on His loving me, whether He would or no. To stop God loving my soul would be to deprive Him of His Godhead; for God is as truly love as He is truth; and as truly as He is goodness, He is love. That is the bare truth, as God lives. There were certain masters[1] who declared that the love that is in us is the Holy Ghost, but that is not true. The bodily food we take is changed into us, but the spiritual food we receive changes us into itself; therefore divine love is not taken into us, for that would make two things. But divine love takes us into itself, and we are one with it. The paint on the wall[2] is maintained by the wall; thus all creatures are maintained in existence by love, which is God. If you took the paint from the wall, it would lose its existence: so all things would lose their existence if deprived of love, which is God.

"God is love and he who dwells in love dwells in God, and God dwells in him".

There is a difference between spiritual things and bodily things. Every spiritual thing can dwell in another; but nothing bodily can exist in another. There may be water in a tub, and the tub surrounds it, but where the wood is, there is no water. In this sense no material thing dwells in another, but every spiritual thing does dwell in another. Every single angel is in the next with all his joy, with all his happiness and all his beatitude as perfectly as in himself; and every angel with all his joy and all his beatitude is in me, and so is God Himself with all His beatitude, though I know it not. Take the lowest angel in his pure nature: the smallest splinter or spark that ever fell from him would suffice to light up the whole world with bliss and joy. Just see how splendid he is in himself! Now I have sometimes said further that the angels are beyond all number and quantity. But now I will leave aside love and come to knowledge: if only we knew them,[3] it would be easy to abandon a whole world. Whatever God ever made or shall yet make — if God were to give all that entire to my soul and God with it, and if so much as a hair's breadth remained behind, it would not satisfy my soul; I should not be happy. If I am happy, then all things are in me, and God. Where I am, there God is; and then I am in God, and where God is, there I am.

"He who dwells in love dwells in God, and God dwells in him". If then I am in God, then where God is, I am and where I am, there God is, unless the scriptures lie. Where I am, there God is: that is the bare truth, and is as truly true as that God is God. "Faithful servant, I will set you over all my goods" (Matt. 25:21). That is to say: inasmuch as God is good in all creatures, so, in accordance with their manifoldness I will "set you over all my goods". Secondly, "I will set you over all my goods" means: whence all creatures derive their blessedness, in the pure unity that is God Himself, whence He draws His own felicity, that is to say: inasmuch as God is good, He will "set us over all His goods". Thirdly, He will set us over all His goods, that is to say: over everything that He is *called*, over everything one can put into words and over everything that one can understand. *Thus* He will set us over all His goods.

"Father, I pray Thee to make them one, as I and Thou

are one"(John 17:20). Where two are to become one, one of them must lose its being. So it is: and if God and your soul are to become one, your soul must lose her being and her life. As far as anything remained, they would indeed be *united*, but for them to become *one*, the one must lose its identity and the other must keep its identity: then they are one. Now the Holy Ghost says: "let them be one as we are one".[4] "I pray Thee, make them *one* in us."

'I pray Thee'. When I pray for aught, my prayer goes for naught; when I pray for naught, I pray as I ought.[5] When I am united with That wherein all things are existent whether past, present or future, they are all equally near and equally one; they are all in God and all in *me*. Then there is no need to think of Henry or Conrad.[6] If one prays for aught but God alone, that can be called idolatry or unrighteousness. They pray aright who "pray in spirit and in truth" (John 4:24). If I pray for someone, for Henry or Conrad, I pray at my weakest. When I pray for nobody and for nothing, then I am praying most truly, for in God is neither Henry nor Conrad. If we pray to God for aught else but God, that is wrong and faithless and a kind of imperfection, for it is to set up something beside God. As I said recently, that is wanting to make a nothing of God, and to make God out of nothing.[7] "God is love, and he who dwells in love is in God, and God is in him".

May we all attain this love of which I have spoken. So help us our beloved Lord Jesus Christ. Amen.

Notes

1. Peter Lombard and St Thomas Aquinas (Q).
2. Miss Evans translates 'the colour from the cloth'. This is a

mistranslation, though the more intimate penetration of cloth by the dye would seem a better image. In another sermon (No.77), Eckhart in fact uses both images.

3. The angels.

4. i.e., as the three Persons of the Trinity are one — a point Eckhart frequently stresses.

5. I have followed Miss Evans's nice play on words here: though not in the original, it hits the sense most happily.

6. Or Tom, Dick and Harry. In modern German 'Hinz und Kunz'.

7. i.e. to make God out of creatures (Q).

SERMON SIX
(Pf 6, Q1, QT1)

INTRAVIT JESUS IN TEMPLUM DEI ET EJICIEBAT OMNES
VENDENTES ET EMENTES
(Matt. 21:12)

We read in the holy gospel that our Lord went into the
Temple and cast out those that bought and sold, and said
to them that sold doves and the like: "Take these things
hence! Take these things away!" Why did Jesus cast out
those that bought and sold and bid those that sold doves
take them hence? His intention was none other than to
have the Temple cleared, just as if he had said: I have a
right to this temple and I want it to myself to be lord
therein. What is the meaning of this? This temple, in which
God would rule with authority, according to His will, is
man's soul, which He has made exactly like Himself, just
as we read that the Lord said: "Let us make man in our
image and likeness" (Gen. 1:26). And this He did. So like
Himself has God made man's soul that nothing else in
heaven or on earth, of all the splendid creatures that God
has so joyously created, resembles God so much as the
human soul. For this reason God wants this temple cleared,
that He may be there all alone. This is because this temple
is so agreeable to Him, because it is so like Him and He is
so comfortable in this temple when He is alone there.

Now then, consider, who were they who bought and
sold there, and who are they still? Take proper note: I will
speak now in this sermon of none but *good* people. Yet
even so, I will now point out who the merchants were —

55

and still are — that thus bought and sold, whom our Lord struck and cast out. He still does so to those who buy and sell in this temple: he would not leave a single one of them therein. See, those are all merchants who, while avoiding mortal sin and wishing to be virtuous, do good works to the glory of God, such as fasts, vigils, prayers and the rest, all kinds of good works, but they do them in order that our Lord may give them something in return, or that God may do something they wish for — all these are merchants. That is plain to see, for they want to give one thing in exchange for another, and so to barter with our Lord. But they are mistaken in the bargain, for if they gave all that they have and have the power to do, for God's sake, and exhausted themselves purely for God's sake, God would not have to give them anything or do anything for them, unless He did it freely and for nothing. For what they are, they are from God, and what they have, they get from God and not from themselves. And so God is in no way bound to requite them for their acts or gifts, unless He freely does so of His grace, and not for what they do or give; for they give not of their own, nor do they act of themselves, as Christ himself says: "Without me you can do nothing" (John 15:5). They are very foolish folk who would bargain thus with our Lord; they know little or nothing of the truth. That is why God cast them out of the Temple and drove them away. Light and darkness cannot exist together. God is the truth, He is the light in Himself. When God enters the Temple He drives out ignorance, which is darkness, and reveals Himself in light and in truth. The merchants must go when truth is revealed, for truth needs no merchandising. God seeks not His own:

He is perfectly free in His acts, which He does out of true love. So does that man who is at one with God: he is perfectly free in all his deeds, he does them for love, without 'why?'[1] – solely to glorify God and not seeking his own therein, and God works in him.

I say further: as long as a man, in all his doings, desires anything at all that God can or will give, still he ranks with these merchants. If you would be free of any taint of trading, so that God may let you enter this temple, then you must do all that you can in all your works, solely to God's glory, and be as free of it as Naught is free, which is neither here nor there.[2] You should ask nothing whatever in return. Whenever you act thus, your works are spiritual and godly, and the merchants are driven right out of the temple, and God is in there alone, for one is thinking only of God. See, that is how your temple is cleared of merchants! The man who considers neither himself nor anything else but God alone and God's glory, he is truly free from all taint of commerce in his deeds, and seeks naught of his own just as God is entirely free in all His works and seeks not His own.

I have also told how our Lord said to those that sold doves: "Take this away! Take this hence!" He did not drive these people out or rebuke them harshly, but said quite mildly "take this away!", as though to say it is not wrong, but it is a hindrance to the pure truth. These are all good people, they work purely for God's sake, not for themselves, but they work with attachment,[3] according ing to time and tide,[4] before and after. These activities hinder them from attaining the highest truth, from being absolutely free and unhindered as our Lord Jesus Christ is absolutely free and unhindered, and conceives himself ever anew without pause and out of time from his heavenly Father, and in that same Now is perpetually born back with praise and thanksgiving, perfect, into the Father's majesty with an equal glory. Thus, to be receptive to the highest truth, and to live therein, a man must needs be without before and after, untrammelled by all his acts or by any images he ever perceived, empty and free, receiving the divine gift in the eternal Now, and bearing it back unhindered in the light of the same with praise and thanksgiving in our Lord Jesus Christ. Then the 'doves' would be gone, that is the hindrance and the attachment to works, good in themselves, in which a man seeks anything of his own. Therefore our Lord said kindly: "Take this hence, take this away!," as if to say, 'It is good, yet it stands in the way.'

When the temple is thus free of obstructions (that is attachment and ignorance), then it glistens with beauty, shining out bright and fair above the whole of God's creation, and through all God's creation, so that none can equal its brilliance but the uncreated God alone. In very truth, there is none like this temple but the uncreated God Himself. Nothing below the angels is the equal of this temple. The very highest angels are like this temple of the noble soul in many ways, but not in all. Their partial likeness to the soul lies in knowledge and in love. But there is a limit set them which they cannot pass. The soul can go further. If a soul, that of a man now living in time, were equal to the highest angel — still that man would have the potential freedom to soar infinitely far above that angel, ever anew, in every Now without number, and that means without mode: above the angelic mode and every created intelligence. God alone is free and uncreated, and thus He alone is like the soul in freedom, though not in uncreatedness, for she is created. And when she emerges into the unmixed light, she falls into her Nothingness[5] and in that Nothingness so far from the created Something, that of her own power she cannot return to her created Something. God with His uncreatedness upholds[6] her Nothingness and preserves her in His Something. The soul has dared to become nothing and so cannot of herself return to herself, for she has departed so far from herself before God comes to the rescue. That must needs be so, for, as I said, Jesus went into the Temple and cast out those who were buying and selling, and said to the others: "Take this hence!"

See, now I have come to the text: "Jesus went in and began saying, 'Take this hence.'" Observe that there was no one there but Jesus when he began to speak in the Temple. Be sure of this: if anyone else would speak in the temple (which is the soul) but Jesus, Jesus is silent, as if he were not at home — and he *is* not at home in the soul, for she has strange guests to talk to. But if Jesus is to speak in the soul, she must be all alone, and she has to be quiet herself to hear what he says. Well then, in he comes and starts speaking. What does the lord Jesus say? He says what he *is*[7]. What is he, then? He is a Word[8] of the Father. In this same Word the Father speaks Himself, all the divine nature and all that God is, just as He knows it, and He knows it as it *is*. And, being perfect in knowledge and power, so too He is perfect in speech. In speaking the Word, He utters the Word and all things in another Person[8] to whom He gives the same nature that He has himself. And he utters all rational spirits in that Word as equal to that Word according to their image as it dwells within (Him). Yet each image as it radiates forth, existing by itself, is not the same in all respects as the Word. Rather, they have received the power to attain to likeness by the grace of the same Word;[9] and this Word as it is in itself was spoken by the Father — the Word, and all that is in that Word.

Since this is spoken by the Father, then what is Jesus saying in the soul? As I have said, the Father speaks the Word; He speaks in this Word and not otherwise, and Jesus speaks in the soul. His manner of speaking is to reveal himself and what the Father said in him, according to the manner in which the spirit is able to receive it. He reveals the Father's authority in the spirit in an equal, immeasurable power. Receiving this power in the Son and through the Son, the spirit waxes mighty in everything it undertakes, so that it becomes equal and mighty in all virtues and in perfect purity, so that neither joy nor sorrow, nor anything God has created in time, can destroy that man, but he stands mightily there as if with divine power, in face of which all things are puny and futile.

Secondly, Jesus reveals himself in the soul in infinite wisdom, which is himself; in that Wisdom the Father knows Himself with all His paternal authority, and that same Word, which is Wisdom itself, and all that is therein, just as it is One. When this Wisdom is united with the soul, all doubt, all error and all darkness are entirely removed, she is set in a bright pure light which is God Himself, as the prophet says: "Lord, in Thy light shall we know the light"(Ps. 36:9). Then God is known by God in the soul; with this Wisdom she knows herself and all things, and this same Wisdom knows her with itself; and with the same Wisdom she knows the power of the Father in fruitful travail, and essential Being in simple unity void of all distinctions.

Jesus reveals himself, too, in infinite sweetness and richness, welling up and overflowing and pouring in from the power of the Holy Ghost, with superabundant richness and sweetness into all receptive hearts. When Jesus reveals himself with this richness and this sweetness, and is united with the soul, the soul flows with this richness and this sweetness into herself and beyond all things, by grace and with power, without means[10] back into her primal source. Then the outer man will be obedient to his inner man until death, and will be at all times at peace in the service of God for ever.

And that Jesus may come into us and clear out and cast away all hindrances of body and soul and make us one, as he is one with the Father and the Holy Ghost, one God, that we may become and remain eternally one with Him, so help us God. Amen.

Notes

1. Following Pfeiffer's text. Cf. in a Latin sermon (*LW* 1V, n. 21): 'Deus et per consequens homo divinus non agit propter cur aut quare' (God, and consequently the divine man, does not act on account of why or wherefore). See No. 43, and cf. Ueda, p. 155.
2. This is the more difficult (and therefore probably authentic) reading adopted by Quint (*als daz niht ledic ist, daz noch hie noch dâ enist*). Miss Evans, following Pfeiffer, has 'as though thou wert not.' See note 5.

3. Eckhart's word is *eigenschaft*, which, as Quint (QT 470) notes, is difficult to render, though perhaps more so into modern German than into English. Literally something like 'own-ness', it is not apparently used by Eckhart in the modern sense of 'quality, characteristic', but rather in that of 'possessiveness'. The idea is, I think, that of *appropriating* what is not really one's own.

4. Lit. 'time and number' *(mit zît und mit zal)*. I have adopted Clark's rendering, using an equivalent phrase that keeps the alliteration.

5. Middle High German *niht* (pronounced like modern German *nicht*) = 'nothing', intensified *nihtes niht*. The positive form *iht* = 'something'. The soul both 'is' and 'is not'. Quint explains that 'Nothing' here is not absolute nullity, but 'not being the soul', i.e. the negation of existence *as soul*.

6. *understât* = Latin *substat*: in scholastic terms, 'gives *substance* to' (Q).

7. Clark renders: 'He says that He is,' and refers to Exodus 3:14. This is grammatically possible, but is less likely in the context. I follow Evans and Quint.

8. This is of course the *Logos* (John 1:1), i.e. the Son in the Trinity.

9. The *Logos* or Word is of one nature with the Father. In so far as the 'images' (or Platonic ideas) of all rational beings are in God, they are one with the Word. In being 'radiated forth' — in the Creation — they are differentiated, but by grace they may regain the likeness with the Word (Q).

10. *âne mitel* (modern German *ohne Mittel*) = 'im-mediately,' with no mediation.

SERMON SEVEN
(Pf 7, Q 76, QT 35)

VIDETE QUALEM CHARITATEM DEDIT NOBIS PATER, UT FILII DEI NOMINEMUR ET SIMUS
(1 John 3:1)

You must know that this is in reality one and the same thing — to know God and to be known by God, to see God and to be seen by God. In knowing and seeing God we know and see that He makes us know and see. And just as the luminous air is not different from the fact of illuminating, for it illumines because it is luminous, so do we know by being known, and because He makes us know. Therefore Christ said: "Again you will see me" (John 16:26). That is to say, by making you see, you know me; and then follows: "Your heart will rejoice," that is in the vision and knowledge of me, and "no one shall rob you of your joy" (John 16:22).

St John says: "See how great is the love that the Father has shown us, that we are called and are the children of God" (1 John 3:1). He says not only "we are called" but "we *are*". So I say that just as a man cannot be wise without wisdom, so he cannot be a son without the filial nature of God's Son, without having the same being as the Son of God has — just as being wise cannot be without wisdom. And so, if you *are* the Son of God, you can only be so by having the same being of God that the Son has. But this is "now hidden from us;" and after that it is written: "Beloved, we are the sons of God." And what do we know? — That is what he adds: "and we shall be like

63

him" (1 John 3:2), that is, the same as he is: the same being, experiencing and understanding -- everything that he is, when we see him as God. So I say God could not make me the son of God if I had not the nature of God's Son, any more than God could make me wise if I had no wisdom. *How* are we God's sons? We do not know yet: "It does not yet appear" to us; all we know is that he says we shall be like Him. There are certain things that hide this knowledge in our souls and conceal it from us.

The soul has something in her, a spark of intellect, that never dies; and in this spark, as at the apex of the mind we place the 'image' of the soul. But there is also in our souls a knowing directed towards externals, the sensible and rational perception which operates in images and words to obscure this from us. How then are we God's sons? By sharing one nature with Him. But to have any realisation of thus being God's Son, we need to distinguish between the outward and the inward understanding. The inward understanding is that which is based intellectually in the nature of our soul. Yet it is not the soul's essence but is, rather, rooted there and is something of the life of the soul. In saying the understanding is the life of the soul we mean her *intellectual* life, and that is the life in which man is born as God's son and to eternal life. This understanding is timeless, without place — without Here and Now. In this life all things are one and all things are common: all things are all in all and all in one.

I will give you an example. In the body, all members are united and one, such that eye belongs to foot and foot to eye. If the foot could speak, it would say that the eye which is in the head was more its own than if it were in the foot, and the eye would say the same in reverse. And so I think that all the grace which is in Mary is more, and more truly an angel's and more in *him* — that which is in *Mary*! — than if it were in him or in the saints. For whatever Mary has, a saint has: the grace in Mary is more his, and he enjoys it more, than if it were in him.

But this interpretation is too gross and carnal, for it depends on bodily imagery. So I will give you another sense, which is more subtle and spiritual. I say that in the heavenly realm all is in all, and all is one, and all ours. The grace of our Lady exists in me (if I am there), not as welling up and flowing out of Mary, but rather as in me and as my own, and not of foreign origin. And so I say that what *one* has there, another has, not as *from* the other or *in* the other, but in *himself*, so that the grace that is in one is entirely in another as his *own* grace. Thus it is that spirit is in spirit. That is why I say that I cannot be the son of God unless I have the very same nature the Son of God has; and having this same nature makes us like him, and we see him as he is God. "But it is not yet revealed what we shall be." And so I say that in this sense there is no *likeness* and no *difference*, but rather, wholly without distinction we shall be the same in essence, in substance and in nature as he is in himself. But that is "not yet revealed": it will be revealed "when we see him as he is God."

God makes us knowing Him, and His being is His knowing, and His making me know is the same as my knowing; so His knowing is mine just as in the master, what he teaches is one and the same as, in the pupil, what he is taught. And since His knowing is mine, and since His substance is His knowing and His nature and His essence, it follows that His essence and His substance and His nature are mine. And if His substance, His being and His nature are mine, then I am the son of God. "See, brethren, what love God has bestowed on us that we should be called and should be the Son of God!"

Note *how* we are the Son of God — by having the same essence that the Son has.

'How can one be the Son of God, or how can one know it, since God is not like anybody?'

That is true, for Isaiah says: "To whom have you likened Him or what image will you give Him?" (Is. 40:18). Since it is God's nature not to be *like* anyone, we have to come to the state of being *nothing* in order to enter in to the same nature that He is. So, when I am able to establish myself in Nothing and Nothing in myself, uprooting and casting out what is in me, *then* I can pass into the naked being of God, which is the naked being of the spirit. All that smacks of *likeness* must be ousted that I may be transplanted into God and become one with Him: one substance, one being, one nature and the Son of God. Once this happens there is nothing hidden in God that is not revealed, that is not mine. *Then* I shall be wise and mighty and all else as He is, and one and the same with Him. Then, Sion will become truly seeing, and true Israel, a God-seeing man, from whom nothing in the Godhead is hidden. Then man is directed into God. But so that nothing may be hidden in God that is not revealed to me, there must appear to me nothing *like*, no image, for no image can reveal to us the Godhead or its essence. Should any image or any *likeness* remain in you, you would never be one with God. To be one with God, there must be in you nothing imagined or imaged forth, so that nothing is covered up in you that is not discovered or cast out.[1]

Observe the nature of defect. It comes from *nothing*.[2] So, what comes of nothing must be expunged from the soul: for so long as there is such defect in you, you are not God's son. Man laments and is sorrowful, solely on account of deficiency. And so, for man to become the Son of God, all *that* must be expunged and driven out, so that there is no more sorrow and lamentation. A man is not stone or wood, for that is all deficiency and nought. We shall not be like Him until this *nothing* is expelled so that we are all in all as God is all in all.

Man has a twofold birth: one *into* the world, and one *out of* the world, which is spiritual and into God. Do you want to know if your child is born, and if he is naked — whether you have in fact become God's son? If you grieve in your heart for anything, even on account of sin, your child is not yet born. If your heart is sore you are not yet a mother — but you *are* in labour and your time is near. So do not despair if you grieve for yourself or your friend — though it is not yet born, it is near to birth. But the child is fully born when a man's heart grieves for nothing: *then* a man has the essence and the nature and the substance and the wisdom and the joy and all that God has. *Then* the very being of the Son of God is ours and in us and we attain to the very essence of God.

Christ says: "Whoever would follow me, let him deny himself and take up his cross and follow me" (Matt. 16:24,

Mk. 8:34). That is, cast out all grief so that perpetual joy reigns in your heart. *Thus* the child is born. And then, if the child is born in me, the sight of my father and all my friends slain before my eyes would leave my heart untouched. For if my heart were moved thereby, the child would not have been born in me, though its birth might be near. I declare that God and the angels take such keen delight in every act of a good man that there is no joy like it. And so I say, if this child is born in you, then you have such great joy in every good deed that is done in the world that this joy becomes permanent and never changes. Therefore he says:"None will deprive you of your joy" (John 16:22). If I am fully transported into the divine essence, then God, and all that He has, is mine. Therefore He says: "I am the Lord thy God" (Ex. 20:2). That is when I have true joy, when neither pain nor sorrow can take it from me, for *then* I am installed in the divine essence, where sorrow has no place. For we see that in God there is no anger or sadness, but only love and joy. Though He seems sometimes to be wrathful with sinners it is not really wrath, it is love, for it comes from the great divine love: those He loves He chastens, for He is love, which is the Holy Ghost. And so God's anger springs from love, for His anger is without passion. And so, when you have reached the point where nothing is grievous or hard to you, and where pain is not pain to you, when everything is perfect joy to you, *then* your child has really been born.

Strive therefore to ensure that your child is not only being born, but is brought to birth, just as in God the Son is always being born and is brought to birth. And that this may be our lot, so help us God. Amen.

Notes

1. This presumably means that the entire contents of the unconscoius must be cleared.

2. cf. No. 6, note 5.

SERMON EIGHT
(Pf 8, Q 2, QT 2)

INTRAVIT JESUS IN QUODDAM CASTELLUM ET MULIER QUAEDAM

EXCEPIT ILLUM ETC.

(Luke 10:38)

I have first quoted this saying in Latin, it is written in the Gospel and in German it means: "Our Lord Jesus Christ went up into a citadel and was received by a virgin[1] who was a wife."[2]

Now mark this word carefully. It must of necessity be a virgin, the person by whom Jesus was received. 'Virgin' is as much as to say a person who is void of alien images, as empty as he was when he did not exist.[3] Now the question may be asked, how a man who has been born and has reached the age of rational understanding can be as empty of all images as he was when he was not; for he knows many things, all of which are images: so how can he be empty of them? Note the explanation which I shall give you. If I were possessed of sufficient understanding so as to comprehend within my own mind all the images ever conceived by all men, as well as those that exist in God Himself — if I had these without attachment, whether in doing or in leaving undone, without before and after but rather standing free in this present Now ready to receive God's most beloved will and to do it continually, then in truth I would be a virgin, untrammelled by any images, just as I was when I was not.

And yet I say that being a virgin by no means deprives a man of works that he has done: he yet remains virgin-free,

71

offering no hindrance to the highest Truth, even as Jesus is empty and free and virginal in himself. Since according to the masters union comes only by the joining of like to like, therefore that man must be a maiden, a virgin, who would receive the virgin Jesus.

Now attend, and follow me closely. If a man were to be ever virginal, he would bear no fruit. If he is to be fruitful, he must needs be a wife. 'Wife' is the noblest title one can bestow on the soul — far nobler than 'virgin'. For a man to receive God within him is good, and in receiving he is virgin. But for God to be fruitful in him is better, for only the fruitfulness of the gift is the thanks rendered for that gift, and herein the spirit is a wife, whose gratitude is fecundity, bearing Jesus again in God's paternal heart.

Many good gifts, received in virginity, are not reborn back into God in wifely fruitfulness and with praise and thanks. Such gifts perish and all comes to naught, and a man is no more blessed or the better for them. In this case his virginity is useless because to that virginity he does not add the perfect fruitfulness of a wife. Therein lies the mischief. Hence I have said, "Jesus went up into a citadel and was received by a virgin who was a wife." It must be thus, as I have shown you.

Married folk bring forth little more than one fruit in a year. But it is other wedded folk that I have in mind now: all those who are bound with attachment to prayer, fasting, vigils and all kinds of outward discipline and mortification. *All* attachment to any work that involves the loss of freedom to wait on God in the here and now, and to follow Him alone in the light wherein He would show you what to do and what not to do, every moment freely and anew, as if you had nothing else and neither would nor could do otherwise — *any* such attachment or set practice which repeatedly denies you this freedom, I call a *year*; for your soul will bear no fruit till it has done this work to which you are possessively attached, and you too will have no trust in God or in yourself before you have done the work you embraced with attachment, for otherwise you will have no peace. Thus you will bring forth no fruit till your work is done. That is what I call 'a year', and the fruit of it is paltry because it springs from attachment to the task and not from freedom. These, then, I call 'wedded folk', for they are bound by attachment. They bring forth little fruit, and paltry at that, as I have said.

A virgin who is a wife, is free and unfettered by attachment; she is always as near to God as to herself. She brings forth many and big fruits, for thay are neither more nor less than God Himself. *This* fruit and *this* birth that virgin bears who is a wife, bringing forth daily a hundred and a thousandfold! Numberless indeed are her labours begotten of the most noble ground or, to speak more truly, of the very ground where the Father ever begets His eternal Word:- it is thence she becomes fruitful and shares in the procreation. For Jesus, the light and splendour of the eternal heart (as St Paul says (Heb. 1:3), that he is the glory and splendour of the Father's heart and illumines the Father's heart with power), this same Jesus is made one with her and she with him, she is radiant and shining with him in one single unity, as one pure brilliant light in the paternal heart.

Elsewhere I have declared that there is a power in the soul[4] which touches neither time nor flesh, flowing from the spirit, remaining in the spirit, altogether spiritual. In this power, God is ever verdant and flowering in all the joy and all the glory that He is in Himself. *There* is such heartfelt delight, such inconceivably deep joy as none can fully tell of, for in this power the eternal Father is ever begetting His eternal Son without pause, in such wise that this power jointly begets the Father's Son and itself, this self-same Son, in the sole power of the Father. Suppose a man owned a whole kingdom or all the goods of this world; then suppose he gave it up purely for God's sake, and became one of the poorest of the poor who ever lived on earth, and that God then gave him as much suffering as He ever imposed on any man, and that he bore all this to his dying day, and that God then gave him one fleeting glimpse of how He is in this power — that man's joy would be so great that all this suffering and poverty would still be insignificant. Yea, though God were never to vouchsafe him any further taste of heaven than this, he would yet be all too richly rewarded for all that he had ever endured, for God is in this power as in the eternal Now. If a man's spirit were always united with God in this power, he would not age. For the Now in which God made the first man and the Now in which the last man shall cease to be, and the Now I speak in, all are the same in God and there is but one Now. Observe, this man dwells in one light with God, having no suffering and no sequence of time, but one equal eternity. This man is bereft of wonderment and all things are in him in their essence. Therefore nothing new comes to him from future things nor any accident, for he dwells in the Now, ever new and without intermission. Such is the divine sovereignty dwelling in this power.

There is another power,[5] immaterial too, flowing from the spirit, remaining in the spirit, altogether spiritual. In this power God is fiery, aglow with all His riches, with all His sweetness and all His bliss. Truly, in *this* power there is such great joy, such vast unmeasured bliss that none can tell of it or reveal it fully. Yet I declare that if ever there were a single man who in intellectual vision and in truth should glimpse for a moment the bliss and the joy therein, then all his sufferings and all God intended that he should suffer would be a trifle, a mere nothing to him — in fact I declare it would be pure joy and comfort to him.

If you would know for certain whether your suffering is your own or God's then you can know by this: If you suffer for yourself, in whatever way, that suffering hurts and is hard to bear. But if you suffer for God and God alone, your suffering does not hurt and is not hard to bear, for God bears the load. In very truth, if there were a man willing to suffer purely for God's sake and for God alone, then although he were suddenly called upon to bear all the suffering that all men have ever endured, the collective sufferings of all the world, it would not hurt him or bear him down, for God would bear the burden. If they put a hundredweight burden on my neck and another were to bear it on *my* neck, I would as willingly bear a hundred pounds as one, for it would not burden me or cause me pain. In brief, whatever a man suffers for God and God alone, He makes light and pleasant. As I said in the beginning, in the opening words of this sermon: 'Jesus went up into a citadel and was received by a virgin who was a wife.' Why? It had to be so, that she was a virgin *and* a wife. Now I have told you that Jesus was received, but I have not yet told you what the citadel is, as I shall now proceed to do.

I have sometimes said that there is a power in the soul which alone is free. Sometimes I have called it the guardian of the spirit, sometimes I have called it a light of the spirit, sometimes I have said that it is a little spark.[6] But now I say that it is neither *this* nor *that*; and yet it is a *something* that is more exalted over 'this' and 'that' than are the heavens above the earth. So now I shall name it in nobler fashion than I ever did before, and yet it disowns the nobler name and mode, for it transcends them. It is free of all names and void of all forms, entirely exempt and free, as God is exempt and free in Himself. It is as completely one and simple as God is one and simple, so that no man can in any way glimpse it. This same power of which I have spoken, wherein God ever blooms and is verdant in all His Godhead, and the spirit in God, in this same power God ever bears His only-begotten Son as truly as in Himself, for verily He dwells in this power, and the spirit gives birth with the Father to the same only-begotten Son, and to itself as the self-same Son, and is itself the self-same Son in this light, and is the Truth. If you could know with my heart, you would understand, for it is true, and Truth itself declares it.

Now pay attention! So one and simple is this citadel in the soul, elevated above all modes, of which I speak and which I mean, that that noble power I mentioned is not worthy even for an instant to cast a single glance into this citadel; nor is that other power I spoke of, in which God burns and glows with all His riches and all His joy, able to cast a single glance inside; so truly one and simple is this citadel, so mode- and power-transcending is this solitary One, that neither power nor mode can gaze into it, nor even God Himself! In very truth and as God lives! God Himself never looks in there for one instant, in so far as He exists in modes and in the properties of His persons. This should be well noted: this One Alone lacks all mode and property. And therefore, for God to see inside it would cost Him all His divine names and personal properties: all these He must leave outside, should He ever look in there. But only in so far as He is one and indivisible, without mode or properties, (can He do this):[7] in that sense He is neither Father, Son nor Holy Ghost, and yet is a Something which is neither this nor that.

See, as He is thus one and simple, so He can enter that One that I here call the citadel of the soul, but in no other mode can He get in: only thus does He enter and dwell therein. In *this* part the soul is the same as God and not otherwise. What I tell you is true: I call the Truth as a witness and offer my soul as pledge.

That we may be such a citadel to which Jesus may ascend and be received to abide eternally in us in such wise as I have said, may God help us to this! Amen.

Notes

1. Eckhart's rendering is very free here: the Latin says nothing about a virgin!
2. The play on the two meanings of *enpfangen*, 'received' and

'conceived', cannot be rendered into English.

3. When he was a (Platonic) idea in God.

4. The higher intellect: cf. 1, note 8.

5. The will. The Franciscans gave the will supremacy, the Dominicans (and therefore Eckhart) the intellect.

6. See Introduction: Note A: *Synteresis*.

7. Supplied (after Miss Evans) to complete the sense.

SERMON NINE

(Pf 9, Q 86, QT 28, Evans II ,2)

INTRAVIT JESUS IN QUODDAM CASTELLUM, ET MULIER
QUAEDAM, MARTHA NOMINE,EXCEPIT ILLUM ETC.
(Luke 10: 38).[1]

St Luke says in his gospel that our Lord Jesus Christ went
into a little town, where he was received by a woman
named Martha, and she had a sister named Mary who sat
at the feet of our Lord and listened to his words, but
Martha moved about, waiting on our Lord. Three things
made Mary sit at our Lord's feet. One was that the goodness of God possessed her soul. The second was unspeakable longing: she desired she knew not what, and wanted
she knew not what. The third was the sweet solace and
joy she gained from the eternal words that flowed from
the mouth of Christ.

With Martha too there were three things that made her
move about and wait on the beloved Christ. One was her
mature age and the ground of her being that was so fully
trained that she thought none could do the work as well
as she. The second was wise understanding, which knew
how to do outward works perfectly as love ordains. The
third was the great dignity of her beloved guest.

The masters say that God is ready to give every man
full satisfaction of all he desires, both of reason and of
the senses. That God gives us satisfaction of mind *and* of
the senses can be clearly distinguished in regard to the
dearest friends of God.[2] Satisfaction of the senses means
that God gives us comfort, joy and contentment — and

79

over-indulgence in these things does not occur in God's true friends in their inner senses. But mental satisfaction is of a spiritual nature. I call that mental satisfaction, when the summit of the soul is not brought so low by any joys as to be drowned in pleasure, but rather rises resolutely above them. Man enjoys mental satisfaction only when creaturely joys and sorrows are powerless to drag down the topmost summit of the soul. 'Creature' I call whatever a man experiences under God.

Now Martha says, "Lord, tell her to help me." This was said not in anger, but it was rather affection that constrained her. We can call it affection or teasing. How so? Observe. She saw how Mary was possessed with a longing for her soul's satisfaction. Martha knew Mary better than Mary knew Martha, for she had lived long and well, and life gives the finest understanding. Life understands better than delight and light (can) whatever, under God, man can attain to in this body, and in some ways more clearly than the eternal light can.[3] For the eternal light makes known oneself and God, not oneself apart from God; but life makes one known to oneself, apart from God. When one sees oneself alone, it is easier to tell what is like and unlike. St Paul makes this plain, and so do the pagan masters. St Paul in his ecstasy saw God, and himself in spiritual fashion, in God, and yet each virtue did not there present itself clearly to his vision, and that was because he had not practised them in deeds.

By practising the virtues, the masters came to such profound discernment that they recognised the nature of each virtue more clearly than Paul or any saint in his first rapture.

Thus it was with Martha. Hence her words, "Lord, tell her to help me," as if to say, 'my sister thinks she is able to do what she *wishes* to do, as long as she sits and receives solace from you. Let her see if it is so: bid her get up and go from you.' The latter part was kindly meant, though she spoke her mind. Mary was filled with longing, longing she knew not why and wanting she knew not what. We suspect that she, dear Mary, sat there a little more for her own happiness than for spiritual profit. That is why Martha said, "Bid her rise, Lord," fearing that by dallying in this joy she might progress no further. Christ answered her, "Martha, Martha, you are fretting and fussing about many things. One thing is needful. Mary has chosen the best part, which shall never be taken away from her." Christ said this to Martha not by way of rebuke, but answering and reassuring her that Mary would become as she desired. Why did Christ say "Martha, Martha," naming her twice? Isidore[4] says there is no doubt that prior to the time when God became man He never called any man by name who was lost; but about those whom He did not call by name it is doubtful. By Christ's 'calling' I mean his eternal knowing: being infallibly inscribed, before the creation of creatures, in the living book of Father, Son and Holy Ghost. Of those named therein and whose name Christ uttered in words, none was ever lost. This is attested by Moses, who was told by God Himself, "I know thee by name" (Ex. 33:12) and by Nathaniel, to whom our beloved Christ said, "I knew you when you lay under the fig-tree" (John 1:50). The fig-tree denotes a spirit that rejects not God and whose name is eternally inscribed in

God.[5] Thus it is demonstrated that no man ever was or will be lost, whom Christ ever named by human mouth out of the eternal Word.

Why did he name Martha twice? He meant that every good thing, temporal and eternal, that a creature could possess was fully possessed by Martha. The first mention of Martha showed her perfection in temporal works. When he said 'Martha' again, that showed that she lacked nothing pertaining to eternal bliss. So he said, "You are careful," meaning: 'You are among things, but they are not in you,' for those who are careful are unhindered in their activity.[6] They are unhindered who organise all their works guided by the eternal light. Such people are with things and not in them. They are very close, and yet have no less than if they were up yonder on the circle of eternity. 'Very close,' I say, for all creatures are 'means'. There are two kinds of means. One means, without which I cannot get to God, is work or activity in time, which does not interfere with eternal salvation. 'Works' are performed from without, but 'activity' is when one practises with care and understanding from within.[7] The other means is to be free of all that.[8] For we are set down in time so that our sensible worldly activity may make us closer and more like to God. St Paul meant this when he said, "Redeem the time, for the days are evil" (Ephes. 5: 16). "Redeeming the time" means the continual intellectual ascent to God, not in the diversity of images but in living intellectual truth. And "the days are evil" should be understood thus: Day presupposes night, for if there were no night, it would not be or be called day — it would all be one light. That was Paul's meaning, for a life of light is too little, being subject to spells of darkness that oppress a noble spirit and obscure eternal bliss. Hence too Christ's exhortation: "Go on while you have the light" (John 12: 35). For he who works in the light rises straight up to God free of all means: his light is his activity and his activity is his light.

Thus it was with dear Martha, and so he said to her: "*One* thing is needful", not two. When *I* and *you* are once embraced by the eternal light, that is *one*. Two-in-one is a fiery spirit, standing over all things, yet under God, on the circle of eternity. This is two, for it sees God but not im-mediately. Its knowing and being, or its knowing and the object of knowledge will never be one. God is not seen except where He is seen spiritually, free of all images. Then one becomes two, two is one: light and spirit, these two are one in the embrace of the eternal light.

Mark now what the circle of eternity means. The soul has three ways into God. *One* is to seek God in all creatures with manifold activity and ardent longing. This was the way King David meant when he said, "In all things have I sought rest" (Eccles. 24:7). The *second* way is a wayless way, free and yet bound, raised, rapt away well-nigh past self and all things, without will and without images, even though not yet in essential being. Christ meant that when he said, "You are blessed, Peter, flesh and blood have not illumined you, but being caught up in the higher mind. When you call me God, my heavenly Father has revealed it to you" (Matt. 16:17). St Peter did not see God unveiled, though indeed he was caught up by the heavenly Father's power past all created understanding to the circle of eternity. I say he was grasped by the heavenly Father in a loving embrace, and borne up unknowingly with tempestuous power, in an aspiring spirit transported beyond all conceiving by the might of the heavenly Father. Then Peter was inwardly called from above in sweet creaturely tones, yet free from all sense-enjoyment, in the single truth of the unity of God and man in the person of the heavenly Father-Son. I make bold to say: if St Peter had seen God unveiled in His own nature, as he did later, and as St Paul did when he was caught up into the third heaven, the most exalted angel's voice would have sounded harsh to him. But thus he spoke many sweet-sounding words, which Jesus had no need of, for *he* sees into the heart and ground of the soul, standing as he does unmediated before God in the freedom of actual unity.[9] *This* is what St Paul meant when he said "a man was caught up and heard such words as may not be uttered by men" (2 Cor. 12:2). You should understand therefore that St Peter stood on the circle of eternity, but was not in unity beholding God in His own being.

The *third* way is called a way, but is really being at home, that is: seeing God without means in His own being. Now Christ says, "I am the way, the truth and the life" (John 14:16): one Christ as Person, one Christ the Father, one Christ the Spirit, three-in-one: three as way, truth and life, one as the beloved Christ, in which he is all. Outside of this way all creatures circle, and are *means*. But led into God on this way by the light of His Word and embraced by them both in the Holy Spirit — that passes all words. Now listen to a marvel! How marvellous, to be without and within, to embrace and be embraced, to see and be the seen, to hold and be held — *that* is the goal, where the spirit is ever at rest, united in joyous eternity!

But to return to our argument, how Martha and all the friends of God are 'with care' but not 'in care'; there temporal work is as noble as any communing with God, for it joins us to Him as closely as the highest that can happen to us except the vision of God in His naked nature. And so he said, "You are with things and with care," meaning that she was troubled and encumbered by her lower powers, for she was not given to indulge in spiritual sweetness: she was with things and not in things...[10]

Three things especially are needful in our works: to be orderly, understanding, and mindful. 'Orderly' I call that which corresponds in all points to the highest. 'Understanding' I call knowing nothing temporal that is better. 'Mindful' I call feeling living truth joyously present in good works. When these three points are one, they bring us just as near and are just as helpful as all Mary Magdalene's joy in the wilderness.[11]

Now Christ says, "You are troubled about *many* things" — not just one thing. That means: when, perfectly simple, wholly unoccupied, she is transported to the circle of eternity, she is troubled if any 'means' intervene to spoil her joy up there. Such a person is troubled by this thing, and is anxious and distressed. But Martha stood maturely and well grounded in virtue, with untroubled mind, not hindered by things, and so she wished her sister to be equally established, for she saw that she was not grounded in her being. *Her* desire came from a mature ground, wishing her all that pertains to eternal bliss. That is why

Christ said, "One thing is needful." What is that? It is the One that is God. That is what all creatures need, for if God took back what is His, all creatures would perish. If God were to withdraw His own from the soul of Christ, where her spirit is united with the eternal Person, Christ would be left merely creature. Therefore that One is truly needful. Martha feared that her sister would stay dallying with joy and sweetness, and wished her to be like herself. Therefore Christ spoke as if to say: 'Never fear, Martha, she has chosen the best part: this will pass. The best thing that can befall a creature shall be hers: she shall be blessed like you.'

Now let me instruct you about virtue. Virtuous living depends in three points on the will. One thing is to resign one's will to God, for it is needful to do fully what one then knows, whether in taking or in leaving. There are three kinds of will.[12] The first is *sensible* will, the second is *rational* will, the third is *eternal* will. The sensible will seeks guidance, so that one needs a proper teacher. The rational will means following in the footsteps of Jesus Christ and the saints, that is, so that words, deeds and way of life are alike directed to the highest end. When all this is accomplished, God will give something more in the ground of the soul, that is, an eternal will consonant with the loving commands of the Holy Ghost. Then the soul says, 'Lord, tell me what thy eternal will is.' And then, if she has satisfied the condition we have just mentioned, and if God so pleases, the Father will speak His eternal Word into the soul.

Now our good people declare that we must be so perfect that no joy can move us, we must be untouched by

weal and woe.[13] They are wrong in this. I say never was
there a saint so great but he could be moved. Yet on the
other hand I hold that it is possible for a saint, even in
this life, to be so that nothing can move him to turn from
God. You may think that as long as words can move you
to joy or sorrow you are imperfect. That is not so. Christ
was not so, as he showed when he cried, "My soul is
sorrowful even unto death" (Matt. 26:38). Words wound-
ed Christ so sorely, that if the collective woe of all creatures were to fall on one single creature, it would not be
so grievous as Christ's woe was, owing to his exalted nature, to the blessed union of divine and human nature.
Therefore I declare that no saint ever lived or ever will
attain to the state where pain cannot hurt him nor pleasure please. Now and then it happens, through love and favour and divine grace, that though a man's faith be impugned or the like, if he were suffused with grace, he
would be indifferent to joy and sorrow. But with the
saints it may well occur that nothing whatever can bring
them from God, so that, although the heart be wrung
while a man is not in a state of grace, yet the will remains
solely with God, saying, "Lord, I am thine and thou art
mine." Whatever then occurs cannot impede eternal bliss,
so long as it does not invade the summit of the soul up
yonder where it is at one with God's sweet will.

Now Christ says, "You are troubled with many things."
Martha was so well grounded in her essence that her activity was no hindrance to her: work and activity she turned to her eternal profit. This was somewhat mediated,
but nobility of nature, industry and virtue in the above
sense help greatly. Mary was a 'Martha' before she was a

'Mary', for when she sat at the feet of our Lord, she was not 'Mary': she was so in name, but not in her being, for she was filled with joy and bliss and had only just entered school, to learn to live. But Martha stood there in her essence, and hence she said, "Lord, bid her get up", as if to say 'Lord, I do not like her sitting there just for joy. I want her to learn life and possess it in essence: bid her arise that she may be perfect.' She was not called Mary when she sat at Christ's feet. Mary I call a well-disciplined body, obedient to a wise soul. By obedient I mean that, whatever understanding dictates, the will accepts.

Now our good people imagine they can reach a point where sensible things do not affect the senses. That cannot be: that a disagreeable noise should be as pleasant to my ear as the sweet tones of a lyre is something I shall never attain to. But this much *can* be attained: that when it is observed with insight, a rational God-conformed will submits to the insight and bids the will stand back from it, and the will answers, 'I will, gladly'. Lo and behold, *then* strife changes to joy. For what a man has gained by heavy toil brings him heart's delight, and *then* it bears fruit.

Again, some people hope to reach a point where they are free of works. I say this cannot be. *After* the disciples had received the Holy Ghost, they began to do good works. And so, when Mary sat at the feet of our Lord, she was learning, for she had just gone to school to learn how to live. But later on, when Christ had gone to heaven and she received the Holy Ghost, she began to serve: she travelled overseas and preached and taught, acting as a servant and washerwoman to the disciples. Only when the saints become saints do they do good works, for then they gather the treasure of eternal life. Whatever is done before, repays old debts and averts punishment. For this we find evidence in Christ. From the very beginning when God became man and man became God, he began to work for our salvation, right to the end, when he died on the cross. Not a member of his body but practised particular virtues. That we may follow him faithfully in the practice of true virtue, may God help us. Amen.

Notes

1. Based on the same text as No 8, but Eckhart's translation of the text is different, as well as his interpretation. The two sermons were probably preached at quite different times. This one, which is probably late in date, treats in typically Eckhartian fashion of Martha and Mary. The text seems to be corrupt in places.

2. This is not, of course, a reference to the later sect known as the 'Friends of God'. Cf. Clark, p. 122 ff.

3. A difficult sentence which I am not sure I have understood. The general sense seems to be that life (experience) teaches us best about worldly things. The meaning of 'delight and light' (*lust unde lieht*) is not totally clear. According to Quint (*DW* III, 494, note 10), life is a better teacher than they are. I suspect the text is still corrupt, even in the version followed by Quint and here translated. The words may mean 'ecstatic vision', since the sense of what follows is that such vision, even that of St Paul, is insufficient for the development of the virtues if they have not previously been practised. The *vita activa* must precede the *vita contemplativa*.

4. (St) Isidore of Seville (d. 636). Quotation untraced (Q).

5. Following QT, p. 282. But in *DW* III, p. 484 and note 21, p.495, Quint agrees with the rendering given by Miss Evans (against Pfeiffer): 'The fig-tree being God in whom his name was inscribed eternally.'

6. Quint has again changed his mind between QT, p. 283 and *DW* III, p. 484 and note 24, p. 496. I originally rendered this, following

QT, 'People who are hindered in their activities are oppressed by care.' The sense of Miss Evan's rendering agrees with that given above.

7. This passage, in Pfeiffer and Evans, follows 'eternal light' above. Transposed by Quint, following better MSS.

8. Miss Evans renders 'selflessness', but *des selben* simply means 'of the same'.

9. *Iresheit*, lit. 'theyness' or 'theirness': the unity of Father and Son.

10. This passage seems corrupt.

11. As narrated in the *Legenda Aurea* of Jacobus a Voragine (ca. 1263–73), ed. Graesse, Leipzig, 1846. Caxton's translation in Temple Classics, 1900.

12. Are these the *three points* in connection with the will? There seems some confusion here.

13. But Eckhart himself had declared this in No 7!

SERMON TEN

(Pf 10, Q 25, QT 38)

MOYSES ORABAT DOMINUM SUUM

(Ex. 32:11ff, Evans II, 11)

I have quoted a text in Latin which is from the lesson appointed for today.[1] In German it means: "Moses besought the Lord his God saying, 'Lord, why is thy wrath kindled against thy people?' Then God answered him, saying, 'Moses, let me alone, grudge not, permit, consent that my wrath be kindled and that I take vengeance on the people.' And God promised Moses, saying, "I will exalt thee and magnify thee and multiply thy seed and make thee ruler over a great nation." Moses said, 'Lord, blot me out of the book of life, or forgive the people.' "

What does he mean by saying, "Moses besought the Lord his God"? Truly if God is your Lord, then you must be His servant, and if you then work for your own good or your own pleasure or your own salvation, then indeed you are not His servant, for you seek not only God's glory but your own profit. Why does he say, "the Lord his God?" If God wills you to be sick and you want to be well; if God wills that your friend should die and you want him to live contrary to God's will, then God is not your Lord. If you love God and are sick: 'In God's name'; if your friend dies: 'In God's name'; if he loses an eye: 'in God's name'. With such a man it would indeed be well. But if you are sick and pray to God for health, then health is dearer to you than God, and He is not *your* God. He is the God of heaven and earth, but not your God.

Now see how God says, "Moses, let my wrath be kindled". You may ask why God is angry. Solely at the loss
of our salvation, for He seeks nothing of His own: God is
so distressed because we jeopardise our salvation. No
greater sorrow could befall God than the martyrdom and
death of our Lord Jesus Christ His only-begotten Son,
which he suffered for our salvation. Note then, God says,
"Moses, suffer my indignation". Just see what a righteous
man can do with God! It is a certain and necessary truth
that he who resigns his will wholly to God will catch God
and bind God, so that God can do nothing but what that
man wills. He who makes his will over wholly to God, to
him God gives His will in return, so wholly and so genuinely that God's will becomes that man's own, and He
has sworn by Himself to do nothing but what that man
wills, for God will never be anyone's own who has not
first become His own: St Augustine says, 'Lord, thou wilt
be no man's own till he has become thine own.'

We deafen God day and night with our cries, 'Lord,
thy will be done', and when God's will *is* done, we are
angry, which is wrong. If our will is God's will, that is
good, but if God's will is our will, that is far better. If
your will is God's will, then if you are sick you will not
desire, against God's will, to be better — though you *would*
wish it were God's will that you were better. And when
things went wrong with you, you would wish it were
God's will that they should go aright. But when God's
will is *your* will, then if you are sick: 'In God's name!', if
your friend dies: 'in God's name!' It is a certain and
necessary truth that though it should entail all the pains
of hell, of purgatory, and the world, the will in union

with God would bear all this eternally, for ever in hellish torment, and take it for its eternal bliss; and resigning in God's will our Lady's bliss and all her perfection and that of all the saints, it would remain for ever in eternal pain and bitterness, not wavering for an instant and with no thought of wishing things were otherwise. When the will is so unified that it forms a single *one*, then the heavenly Father bears His only-begotten Son in Himself — in me. Why in Himself, in me? Because then I am one with Him, He cannot shut me out, and in that act the Holy Ghost receives his being, his becoming, from me as from God. Why? Because I am *in* God. If he does not receive it from me, he does not receive it from God: he cannot in any way exclude me.

Moses' will had become so fully God's will that God's honour with the people was dearer to him than his own felicity. God held out promises to Moses which Moses brushed aside: had He promised him His whole Godhead, Moses would not have consented. But Moses besought God, saying, "Lord, blot me out of the book of life." The masters ask, 'Did Moses love the people more than himself?' They answer, No! For Moses well knew that by seeking God's honour among the people, he came closer to God than by being careless of God's honour and seeking his own salvation. And so it behoves a righteous man not to seek his own in all he does, but only God's honour. While in all your doings you are turned more towards yourself, or towards one person more than another, God's will has not truly become your will.

Our Lord says in the Gospel: "My teaching is not mine but His who sent me" (John 7:16). And so it should be with a good man: 'my work is not my work, my life is not my life.' And if I am thus, then all the perfection and bliss that St Peter has, and that St Paul stretched out his head (in martyrdom), and all the felicity they gained thereby, this *I* enjoy as well as they, and I look to enjoy it eternally as if it had been my own doing. More: all the works that all the saints and all the angels and Mary, God's mother, too, ever did, from this I hope to reap eternal joy as if I had done it all myself.

I say humanity and man are different.[2] Humanity in itself is so noble that the highest peak of humanity is equal to the angels and akin to God. The closest union that Christ had with the Father, that is possible for me to win, could I but slough off what there is of *this* and *that*, and realise my humanity. All that God ever gave His only-begotten Son He has given me as perfectly as him, no less. He has given me more: He gave more of my humanity in Christ than to him, for to him He gave nothing: he had it eternally in the Father. If I hit you, I hit first a Burkhard or a Heinrich, and only then a man. But God did not do thus. He *first* took on humanity. Who is a man? One who has his name from Jesus Christ. Hence our Lord says in the Gospel, "He that touches one of these, touches the apple of my eye" (Zach. 2:8, cf. Matt. 25:40).

Now I repeat: "Moses besought the Lord his God". Many people pray to God to do all He can for them, but they do not want to give God all *they* can. They want to share with God and give Him the worst part, and not much at that! But the first thing God gives is Himself. And when you have God, you have all things *with* God. I have sometimes said, he who has God and all things with

God, has no more than one who has God alone. I say too, a thousand angels in eternity are no more than two or one, for there is no number in eternity, it transcends number.

"Moses besought the Lord his God". Moses means one who was lifted out of the water. But now I will speak again of the will. To give a hundred marks of gold for God is a noble deed, and appears as such. Yet I declare that if I have the *will* that I should give a hundred marks if I had them — if the will is perfect, then in fact I have paid God and He must give account to me as if I had really given Him a hundred marks. I say further: If I had the will to give up a whole world did I possess it, then I *have* made over to God a whole world, and He must render account to me as if I had given a whole world to Him. I say, if the Pope had been slain by my hand, and if it had not occurred with my will, I would go up to the altar and say mass as usual. I say humanity is as perfect in the poorest and most wretched as in pope or emperor, for I hold humanity more dear in itself than the man I carry about with me.

That we may be thus united with God, may the truth of which I have spoken help us. Amen.

Notes

1. Eckhart's scriptural quotation is, as often, free. It is also exceptionally lengthy. This is the lesson for the Tuesday after the 4th Sunday in Lent.

2. Human nature as distinct from the individual man. Christ assumed human nature, not a person (see No. 13a).

SERMON ELEVEN
(Pf 11, Q 26, QT 49)

MULIER, VENIT HORA ET NUNC EST, QUANDO VERI ADORATORES
ADORABUNT PATREM IN SPIRITU ET VERITATE
(John 4:23).

This is found in St John's Gospel. I take one sentence from a long story. Our Lord said, "Woman, the time shall come and now is, when true worshippers shall worship the Father in spirit and in truth, and such the Father seeks."

Take note of the first thing he says: "The time shall come and now is." He who would worship the Father must betake himself into eternity in his desires and hopes. There is one, the highest peak of the soul which stands above time and knows nothing of time or of the body. All that happened a thousand years ago, the day that was a thousand years ago, is in eternity no further off than this moment I am in now; or the day which shall be a thousand years hence, or in as many years as you can count, is no more distant in eternity than this moment I am in.

Now he says, "That the true worshippers shall worship the Father in spirit and in truth". What is truth? The truth is such a noble thing that if God were able to turn away from truth, I would cling to truth and let God go; for God is truth, and all that is in time, and that God created, is not truth.

Now he says, "they shall worship the Father". Alas, how many are there who worship a shoe or a cow and

97

encumber themselves with them — they are foolish folk! As soon as you pray to God for creatures, you pray for your own harm, for creature is no sooner creature than it bears within itself bitterness and trouble, evil and distress. So they get their deserts, these people who reap distress and bitterness. Why? They prayed for it.

I have sometimes said whoever seeks God and seeks anything *with* God, does not find God; but he who seeks God alone in truth finds God but he does not find God alone — for all that God can give, that he finds with God. If you seek God and seek Him for your own profit and bliss, then in truth you are not seeking God. And so he says that true worshippers worship the Father, and that is well said. Ask a good man, 'Why do you seek God?' (and he will answer) 'Because He is God'. — 'Why do you seek truth?' — 'Because it is truth'. — 'Why do you seek right-eousness?' — 'Because it is righteousness.' With such, all is well.

All things that are in time have a 'Why?'. Ask a man why he eats: 'For strength'. — 'Why do you sleep?' — 'For the same reason'. And so on with all things that are in time. But if you should ask a good man, 'Why do you love God?' — 'I don't know — for God's sake'. — 'Why do you love truth?' — 'For truth's sake'. — 'Why do you love righteousness?' — 'For righteousness' sake'. 'Why do you live?' — 'Indeed I don't know — I *like* living!'

A master says, 'He who has once been touched by truth, justice and goodness, though it entailed all the pangs of hell, that man could never turn from them even for an instant.' He goes on: 'That man, whoever he may be, who is touched by these three — truth, justice and goodness — can no more quit these three than God can quit His Godhead.'

A master says goodness has three branches. The first branch is utility, the second enjoyment, the third seemliness. Hence he says, "They worship the Father". Why does he say "the Father"? When you seek the Father, that is God alone, you will find with God all that He has to give. It is a certain and necessary truth, a declared truth — and if it were not declared it would still be true — that if God had still more He could not hide it from you, He would *have* to show it to you and give it to you, and I sometimes say that He *does* give it to you, and gives it to you as a birth.

The masters[1] say the soul has two faces: her upper face gazes at God all the time, and the lower face looks down somewhat and guides the senses. The upper face, which is the apex of the soul, is in eternity and has nothing to do with time: it knows nothing of time or of the body. I have sometimes said that in this lies hidden the fount, as it were, of all goodness, as a shining light that is always shining, a burning brand that is ever burning, and the brand is none other than the Holy Ghost.

The masters say that out of the peak of the soul there flow forth two powers. The one is will, the other intellect, and her powers' perfection lies in the highest power, which is the intellect.[2] This never rests. It does not want God as the Holy Ghost nor as the Son: it flees the Son. Nor does it want God, as He is God. Why? There He has a name, and if there were a thousand Gods it would go on breaking through, it wants to have Him there where He has no name: it wants a nobler, better thing than God as having a name. What does it want, then? It does not know: it would have Him as He is Father. And so St Philip says, "Lord, show us the Father, and we shall be content" (John 14:8). It wants Him as the marrow from which goodness comes, it wants Him as the kernel from which goodness flows, it wants Him as a root, as a vein whence goodness springs: only there is He Father.

Now our Lord says, "None knows the Father but the Son, nor the Son but the Father" (Matt. 11:27). In truth, to know the Father we must be the Son. I have once spoken three words: now take them like three bitter muscat-seeds, and then drink. First, if we are to be the Son, we must have a Father, for none can say he is a son unless he has a father, and no one is a father unless he has a son. If his father is dead, he says, 'He was my father'. If his son is dead, he says, 'He was my son'. For the son's life depends on the father and the father's on the son, so no man can say 'I am a son' unless he has a father, and that man is truly a son whose every work is done for love. The second thing that most makes a man a son is equanimity. If he is sick, he would as lief be sick as well, well as sick. If his friend dies: 'In God's name!' If he loses an eye: 'In God's name!' — The third thing a son should possess is that he can bow his head to none but the Father. Oh, how noble is that power that transcends time and transcends place![3] For, being above time it both contains all time and is all time, and however little a man might have of that which transcends time, he would be rich indeed, for what lies beyond the sea is no more distant to this power than what is here present. And therefore he says: "such the Father seeks".

See, God loves us so, God importunes us so, and God cannot wait till the soul has turned away and stripped off all creatures. It is a certain and necessary truth that God must needs seek us, as though His Godhead were at stake — which it is! And God can no more do without us than we without Him, for even if we were able to turn from God, God still could not turn from *us*. I declare that I will not pray to God to give to me, nor praise Him for what He has given me, but I will pray to Him to make me worthy to receive, and I will praise Him because He is of such nature and essence that He *must* give. He who would deprive God of this would deprive Him of His own being, of His very life.

That we may thus in truth become the Son, may that truth help us, of which I have spoken. Amen.

Notes
1. St Augustine and Avicenna (Q).
2. Cf. No. 8, note 5.
3. Cf. No. 1, note 8.

SERMON TWELVE

(Pf 12, Q 27, QT 50)

HOC EST PRAECEPTUM MEUM, UT DILIGATIS
INVICEM SICUT DILEXI VOS
(John 15:12ff.)

I have quoted three words in Latin from the Gospel. The first word that our Lord says is: "This is my commandment, that you love one another as I have loved you." The second is: "I have called you my friends, for all the things that I have heard from my Father I have made known to you." The third is, "I have chosen you that you should go and bring forth fruit and that your fruit should remain."

Now observe the first word that he says: "This is my commandment." I would say a word to you about this, that "should remain with you". "This is my commandment, that you love." What does he mean when he says, "that you love"? He wants to say one thing that you should note: Love is quite pure, quite bare, quite detached in itself. The greatest masters[1] say that the love with which we love is the Holy Ghost. There were some[2] who would dispute this. That is eternally true: in all the motion with which we are moved to love, we are moved by nothing but the Holy Ghost. Love at its purest and at its most detached is nothing but God. The masters say that the goal of love, towards which love does all its works, is goodness, and goodness is God. Just as my eye cannot speak and my tongue cannot recognise colours, so love cannot incline to anything but goodness and God.

Now pay attention. What does he mean when he so earnestly enjoins us to love? He means that the love with which we love must be so pure, so bare, so detached that it is not inclined towards myself nor towards my friend nor anywhere apart from itself. The masters say we cannot call any work a good work, or any virtue a virtue, unless it is performed in love. Virtue is so noble, so detached, so pure, so bare in itself that it knows nothing better than itself and God.

Now he says: "This is my commandment." If anyone commands me to do that which is pleasant, which avails me or on which my bliss depends, that is exceedingly sweet to me. When I am thirsty, the drink commands me; when I am hungry, the food commands me. And God does the same: He commands me to such sweetness that the whole world cannot equal. And if a man has once tasted this sweetness, then indeed he can no more turn away with his love from goodness and from God, than God can turn away from His Godhead: in fact it is easier for him to divest himself of self and all bliss and to remain with love close to goodness and God.

Now he says: "that you love one another". Oh, what a noble and blessed life that would be! Would not that be a noble life, if every man were devoted to his neighbour's peace as well as to his own, and his love were so bare and pure and detached in itself that its goal was nothing but goodness and God? If you were to ask a good man, 'Why do you love goodness?' — 'For goodness' sake'. 'Why do you love God?' — 'For God's sake'. And if your love really is so pure, so detached and so bare in itself that you love nought but goodness and God, then it is a certain truth that all the virtuous deeds performed by all men are yours as perfectly as if you had performed them yourself, and even purer and better. For the Pope has often tribulation enough for being Pope. But you have *his* virtues more purely and with greater detachment and peace, and they are more yours than his, if your love is so pure and bare in itself that you desire and love nothing but goodness and God.

Now he says: "As I have loved you". How has God loved us? He loved us when we were not,[3] and when we were His foes. God needs our friendship so much that He cannot wait for us to pray to Him: He approaches us and begs us to be His friends, for He desires of us that we should want His forgiveness. That is why our Lord rightly says: "It is my will that you beg them that harm you" (cf. Luke 6:27). That is how important it is that we should beg them that harm us. Why? That we may do God's will, that we should not wait till they beg us: we should say, 'Friend, forgive me that I have made you sad'. And that is how serious we should be in our practice of virtue: the greater our pain, the more seriously we should strive for virtue. So much should your love be *one*, for love does not wish to be anywhere but where there is likeness and oneness. Where there is a master and servant there is no peace, for there is no likeness. A woman and a man are unlike, but in love they are alike. And so scripture rightly says that God took woman from the man's rib and side and not from the head or from the feet; for where there are two, there is a lack. Why? One is not the other, for the *not* that makes the difference is nothing but bitterness, because there is no peace. If I hold an apple

105

in my hand, that delights my eyes, but my mouth is deprived of the sweetness. But if I eat it, I deprive my eyes of the pleasure I have from that. Thus two cannot co-exist, for one must lose its being.

That is why he says: "Love one another", that is, *in* one another. Scripture expresses this very well. St John says, "God is love, and whoever dwells in love, is in God and God is in him" (1 John 4:16). He speaks very truly: for if God were in me and I were not in God, or if I were in God and God were not in me, there would be two. But if God is in me and I am in God, then I am not meaner and God is not higher. Now you might say, 'Sir, you bid me love, but I *can't* love!' Our Lord put this well when he said to St Peter, "Peter, do you love me?" — "Lord, you know well that I love you" (John 21:15). If you have given it to me, Lord, I love you; if you have not given it to me, then I do not love you.

Now note the second text: "I have called you friends, for all the things I have heard from the Father I have made known to you." Note that he says, "I have called you my friends." In the same source where the Son takes rise, where the Father speaks His eternal Word, and from the same heart, the Holy Ghost also takes rise and flows forth. And if the Holy Ghost had not flowed forth from the Son (and from the Father),[4] there would have been no distinction between the Son and the Holy Ghost. When I preached at Trinity,[5] I quoted a text in Latin that the Father gave His only-begotten Son all that He has to offer, all His Godhead, all His bliss, holding nothing back. The question then arose, did God give him His true nature? And I said 'Yes', for the nature of God, which is to

106

give birth, is not different from God, and I have said that He holds nothing back. In fact I declare: He utters the root of the Godhead completely in the Son. And so St Philip said, "Lord, show us the Father, and it will suffice us" (John 14:8). A tree that bears fruit gives forth its fruits. Whoever gives me the fruit does not give me the tree. But whoever gives me the tree and the root and the fruit has given me more.

Now he says: "I have called you my friends." Truly, in that self-same birth in which the Father bears His only-begotten Son and gives him the root and all His Godhead and all His bliss, holding nothing back, in that self-same birth He calls us His friends. Even if you hear and understand nothing of His speaking, yet there is a power in the soul (I mentioned it when I recently preached here),[6] which is so detached and pure in itself and is akin to the divine nature, and in *that* power it is understood. Therefore he truly says: "All the things I have heard from the Father I have made known to you." Now he says, "that I have heard". The Father's speaking is His giving birth, the Son's hearing is his being born. Now he says, "All that I have heard from my Father." Truly, all that he has eternally heard from his Father, he has revealed and not concealed from us. I say if he had heard a thousand times more, he would have revealed it and not concealed it from us. And so we should conceal nothing from God, we should reveal to Him all that we can do. For if you were to hold back anything for yourself, you would thereby lose your eternal bliss, for God has withheld nothing of His own from us. This seems to some a hard saying. But nobody should despair on that account.

The more you give of yourself to God, the more God gives Himself to you in return, and the more you divest yourself of self, the greater your eternal bliss. It occurred to me just now as I was saying my Paternoster (which God Himself taught us), that when we say 'Thy kingdom come, thy will be done',[7] we are praying to God to deprive us of ourselves.

Concerning the third text I will not now speak, when he says: "I have chosen you, fed you, stilled you, established you that you may go forth and bring forth fruit and that your fruit shall remain".[8] And the fruit is known to none but God alone. And that we may come to this fruit, may the eternal truth help us, of which I have spoken. Amen.

Notes

1. Peter Lombard among others.
2. St Thomas Aquinas held that the Holy Ghost is the *cause* of our love.
3. Cf. No. 8, note 3.
4. Supplied from the Basle Tauler print, not in the MSS.
5. *LW* IV, 5.
6. See No. 11, note 2.
7. Eckhart's rendering of *Fiat voluntas tua* as 'may (my) will be thine' recurs in No. 18 and elsewhere.
8. I have not rendered the strange repetitions of verbs in this sentence. For discussion of this third point, see No. 17.

SERMON THIRTEEN (a)
(Q 5a)

IN HOC APPARUIT CHARITAS DEI IN NOBIS, QUONIAM FILIUM SUUM
UNIGENITUM MISIT DEUS IN MUNDUM UT VIVAMUS PER EUM
(1 John 4:9).[1]

St John says, "God's love was disclosed to us in this, that
He sent His Son into the world that we should live
through him", and with him. And thus our human nature
has been immeasurably exalted because the Highest has
come and taken on human nature. A master says, 'When I
consider that our nature is exalted over all creatures and
sits in heaven above the angels, and is adored by them, I
must ever rejoice in my heart, for Jesus Christ, my dear
Lord, has made mine all that he has himself.' He says
further that in all that the Father ever gave His Son Jesus
Christ in human nature, He meant it more for me, and
loved me more, and gave it to me rather than to him.
How is this? He gave it to him for my sake, for I needed
it. Therefore, whatever He gave him, he meant for me and
gave it to me as well as to him. I except nothing, neither
union nor the holiness of the Godhead nor anything else.
All that He ever gave him in human nature is no more
alien or distant from me than from him, for God cannot
give a little: He must give either everything or nothing.
His giving is utterly simple and perfect, undivided, and
not in time but all in eternity. Be assured of this as I live:
if we are to receive thus from Him, we must be raised up
in eternity, above time. In eternity all things are present.
That which is above me is just as near and present to me

109

as that which I have here by me, and *there* we shall receive whatever we are to get from God. God knows nothing[2] outside of Himself, His eye is always turned inwards into Himself. What He sees, He sees entirely within Himself. Therefore God does not see us when we are in sin. Therefore, in as far as we are *in* Him, God knows us; that is, in as far as we are without sin. And all the works that our Lord ever did he has given me for my own, to be as meritorious to me as the works I did myself. Now since all his nobility belongs equally to us all and is equally near to us, why do we not receive equally? Ah, this you must understand! Whoever wants to come to this giving so as to receive this good equally, to receive that human nature which is common and equally close to all men, then, just as in human nature nothing is strange and nothing is further or nearer, so it is necessary that you should make no distinction in the family of men, not being closer to yourself than to another. You must love all men equally, respect and regard them equally, and whatever happens to another, whether good or bad, must be the same as if it happened to you.

Now this is the second meaning: "He sent him into the world." By this we must understand the great world into which the angels look. How should we be? We should be there with all our love and all our desire. St Augustine says, what a man loves, that he becomes in love. Should we now say that if a man loves God he becomes God? That sounds as if it were contrary to faith. In the love that a man gives there is no duality but one and unity, and in love I am God more than I am in myself. The prophet says, 'I have said you are gods and children of the Most High' (Ps. 82:6). That sounds strange, that man can become God in love, but so it is true in the eternal truth, and our Lord Jesus Christ possesses it.

"He sent him into the world (*mundum*)." *Mundum* means in one sense 'pure'. Note this: God has no place more His own than a pure heart and a pure soul. *There* the Father begets His Son, just as He begets him in eternity — neither more nor less. What is a pure heart? That is pure which is separated and parted from all creatures , for all creatures produce impurity, because they are nothing,[3] and nothing is a lack and tarnishes the soul. All creatures are mere nothing, neither angels nor creatures are anything. They touch everything (?)[4] and soil it, for they are made out of nothing, they are and were nothing. Whatever is opposed to all creatures and displeases them, is nothing. If I placed a burning coal on my hand it would hurt. That is purely from nothing, and if we were free of nothing, we would not be soiled.

Now: "We live in him", with him. We desire nothing more than life. What is my life? That which is moved from within by itself. What is moved from without is not alive. So if we live with him, we must also co-operate with him from within, so that we do not work from without, we must be moved from that out of which we live, which is by him. We can and must work from our own power from within. If then we are to live in him and through him, he must be our own, and we must work from our own: just as God does all things of His own and through Himself, so we must work from our own, which is He, in us. He is altogether our own, and all things are our own in Him. Whatever all angels and all saints and our Lady have, that is my own in Him, and is no stranger or further from me than what I have myself. All things are equally my own in him, and if we are to come to the very own, in which all things are our own, we must take Him equally in all things, in one not more than in another, for He is alike in all things.

We find people who like the taste of God in one way but not in another, and they want to have God only in one way of contemplation, not in another. I raise no objection, but they are quite wrong. If you want to take God properly, you should take Him equally in all things, in hardship as in comfort, in weeping as in joy, it should be all the same to you. If you think you have no devotion or earnestness, and have not caused this through mortal sin, when you want to have devotion and earnestness, and that therefore you have not got God — then, if you regret this lack of devotion and earnestness, that *is* devotion *and* earnestness. So you should not bind yourself to any mode, for God is not in any mode, neither this nor that. So those who take God this way are wrong. They take the mode and not God. So remember this: love and seek God purely, and whatever the way of it, be content. For your intention should be purely God and nothing else. What you then like or dislike, that is right, and you must know that anything else is wrong. Those who want so many ways push God under the bench: whether it is weeping or sighing or anything of the sort — it is all *not God*. If it comes so, take it and be content — if it does not come, be likewise content and take whatever God wants to give you at the time, and remain always in humble self-naughting and rejection, considering always

112

that you are unworthy of any good that God could do you, if He would.

Now I have explained to you the words of St John: "God's love was disclosed to us in this." If we were in such case, this good would be revealed in us. That it is hidden from us has no other cause than ourselves. We are the cause of all our hindrances. Guard yourself against yourself, then you will have guarded well. And if it is the case that we do not want to take it, still He has chosen us for this. If we do not take it, we shall regret it and we shall be sorely punished. If we do not come to where this good may be got, that is not His fault, but ours...[5]

Notes

1. This somewhat fragmentary text was discovered by Quint. Its relation to 13b is discussed by him in *Zeitschrift für deutsche Philologie* 60 (1935), 173-192.

2. Clark (p. 234) makes one of his rare mistakes in translating here. He has rendered *nütz* as 'what is useful'; it is in fact a dialect form of *niht* 'nothing'.

3. Cf. No 6, note 5. This 'nothing' is therefore not 'seen' by God (note 2).

4. *Sy hand all in all* seems to mean, as Clark translates, 'they have all in all', but this makes little sense and Quint is probably right in believing the text to be corrupt.

5. The normal conclusion of a sermon is lacking. It is not possible to say how much more may be missing.

IN HOC APPARUIT CARITAS DEI IN NOBIS

(1 John 4:9)[1]

"God's love was disclosed and revealed to us in this, that God sent His only-begotten Son into the world, that we might live with the Son and in the Son and through the Son", for all who do not live through the Son, are indeed in the wrong.

Suppose there were a mighty king who had a beautiful daughter, if he gave her to the son of a poor man, all those who belonged to that family would thereby be raised up and ennobled. Now a master says, 'God became man, and thereby the whole human race is raised up and ennobled. We must all rejoice that Christ, our brother, has risen of his own power above all the choirs of angels and sits at the right hand of the Father.' This master has spoken truly, but still I care little about it. What good would it do me to have a brother who was a rich man if I were a poor man? What good would it do me to have a brother who was a wise man if I were a fool?

I say something different and more to the point: God not only became man, but he took on human nature.

The masters agree in saying that all men are equally noble by nature. But I say in truth, all the goodness that all the saints have possessed, and Mary, God's mother, and Christ according to his humanity — that is *my own* in this nature. Now you might ask me, since I have everything in this (human) nature that Christ can perform according to his humanity, why then do we praise and magnify Christ as our Lord and our God? That is because he was a messenger from God to us and has brought our blessedness to us. The blessedness he brought us was our own. Where the Father bears His Son in the innermost ground, *this* nature flows in there. This nature is one and simple. Something may here peep out or hang on it, but that is not this One.

I say something else, and even harder. Whoever would exist in the nakedness of this nature, free from all mediation, must have left behind all distinction of person, so that he is as well disposed to a man who is across the sea, whom he never set eyes on, as to the man who is with him and is his close friend. As long as you favour your own person more than that man you have never seen, you are assuredly not right and you have never for a single instant looked into this simple ground. You may indeed have seen a derived image of the truth in a picture, but it was not the best! And secondly, you must be pure of heart, for that heart alone is pure that has abolished creatureliness.

Thirdly, you must be free of *nothing*. The question is asked, what burns in hell. The masters generally say it is self-will. But I declare in truth: *nothing*[2] burns in hell. Here is a simile. Take a burning coal and put it on my hand. If I said the coal burnt my hand, I would do it injustice. Were I to say truly what burns me, it is negation, for the coal contains something that my hand has *not*. It is this *not* that burns me. But if my hand contained all that the coal has or can effect, it would be all of the nature of fire. Then, if anyone were to take all the fire

116

that ever burnt, and poured it out on to my hand, that could not hurt me. In the same way, I say, just because God and all those who stand before His face have on account of their true blessedness something which they who are separated from God have *not*, this very *not* torments the souls in hell more than self-will or any fire. I say truly, in so far as *not* adheres to you, to that extent you are imperfect. Therefore, if you want to be perfect, you must be rid of *not*.

This is what the text I have given you is concerned with: "God sent His only-begotten Son into the world." You should not take this to mean the external world, as when he ate and drank with us, but you should understand it of the inner world. As surely as the Father in His simple nature bears the Son naturally, just as surely He bears him in the inmost recesses of the spirit, and *this* is the inner world. Here God's ground is my ground and my ground is God's ground. Here I live from my own as God lives from His own. For the man who has once for an instant looked into this ground, a thousand marks of red minted gold are the same as a brass farthing. Out of this inmost ground, all your works should be wrought without Why. I say truly, as long as you do works for the sake of heaven or God or eternal bliss, from without, you are at fault. It may pass muster, but it is not the best. Indeed, if a man thinks he will get more of God by meditation,[3] by devotion, by ecstasies or by special infusion of grace than by the fireside or in the stable — that is nothing but taking God, wrapping a cloak round His head and shoving Him under a bench. For whoever seeks God in a special way gets the way and misses God, who lies

117

hidden in it. But whoever seeks God without any special way gets Him as He is in Himself, and that man lives with the Son, and he is life itself. If a man asked life for a thousand years, 'Why do you live?', if it could answer it would only say, 'I live because I live.' That is because life lives from its own ground, and gushes forth from its own. Therefore it lives without Why, because it lives for itself. And so, if you were to ask a genuine man who acted from his own ground, 'Why do you act?', if he were to answer properly he would simply say, 'I act because I act.'

Where creature stops, God begins to be. Now all God wants of you is for you to go out of yourself in the way of creatureliness and let God be within you. The least creaturely image that takes shape in you is as big as God. How is that? It deprives you of the whole of God. As soon as this image comes in, God has to leave with all His Godhead. But when the image goes out, God comes in. God desires you to go out of yourself (as creature) as much as if all His blessedness depended on it. My dear friend, what harm can it do you to do God the favour of letting Him be God in you? Go right out of yourself for God's sake, and God will go right out of *Himself* for your sake! When these two have gone out, what is left is one and simple. In this One the Father bears His Son in the inmost source. Out of that the Holy Ghost blossoms forth, and *then* there arises in God a will which belongs to the soul. As long as this will stands untouched by all creatures and all that is created, this will is free. Christ says, "No man comes to heaven but he who came from heaven" (John 3:13). All things are created out of nothing, therefore their true source is nothing, and as far as this noble

118

will inclines to creatures, it is dissipated with creatures in their nothing. The question arises, whether this noble will can be so dissipated that it can never return. The masters generally declare that it can never return in so far as it is dispersed in time. But *I* say: whenever this will turns back from itself, and from all creation for a moment into its primal source, then the will has its true birthright of freedom and is free, and in this moment all time lost is recovered.[4]

People often say to me 'Pray for me'. And I think, 'Why do you go out? Why do you not stay within yourself and draw on your own treasure? For you have the whole truth in its essence within you.' That we may thus truly stay within, that we may possess all truth immediately, without distinction, in true blessedness, may God help us. Amen.

Notes

1. Quint considers this to be a toned-down version of 13a, to which the censors had taken exception. It might, however, be an independent reconstruction, from notes, of the same sermon.

2. Cf. No. 6, note 5, and No. 13a, note 2. Eckhart plays on the two senses of Middle High German *niht* which means both 'not' (Modern *nicht*) and 'nothing' (Modern *nichts*).

3. *Innerkeit* 'inwardness'.

4. Cf. No. 15.

SERMON FOURTEEN (a)
(Q 16a)[1]

A master says, if all mediation were gone between me and this wall, I would be *on* the wall, but not *in* the wall. It is not thus in spiritual matters, for the one is always in the other: that which embraces is that which is embraced, for it embraces nothing but itself. This is subtle. He who understands it has been preached to enough. But now a little on the image of the soul.[2]

There are many masters who claim that this image is born of will and intellect, but this is not so. I say rather that this image is an expression of itself without will and without intellect. I will give you a simile. Hold up a mirror before me, and whether I want to or not, without will and without intellectual knowledge of myself I am imaged in the mirror. This image is not of the mirror, and it is not of itself, but this image is most of all in him from whom it takes its being and its nature. When the mirror is taken away from me, then I am no longer imaged in the mirror, for I am myself the image.

Another simile. When a branch grows out of a tree, it bears both the name and the essence of the tree. What comes out is what stays within, and what stays within is what comes out. Thus the branch is an expression of itself.

Thus too I say of the image of the soul: what comes out is what stays within, and what stays within is what comes out. This image is the Son of the Father, and I myself am this image, and this image is wisdom. Therefore God be praised now and evermore. Whoever does not

121

understand, let him not worry.

Notes

1. This fragment from the British Library (formerly British Museum) MS. Egerton 2188, f. 104^V, was printed by Priebsch in his *Deutsche Handschriften in England* II, Erlangen 1901, p. 82. It was shown by Brethauer to be in close agreement with Art. 8 of the Supplementary Accusation.

2. For further notes, see No. 14b.

SERMON FOURTEEN (b)
(Pf 14, Q 16b)

QUASI VAS AUREUM SOLIDUM ORNATUM
OMNI LAPIDE PRETIOSO
(Eccl. 50:10)

I have quoted a text in Latin which is read today in the epistle,[1] that can be applied to St Augustine or to any virtuous and holy soul. Such are likened to "a gold vessel which is strong and firm and is adorned with the noble nature of all precious stones". It is on account of the noble nature of the saints that we cannot do justice to them with any one likeness, and therefore they are likened to trees, to the sun and the moon.[2] So here St Augustine is likened to a golden vessel, strong and firm, adorned with the noble nature of all precious stones. Indeed, the same may be said of any virtuous and saintly soul who has abandoned all things to possess them where they are eternal. Who ever leaves things in so far as they are contingent, possesses them there, where they are pure being and eternal.

Every vessel has two properties: it receives and it contains. Spiritual vessels are different from physical vessels. The wine is in the cask, the cask is not in the wine. And the wine is not in the cask as it is in the staves, for if it were in the cask as it is in the staves, we could not drink it. With a spiritual vessel it is different. Whatever is received in *that* is in the vessel and the vessel in it, and it is the vessel itself. Whatever the spiritual vessel receives, is its own nature. God's nature is to give Himself to every

123

virtuous soul, and the soul's nature is to receive God, and this can be said in regard to the soul's noblest achievement. *There*, the soul bears God's image and is like God. There can be no image without likeness, but there *can* be likeness without images. Two eggs are equally white, but one is not the image of the other, for that which is the image of another must have come from its nature and be born of it and be like it.[3]

Every image has two properties. One is that it takes its being im-mediately from that of which it is the image, involuntarily, for it is a natural product, thrusting forth from nature like the branch from the tree. When a face is cast before a mirror, the face must be imaged in it whether it will or not. But its *nature* does not appear in the mirror-image, though the mouth and eyes and all the features of the face appear in the mirror. God has reserved this to Himself that, in whatever reflects Him, there His nature and all that He is and can perform, is at once involuntarily reflected. For the image precedes the will and the will follows the image, the image first breaking forth from His nature and drawing into itself all that nature and essence can perform: all His nature pours out into His image while yet remaining intact within itself; For the masters locate this image not in the Holy Ghost but rather in the middle Person; for the Son is the first issue of His nature, and therefore he is properly called an image of the Father, but the Holy Ghost is not this — he is simply an efflorescence of the Father and the Son, yet having one nature with them. But the will is not a mediator between image and nature, indeed neither understanding nor knowledge nor wisdom can be a mediator here, for the divine image breaks forth from the fecundity of nature without mediation. But if there is any mediator of wisdom, that is the image itself. Therefore, in the Godhead the Son is called the Wisdom of the Father.

You should know that this simple divine image which is impressed on the soul's inmost nature is received without means. It is the inmost and noblest part of the (divine) nature that is most truly patterned in the image of the soul, and here neither will nor wisdom is a means; as I have said, if wisdom is a means, it is the image itself. God is here in the image without means, and the image is without means in God. But God is in far nobler fashion in the image than the image is in God. The image does not receive God as the creator, but as He is a rational being, and the noblest part of the divine nature is most truly patterned in the image. This is a natural image of God which God has impressed by nature in every soul. More than this I cannot ascribe to the image; to ascribe more to it would make it God Himself, which is not the case, for then God would not be God.

The second property of the image is to be observed in the image's likeness. And here especially note two things; an image is, firstly, not *of* itself, and (secondly), not *for* itself. In the same way that the image received in the eye is not the eye's and has no existence in the eye, but merely depends on and is attached to that of which it is the image. Therefore it is not *of* itself or *for* itself, but really belongs to that of which it is the image, is its property, takes its being therefrom and is the same being.

Now listen carefully. What an image really is can be seen from four things, or maybe there will be more. An image is not of itself or for itself, it is solely that thing's whose image it is and all that it is belongs to that. Whatever is alien to that which it represents, it is not and does not belong to. An image takes its being solely from that of which it is the image without means, has one essence with it and is the same essence. I am not speaking here of matters discussed in the schools, but they can well be spoken of from the pulpit as doctrine.[4]

You often ask how you ought to live. Now pay close attention. Just as I have told you about the image — that is the way you should live! You should be His and for Him, you should not be your own or for yourself, or belong to anyone. When I came to this convent yesterday, I saw sage and herbs on a grave, and I thought, here lies someone's dear friend, and he loves this plot of earth the more on that account. Whoever has a very dear friend, loves whatever belongs to him, and can do nothing against his friend's interests. Take the dog, an irrational beast, as an example. He is so faithful to his master that he hates whatever opposes his master, and whoever is his master's friend he likes, taking no heed of riches or poverty. If a blind beggar were his master's bosom friend, the dog would like him better than a king or emperor who was his master's foe. In fact, I tell you that if it were possible for half the dog to be unfaithful to his master, he would hate half himself.

But now some complain that they have no inwardness nor devotion nor rapture nor any special consolation from God. Such people are still not on the right way: one can bear with them but it is second-best. I declare truly that, as long as *anything* is reflected in your mind which is not the eternal Word, or which looks away from the eternal Word, then, good as it may be, it is not the right thing. For he alone is a good man who, having set at naught all created things, stands facing straight, with no side-glances towards the eternal Word, and is imaged and reflected there in righteousness. That man draws from the same source as the Son, and is himself the Son. Scripture says, "No man knows the Father but the Son" (Matt. 11:27). Therefore, if you would know God, you must not merely be *like* the Son, you must *be* the Son yourself. But some people want to see God with their own eyes as they see a cow, and they want to love God as they love a cow. You love a cow for her milk and her cheese and your own profit. That is what all those men do who love God for outward wealth or inward consolation — and they do not truly love God, they love their own profit. I truly assert that *anything* you put in the forefront of your mind, if it is not God in Himself, is — however good it may be — a hindrance to your gaining the highest truth.

And as I said before that St Augustine is compared to a gold vessel, closed at the bottom and open at the top — see, that is how *you* should be! If *you* would stand with St Augustine and in the sanctity of all the saints, your heart must be closed to all created things and receive God as He is in Himself. Thus men are compared to the higher powers because they always go bareheaded, and women to the lower powers because their head is always covered. The higher powers transcend time and space, springing im-mediately from the soul's essence, so they are comp-pared to men, who always go uncovered. Hence their activity is eternal. A master[5] says that all the lower

127

powers of the soul, in so far as they are touched by time and space, have to that extent lost their virginal purity, and can never be so finely attenuated or sifted that they can reach the highest powers. Yet they *can* receive the imprint of a similar image.

You should be firm and steadfast, that is, you should be the same in weal and woe, in fortune and misfortune, having the noble nature of precious stones;[6] that is: all virtues should be enclosed in you and flow out of you in their true being. You should traverse and transcend all the virtues, drawing virtue solely from its source in that ground where it is one with the divine nature. And, inasmuch as you are more united to the divine nature than are the angels, *they* must get it from you. That we may be One, may God help us. Amen.

Notes

1. St Augustine's Day (28 August).
2. In the Dominican missal (Q).
3. If B is derived from A, it is the image of A. But if C is also derived from A, it may resemble B, but is the *image* of A, not B.
4. i.e., this is not just a point for academic discussion, but has a practical value for instruction. This follows.
5. Avicenna (Ibn Sina, 980-1037).
6. Precious stones were believed to have magic powers.

MORTUUS EST ET REVIXIT, PERIERAT ET INVENTUS EST

(Luke 15:32)

"He was dead and has come back to life. He was lost and has been found again." I have said in a sermon that I wanted to teach a man who had done good works while in mortal sin, how these works come to life again with the time in which they were done.[1] And this I will now show as it truly is, because I have been asked to make my meaning clear. I will do so, although it is in opposition to all masters now living.

The masters all say that as long as a man is in a state of grace, all his works are worthy of eternal reward, and that is true, for God does the works in grace, and I agree with them. But the masters concur in saying that if a man falls into mortal sin, all the works that he does while in mortal sin are dead, just as he himself is dead, and they are not worthy of eternal reward, because he is not living in a state of grace. And in this sense it is true, and I agree with them. Now the masters say: if God restores to grace a man who repents his sins, all the works he ever did in a state of grace before he fell into mortal sin — these all arise again in the new state of grace and live, as they did before. And I agree with them. But, they say, those works the man did while he was in mortal sin are eternally lost — the time and the works together. And *that* I, Master Eckhart, totally deny, and I say this. Of all the good works that a man did while he was in mortal sin,

129

not a single one is lost, nor the time in which they occurred, if he is restored to grace. Observe, this is contrary to all masters now living!

Now pay close attention to what my words imply, then you will grasp my meaning. I declare roundly: *all* good works that man ever did or ever will, as well as the time in which they occurred or ever will occur — works *and* time are totally lost, works as works, time as time. I say further, *no* work was ever good or holy or blessed. I say also that time was never holy or blessed or good, nor ever will be, neither the one nor the other. How then could it be preserved, since it is not good, blessed, or holy? And so, since *good* works, and also the time in which they occurred, are altogether completely lost, how could those works be preserved that took place in mortal sin and the time in which they occurred? But I declare: they are lost altogether, works *and* time, evil *and* good, works as works, time as time — they are altogether lost eternally.

Now the question arises: *Why* is a work called 'a holy work', 'a blessed work', and 'a good work', and likewise the time in which the work occurred? Note, as I said: the work and the time in which it occurred is neither holy, nor blessed, nor good. Goodness, holiness and blessedness — that is a *name attached* to the work and the time, and not its possession. Why? — A work *as* a work is not of itself, it is not there for its own sake, it does not occur of its own accord, or for its own sake, and it knows nothing of itself. And therefore it is neither blessed nor unblessed: rather, the spirit out of which the work proceeds rids itself of the 'image', and that never comes in again.[2] For the work, as work, perished at once, and likewise the time in which it occurred, and is neither here nor there, for the spirit has nothing more to do with the work. If it is to work any more, it must be with other works, and in another time. Therefore works and time are altogether lost, evil and good are equally lost, for they have not resting-place in the spirit, nor have they any being or place in themselves, and God too has no need of them. And so, in themselves, they are lost and perish.

If a good work is done by a man, he *rids* himself with this work, and by this *ridding* he is more like and closer to his origin than he was previously, before the ridding occurred, and by that much he is the more blessed and better than previously, before the ridding occurred. *That* is why the work is *called* holy and blessed, as well as the time in which the work occurred; but it is not really true, for the work has no being, nor has the time in which it occurred, since it perishes in itself. Therefore it is neither good nor holy nor blessed, but rather the *man* is blessed in whom the *fruit* of the work remains, neither as time nor as work, but as a good disposition which is eternal with the spirit as the spirit is eternal in itself, and it *is* the spirit itself. Observe, in *this* way no good deed was ever lost, nor the time in which it occurred; not that it was preserved *as* work and as time, but rather as being *freed* of work and time with the disposition in the spirit, in which it is eternal as the spirit is eternal in itself.

Now let us consider those works done while in mortal sin. As you have heard (those of you who have understood me), as works and as time, those good works done in mortal sin are lost, works and time together. But I have *also* said that works and time are nothing in themselves.

131

But if works and time are nothing in themselves, then, see, he who loses them loses *nothing*. That is true. But I have said further: Works and time have no being and place in themselves; as a work it has been *dropped* by the spirit in time. If the spirit is to perform further, this must needs be another work and in a different time. And therefore it can never enter the spirit, as far as it was work and time. And it can in no way enter God, for *no* time or temporal work ever came into God. And therefore it must needs perish and be lost.

And *yet* I have said that all good works a man does while he is in mortal sin are none of them lost, neither time nor works. And that is true, in the sense which I shall explain. And, as I said before, it is contrary to all masters now living.

Now observe, in brief, the true sense of the matter. If a man does *good* works while he is in mortal sin, he does not do the works from out of that mortal sin, for these works are *good* and mortal sins are *evil*. He does them rather out of the ground of his spirit, which is good in itself by nature, although he is not in a state of grace, and the works do not, in themselves, merit heaven at the time of their occurrence. Nevertheless, it does not harm the spirit, for the *fruit* of the work, free from work and time, remains with the spirit and is spirit with the spirit, and perishes as little as the essence of the spirit perishes. But the spirit frees its being by working out these images, which are *good*, just as truly as it would were it in a state of grace (even though it does not gain heaven by these works, as would be the case in a state of grace), for in this way it creates the same readiness for union and likeness, work and time being of use only to enable man to work himself *out*. And the more a man frees himself and works himself out, the more he approaches God, who is free in Himself; and inasmuch as a man frees himself, to that extent he loses neither works nor time. And when grace returns, whatever was in him by nature is now entirely in him by grace.

And to the extent that he has freed himself with good works while he was in mortal sin, just so far does he leap forward to unite with God — which he would not have been able to do unless he had freed himself with these works while he was in mortal sin. If he had to work them off now, he would have to take time for this. But since he freed himself in the previous period while in mortal sin, he has gained for himself the time in which he is now free. Accordingly, the time in which he is now free is not lost, because he has gained this time and can do other works in this time, which will bring him into still closer union with God. The fruits of the works that he did in the spirit remain in the spirit, and are spirit with the spirit. Although the works and the time have passed away, the spirit, out of which they were done, still lives, and the fruit of the works, free from works and time, full of grace as the spirit is full of grace.

See, thus we have proved the truth of my assertion, as it truly is. And all those who contradict it, I contradict them and care not a jot for them, for what I have said is true, and truth itself declares it.[3] If they understood what spirit is, and what work and time are *in themselves*, and in what manner the work corresponds to the spirit, then they would certainly not declare that any good deed or disposition would or could ever be lost. Although the work passes away with time and perishes, yet in that it corresponds to the spirit in its essence, it never perishes. The correspondence consists just in this, that the spirit is freed[4] by the disposition which takes effect in the works. That is the power of the work, for the sake of which the work occurred. *This* remains in the spirit and has never come out, and it can no more perish than the spirit in itself, because it *is* that spirit. Now see, if a man were able to understand this, how could he say that any good work could ever perish as long as the spirit has its being and lives in the new grace?

That we may become one spirit with God, and that we may be found in a state of grace, may God help us. Amen.

Notes

1. Cf. No. 13, note 4.
2. The mind that conceived the idea has thereby become 'free' of it.
3. This expression normally means that there is biblical confirmation for a statement. But no text is quoted, and Quint does not adduce any.
4. Reading *gelediget* with Quint. Pfeiffer has *geedelt* 'ennobled'.

SERMON SIXTEEN

(Q 29, Pf 74)

CONVESCENS PRAECEPIT EIS, AB IEROSOLYMIS
NE DISCEDERENT ETC.

(Acts 1:4)

These words which I have quoted in Latin are read in the mass for this feast-day.[1] St Luke writes here how our Lord, when he was about to ascend into heaven, ate with his disciples and bade them not to leave Jerusalem, but to await the promise of the Father which they had heard from his lips, for within a few days they would be baptized in the Holy Ghost.

He speaks there of the promise or pledge of the Father. This pledge was also given to us, that we should be baptized in the Holy Ghost and receive the gift from him of dwelling above time in eternity. In things temporal, the Holy Ghost can be neither received nor given. When a man turns from temporal things and into himself, he there perceives a heavenly light, a light that comes from heaven. It is beneath heaven, but it comes from heaven.[2] In this light man finds satisfaction, and yet it is corporeal: they say it is material. A piece of iron, whose nature is to fall, will rise against its nature and hang suspended to a lodestone in virtue of the master-force the stone has received from heaven. Wherever the stone turns, the iron will turn with it. The spirit does the same: not fully satisfied with this light, it presses right through the firmament and drives through heaven till it reaches that spirit that revolves the heavens, and from the revolution of the

135

heavens all things in the world grow and green. Still the mind is not satisfied till it pierces to the apex, to the primal source where spirit has its origin. This (human) spirit knows neither number nor numberlessness: there is no numberless number in the malady of time. No one has any other root in eternity, where there is 'nobody' without number.[3] This spirit must transcend number and break through multiplicity, and God will break through him: and just as He breaks through into me, so I break through in turn into Him. God leads this spirit into the desert and into the unity of Himself, where He is simply One and welling up in Himself. This spirit is in unity and freedom.

Now the masters declare that the will is so free that none can bind it except God alone. God does not bind the will, He sets it free in such a fashion that it wills naught that is not God Himself, and that is real freedom. And the spirit *cannot* will otherwise than as God will, and that is not its bondage but its true liberation.[4] Some people say, 'If I have God and the love of God, then I can do what I like.' They have not grasped this aright. So long as you are capable of doing anything that is against God and His commandment, you have not the love of God, though you may deceive the world into thinking you have.[5] The man who is in God's will and in God's love is fain to do whatever is pleasing to God and to leave undone whatever is opposed to God; and he can no more leave undone a thing that God wants done than he can do a thing that God abhors, just like a man whose legs are tied so that he cannot walk, so a man who is in the will of God can do no wrong. Someone said, 'Though God should bid me do evil and shun virtue, yet I would be incapable of wrongdoing.' For none loves virtue but he who is virtue itself. He who has abandoned self and all things, who seeks not his own in any thing, and does all he does without Why and in love, that man being dead to all the world is alive in God and God in him.

Here some folk will say, 'You are telling us wondrous things, but we perceive them not.' I regret that too. This state [6] is so noble yet so common, that you have no need to purchase it for a penny or a halfpenny. If your intention is right and your will is free, you have it. He who has thus abandoned all things on the lower plane where they are mortal, will recover them in God, where they are reality. Whatever is dead here is alive there, and all that is dense matter here is spirit there in God. Just as, if one were to pour clean water into a clean basin, absolutely bright and clean, and stood it quite still, then, if a man held his face over it, he would see it at the bottom as it was in itself. That is because the water is pure and clean and still. It is just the same with all people who are in a state of freedom and unity in themselves. If they can receive God in peace and quiet, they should receive Him too in turmoil and disquiet, and then all is well. But if they receive Him less in turmoil and disquiet than in peace and quiet, that is not right. St Augustine says, 'When you are weary of the day and the time is long, turn to God where no "long" exists and all things are at rest.' Whoever loves justice is possessed with justice, and he becomes justice itself.

Now our Lord said, "I have not called you servants, I have called you friends, for the servant does not know his master's will" (John 15:15). My friend, too, may know something I am ignorant of, if he did not want to reveal it to me. But our Lord said, "All that I have heard from my Father, I have revealed to you." I marvel how some priests, learned men with pretensions to eminence, are so easily satisfied and are misled by these words, that our Lord spoke, "All that I have heard from my Father, I have revealed to you." They want to take it this way and declare that he has revealed to us 'on the way' just so much as is needful to our eternal bliss. I do not accept this interpretation, for it is not the truth. Why did God become man? That I might be born God Himself. God died that I might die to the whole world and all created things. It is in this sense that we should understand the saying of our Lord: "All that I have heard from my Father, I have revealed to you." *What* does the Son hear from his Father? The Father can only give birth, the Son can only be born. All that the Father has and is, the profundity of the divine being and the divine nature, He brings forth all at once in His only-begotten Son. *That* is what the Son "hears" from the Father, that is what he has revealed, that we may be the same Son. All that the Son has he has from his Father: essence and nature, that we may be the same only-begotten Son. No one has the Holy Ghost unless he is the only-begotten Son. Father and Son inspire the Holy Spirit, where the Holy Spirit is inspired, for that is essential and spiritual.

It is true that you may receive the gifts of the Holy Ghost, or the *likeness* of the Holy Ghost, but it does not abide with you — it is impermanent. In the same way a man may blush for shame or blench, but that is accidental

138

and it passes. But a man who is by nature ruddy and fair, remains so always. So it is with a man who is the only-begotten Son, the Holy Ghost remains in his being. Therefore it is written in the Book of Wisdom: "This day I have born you in the reflection of my eternal light, in the fullness and glory of all the saints" (Psalm 2:7+109:3). He bears him now, today. There is 'childbed in the Godhead', there they are baptized in the Holy Ghost, that is the promise made by the Father. "After these days, which are not few or many", that is the 'fullness of the Godhead' wherein is neither day nor night. In that, what is a thousand miles away is as near to me as the place where I stand now. There is fullness and full enjoyment of the Godhead, there is one unity. As long as the soul perceives any distinction, that is not right. As long as anything peeps out or peeps in, there is no oneness. Mary Magdalene sought our Lord within the tomb; seeking one dead man she found two living angels, but still was unconsoled. Then the angels said, "Why are you troubled? Whom do you seek? One dead man, and you find two living." And she said, "That is just my disappointment, that I find two where I sought only one." As long as any distinction of any created things can look into the soul, she is disconsolate. I say, as I have often said it before, so far as the soul's created nature goes, there is no such thing as truth. I say there is something higher than the soul's created nature. But some priests cannot understand how there can be anything so nearly akin to God, and so *one*. It has naught in common with anything. All that is created or creaturely is alien. It is a single one in itself, and takes in nothing from outside.

Our Lord ascended into heaven, beyond all light, beyond all understanding and all human ken. The man who is thus translated beyond all light, dwells in eternity.[7] Therefore St Paul says, "God dwells in a light to which there is no approach" (1 Tim. 6:16), and that is in itself pure unity. Therefore a man must be slain and wholly dead, devoid of self and wholly without likeness, like to none, and then he is really God-like. For it is God's character, His nature, to be peerless and like no man.

That we may be thus one in the oneness that is God Himself, may God help us. Amen.

Notes

1. Ascension Day.
2. The light of the highest peak, or spark of the soul (Q).
3. The text is corrupt. I follow Quint's reconstruction. The general sense, that multiplicity must be transcended, is clear.
4. The seeming paradox was not invented by Eckhart, it is orthodox Thomism.
5. According to Karrer (quoted by Quint), an allusion to St Augustine's "Love, and do what you will". The people referred to may be the so-called Brethren of the Free Spirit.
6. Reading *wesen* with Quint, who considers Pfeiffer's reading *wizzen* 'knowing' as meaningless. This is not quite true, but Quint's reading is the more pregnant.
7. Following Quint's reading *êwicheit* against Pfeiffer's *einekeit* 'unity', which, however, would also make sense.

SERMON SEVENTEEN

(Pf 81, Q 28, QT 31)

EGO ELEGI VOS DE MUNDO
(John 15:16)

These words which I have quoted in Latin are read today in the holy Gospel for the feast of a saint, Barnabas by name,[1] who is commonly referred to in the scriptures as being an apostle. And our Lord says, "I have chosen you, I have selected you from all the world, picked you out from the entire world and from all created things, that you should bring forth much fruit and that your fruit should remain" (John 15:16), for it is very delightful to bring forth fruit and for the fruit to remain, and the fruit *does* remain to him who dwells in love. At the end of this gospel our Lord says, "Love one another as I have ever loved you; and as my Father eternally loved me, so I have loved you. Keep my commandments, then you will remain in my love" (John 15:12 + 9/10).

All God's commandments come from love and from the goodness of His nature, for if they did not come from love they would not be God's commandments. For God's commandment *is* the goodness of His nature, and His nature is His goodness in His commandment. Now, whoever dwells in the goodness of his nature, dwells in God's love: but love is without Why. If I had a friend and loved him for benefits received and because of getting my own way, I should not be loving my friend, but myself. I ought to love my friend for his own goodness, for his virtues and for all that he is in himself. Only then would I

141

love my friend aright, if I loved him as I have said. It is just the same with the man abiding in God's love, seeking not his own in God or in himself or in any thing, but loving God solely for His goodness and for the goodness of His nature, and for all that He is in Himself. That is genuine love.

Love of virtue is a flower, an ornament, the mother of all virtue, of all perfection, of all blessedness, for it is God; for God is the fruit of virtues (God begets all virtues and is a fruit of the virtues), and it is this fruit that remains to man. A man who should work for the fruit would rejoice greatly if the fruit remained with him. If a man had a vineyard or a field, and made it over to his servant to till, letting him keep the produce, at the same time giving him all that was necessary, the servant would be very pleased to have the fruits at no expense. Thus too a man rejoices who dwells with the fruit of virtue, for he has no worries or vexations because he has relinquished himself and all things.

Now our Lord says, "Whoever abandons anything for me and for my name's sake, I will return it to him a hundredfold, with eternal life to boot" (Matt. 19:29). But if you give it up for the sake of that hundredfold and for eternal life, you have given up nothing, even if you give it up for a thousandfold reward you are giving up nothing. You must give up yourself, altogether give up self, and then you have really given up.

A man once came to me — it was not long ago — and told me he had given up a great deal of property and goods, in order that he might save his soul. Then I thought: Alas! how little and how paltry are the things you have given up. It is blindness and folly, so long as you care a jot for what you have given up. But if you have given up self, then you have really given up.

The man who has resigned himself is so purified that the world will have none of him. I said here once — it was not long ago — he who is devoted to justice is taken up by justice, seized of justice, becomes one with justice.[2] I once wrote in my book:[3] The just man serves neither God nor creatures, for he is free, and the closer he is to justice, the closer he is to freedom, and the more he is freedom itself. Whatever is created, is not free. So long as there is anything at all above me, that is not God, that oppresses me, however small it may be or whatever its nature; even though it were reason and love, as long as this is something created and not God Himself, it oppresses me, for it is not free. The unjust man is the servant of truth,[4] whether he likes it or not, and he serves the world and creatures, and is a bondman of sin.

I once thought — it was not long ago — : That I am a man is something other men share with me; that I see and hear and eat and drink, that is the same as with cattle; but that I am, that belongs to no man but myself, not to a man, not to an angel, not even to God except in so far as I am one with Him. It is one purity and one unity. All God works, He puts into the one that is like Himself. God gives equally to all things, though their works are unequal, yet they tend in their operation to reproduce themselves. Nature wrought in my father the work of nature. Nature's intention was that I too should be a father as he was. He performs all this work for the sake of his own likeness and his own image, so that his work shall

143

be himself. The intention is always the man.[5] But when nature is shifted or hindered so as not to operate with full power, the result is woman; and when nature ceases her operation, God begins to work and create, for without women, there would be no men. When the child is conceived in the mother's womb, it has image, form and material being: that is the work of nature.[6] That lasts for forty days and nights, and on the fortieth day God creates the soul in less than an instant, so that the soul is form and life for the body. Now ends the work of nature with all that nature can contrive in form, image and material being. The work of nature goes out altogether, and as nature's activity withdraws, it is fully replaced in the rational soul. This is now a work of nature *and* a creation of God.

In created things — as I have said before — there is no truth. There is something that transcends the created being of the soul, not in contact with created things, which are nothing; not even an angel has it, though he has a clear being that is pure and extensive: even that does not touch it. It is akin to the nature of deity, it is one in itself, and has naught in common with anything. It is a stumbling-block to many a learned cleric. It is a strange and desert place, and is rather nameless than possessed of a name, and is more unknown than it is known. If you could naught yourself for an instant, indeed I say less than an instant, you would possess all that this is in itself. But as long as you mind yourself or any thing at all, you know no more of God than my mouth knows of colour or my eye of taste: so little do you know or discern what God is.

Now Plato, that great priest,[7] begins to speak and would discourse on weighty matters. He speaks of something pure that is not in the world, it is neither in the world not out of the world, neither in time nor in eternity, having neither inside nor outside. Out of this God, the eternal Father, derives the plenitude and depth of all His Deity. This He bears here in His only-begotten Son, so that we are that very Son, and His birth is His indwelling and His indwelling is His birth. It remains ever the One, that continually wells up in itself. *Ego*, the word 'I', is proper to none but God in His oneness. *Vos*, this word means 'you', that you are one in unity, so that *ego* and *vos*, I and you, stand for unity.

That we may be this same unity and remain this unity, may God help us. Amen.

Notes

1. 11 June.
2. See No. 16.
3. What book this was is unknown.
4. Quint has restored the MS reading *wârheit*, instead of Pfeiffer's conjecture *unwârheit*: Eckhart means that the unjust man cannot help serving truth.
5. Woman was considered an 'incomplete man'.
6. Nature is conceived as the handmaid of God. She can make the body, but not the soul.
7. Cassiodorus called Plato the 'theologian'. Aristotle the 'logician' (Q).

SERMON EIGHTEEN
(Q 30, Pf 66)

PRAEDICA VERBUM, VIGILA, IN OMNIBUS LABORA

(2 Tim. 4:2)

We read a text today and tomorrow for my lord St Dominic,[1] which St Paul writes in the epistle, and in German it means: "Speak the Word, publish it, proclaim it, bring it forth and propagate it." It is a remarkable thing that anything should pour forth and yet remain within. That the Word should pour forth and still remain within is very wonderful;[2] that all creatures should pour forth and remain within is very wonderful; what God has given and has promised to give is most wonderful, incomprehensible, incredible. And that is right so, for if it were comprehensible and credible, it would not be fitting. God is in all things. The more He is in things, the more He is out of things: the more in, the more out, and the more out, the more in. I have often said, God is creating the whole world now this instant. Everything God made six thousand years ago and more when He made this world, God is creating now all at once. God is in all things; but as God is divine and intelligible, so God is nowhere so truly as in the soul, and in the angels if you will, in the inmost soul, in the summit of the soul. And when I say the inmost, I mean the highest, and when I say the highest, I mean the inmost part of the soul. In the inmost and the highest part of the soul — there I mean them both together in one. Where time never entered, where no image ever shone in, in the inmost and highest part of the soul, God

147

is creating the whole world. All that God created six thousand years ago, when He made the world, and all that God will create in the next thousand years, if the world lasts so long, is being wrought by God in the inmost recesses, at the apex of the soul. All that is past, all that is present and all that is to come, God creates in the inmost part of the soul. All that God works in all the saints, that He works in the inmost part of the soul. The Father bears His son in the inmost part of the soul, and bears you with his only-begotten Son, no less. If I am to be the Son, then I must be Son in the same essence as that in which he is Son, and not otherwise. If I am to be a man, I cannot be a man in the essence of an animal. But if I am to be this man, then I must be this man in this essence. Now St John says, "You are the children of God" (1 John 3:1).

"Speak the Word, tell it abroad, pronounce it, bring forth and propagate the Word." "Tell it forth!" What is spoken in from without is gross, but *that* Word is spoken within. "Tell it forth!", that implies that you have it within you. The prophet says, "God spoke one, and I heard two" (Psalm 61:12). That is true: God spoke but once. His utterance is but one. In His Word He speaks His Son and the Holy Ghost and all creatures, which are all but one utterance in God. But the prophet says,'I heard two', that is, I heard God and creatures. There where God speaks it, it is God, but here it is creature. People think God only became man *there*, but that is not true, for God became man here as well as there,[3] and the reason why He became man was that He might bear *you* as His only-begotten Son, no less.

Yesterday I sat in a certain place and quoted a text from the Lord's Prayer, which is: "Thy will be done". But it would be better to say: "Let will be thine",[4] for what the Lord's Prayer means is that my will should become His, that I should become He. This text means two things. One is, 'Be asleep to all things', that is, to know nothing of time or creatures or images. The masters declare that if a man truly slept for a hundred years, he would have no knowledge of creatures, he would know nothing of time or of images — and *then* you would understand what God wrought in you. Therefore it says in the Book of Love, "I sleep but my heart wakes" (Cant. 5:2). And so, when all *creatures* are asleep in you, you can know what God works in you.[5]

The words "Labour in all things" (2 Tim. 4:5) has three meanings. It means 'Turn all things to your advantage', that is, see God in all things, for God is in all things. St Augustine says God made all things, not that He might let them come into existence while He went His way, but He stayed in them. People imagine they have more if they have things together with God than if they have God without the things. That is wrong, for all things with God are no more than God alone. Anyone who thought that if he had the Son and the Father with him he had more than if he had the Son without the Father would be wrong. For the Father with the Son is no more than the Son alone, and the Son with the Father is no more than the Father alone. Therefore, accept God in all things, and that is a sign that He has born you as His only-begotten Son, no less. The second sense of "Turn all things to your advantage" is: "Love God above all things

149

and your neighbour as yourself" (Luke 10:27). This is a
commandment from God. But I say it is not only a
commandment, but it is also what God has given and has
promised to give. And if you love a hundred marks more
in yourself than in another, you are wrong. If you prefer
one person to another, that is wrong; if you love your
father and mother and yourself more than another, that
is wrong; if you love blessedness for yourself more than
for another, that is wrong. "God bless us! What are you
saying? Should I not love blessedness for myself more
than for another?" There are many learned folk who
cannot grasp this, and it seems hard to them, but it is not
hard, it is quite easy. See, nature has two purposes for
every member to fulfil in every man. The first purpose of
its activities is that it should serve the body as a whole,
and after that, each particular member separately, just like
itself and no less than itself, not being concerned in its
activities for itself any more than for any other member.
All the more should this apply to grace! God should be a
rule and a foundation of your love. The first object of
your love should be God alone, and after that your
neighbour as yourself, and no less than yourself. And if
you love blessedness in yourself more than in another,
that is wrong; for if you love blessedness in yourself more
than in another, you love yourself; and if you love
yourself, then God is not your sole love, and that is
wrong. For, if you love the blessedness in St Peter and St
Paul as much as in yourself, then you will possess the
same blessedness that they have. And if you love the
blessedness in the angels as much as in yourself, and if
you love the blessedness in our Lady as much as in

yourself, you will enjoy in truth the same blessedness that they do, it will be yours as much as theirs. Hence it says in the Book of Wisdom: "He made him like His saints" (Eccl. 45:2).

The third sense of "Turn all things to your advantage" is, "Love God equally in all things", that is, Love God in all things equally: Love God as much in poverty as in riches, love Him as much in sickness as in health; love Him as much in temptation as without temptation, love Him as much in suffering as without suffering. Indeed, the greater the suffering, the lighter the suffering, just as with two buckets: the heavier the one, the lighter the other, and the more a man gives up the easier it is to give up. A man who loves God could give up the whole world as easily as an egg. The more he gives up, the easier it is to give up, as it was with the Apostles: the more they had to suffer, the easier it was to bear.

"Labour in all things" means: When you stand on manifold things and not on bare, pure, simple being, let this be your labour, strive in all things, and fulfil your service. This means as much as "Lift up your head!", which has two meanings. The first is: Put off all that is your own, and make yourself over to God. Then God will be your own, just as He is His own, and He will be God to you just as He is God to Himself, no less. What is mine I have from nobody, but if I have from another, it is not mine but belongs to him from whom I got it. The second meaning of "Lift up your head" is "Direct all your works to God". There are many who cannot understand this, and this does not surprise me, for he who would understand this must be very detached and raised above all

things. That we may attain to this perfection, may
God help us. Amen.

Notes

1. 5 August.
2. See No 17, at end.
3. 'There' refers to the historical birth of Jesus, 'here' to the birth
of Christ in the soul. (Q).
4. This is Eckhart's own particular rendering of *fiat voluntas tua.*
5. 'God's working' seems to be the second meaning. But Quint
considers the second meaning is what follows.

SERMON NINETEEN
(Pf 19, Q 71, QT 37)

SURREXIT AUTEM SAULUS DE TERRA APERTISQUE
OCULIS NIHIL VIDEBAT

(Acts 9:8)

This text which I have quoted in Latin is written by St Luke in *Acts* about St Paul. It means:"Paul rose from the ground and with open eyes saw nothing."

I think this text has a fourfold sense. One is that when he rose up from the ground with open eyes he saw Nothing, and the Nothing was God; for when he saw God he[1] calls that Nothing. The second: when he got up he saw nothing but God. The third: in all things he saw nothing but God. The fourth: when he saw God, he saw all things as nothing.

He previously told how a light came suddenly from heaven and felled him to the ground. Note, he says that a light came from heaven (Acts 9:3). Our best masters[2] say that heaven has light within itself, and yet does not shine. The sun also has light within itself, and does shine. The stars too have light, though it is conveyed to them.[3] Our masters say fire in its simple, natural purity gives no light at its highest place. Its nature (there) is so pure that no eye can see it in any way. It is so subtle and so alien to the eyes, that if it were down here before the eyes, they could not touch it by the power of sight. But in an alien object one can easily see it, where it has been caught by a piece of wood or a lump of coal.

By the light of heaven we mean the light that is God,

to which no man's senses can attain. Hence St Paul says, "God dwells in a light that no man can approach" (1 Tim. 6:16). He says God is a light to which there is no approach. There is no way in to God. No man still on the way up, still on the increase in grace and light, ever yet got into God. God is not a growing light, yet one must have got to Him by growing. During the growing we do not see God. If God is to be seen, it must be in the light that is God Himself. A master says, 'In God there is no less or more, no this or that'. As long as we are on the approaches, we cannot get in.

Now he says: "A light from heaven shone about him". That means that everything pertaining to his soul was enveloped. A master says that in this light all the soul's powers are lifted up and exalted: the outer senses we see and hear with, and the inner senses we call thoughts. The reach of these and their profundity is amazing. I can think as easily of a thing overseas as of something close at hand. Above thoughts is the intellect which still seeks. It goes about looking, spies out here and there, picks up and drops. But above the intellect that seeks there is another intellect which does not seek, but stays in its pure, simple being, which is embraced in that light. And I say that it is in this light that all the powers of the soul are exalted. The senses rise up into the thoughts. How high and how fathomless these are, none knows but God and the soul.

Our masters say — and it is a knotty question — that even the angels know nothing about thoughts unless they break out and rise into the questing intellect,[4] and this seeking intellect springs up into the intellect that does not seek, which is pure light in itself. This light embraces in itself all the powers of the soul. Therefore he says: "The light of heaven shone about him".

A master says that all things that have an emanation receive nothing from things below them. God flows into all creatures, and yet remains untouched by them all. He has no need of them. God gives nature the power to work, and her first work is the heart. And so some masters held that the soul is entirely in the heart and flows out thence, giving life to the other members. That is not so. The soul is entire in every single member. It is true that her first work is in the heart. The heart lies in the middle, and needs protecting on all sides, just as heaven suffers no alien influence and receives nothing from anywhere, for it possesses all things. It touches all things and remains untouched. Even fire, exalted as it is in its highest part, cannot touch heaven.

In the encircling light he fell to earth and his eyes were opened, so that with open eyes he saw all things as naught. And when he saw all things as naught, he saw God. Now note a word spoken by the soul in the Book of Love: "In my bed at night I have sought him whom my soul loves, and not found him" (Cant. 3:1). She sought him in her bed, which means that whoever clings or hangs on to anything less than God, his bed is too narrow. All that God can create is too narrow. She says, "I sought him all through the night". There is no night that is without light, but it is veiled. The sun shines in the night, but is hidden from view. By day it shines, and eclipses all other lights. So does the light of God, it eclipses all other lights. Whatever we seek in creatures, all that is night. I mean this: whatever we seek in any creature, is but a shadow and is night. Even the highest angel's light, exalted though it be, does not illumine the soul. Whatever is not the first light is all darkness and night. Therefore she cannot find God. "I arose and sought him all about, and ran through the broad ways and the narrow. Then the watchmen — they were the angels — found me, and I asked them if they had seen him whom my soul loves. But they were silent." Perhaps they could not name him. "When I had passed on a little further, I found him that I sought." The little, the trifle that she missed him by is a thing I have spoken of before. He to whom all transient things are not trivial and as nothing will not find God. Hence she said: "Having passed on a *little* further, I found him that I sought." When God takes form in the soul and infuses it, if you then take Him as a light or a being or as goodness — if you recognise anything of Him — that is not God. See, we have to pass over that *little* and discard all that is adventitious and know God as One. Therefore she says: "When I had passed on a little further, I found him that my soul loves."

We very often say, 'Him my soul loves'. Why does she say, 'Him my soul loves'? For He is far above the soul, and she did not name Him she loved. There are four reasons why she did not name Him. One reason is that God is nameless. Had she given Him a name, that would have had to be imagined.[5] God is above all names, none can get so far as to be able to express Him. The second reason why she gave Him no name is that when the soul swoons away into God with love, she is aware of nothing but love. She thinks that everyone knows Him as she does. She is amazed that anyone should recognise anything *but* God. The third reason is, she had no time to name Him. She cannot turn away from love for long enough to utter another word but 'love'. The fourth is, perhaps she thinks He has no other name but 'love'.With 'love' she pronounces all names. Therefore she says: "I rose up, I went through the broad ways and the narrow. And when I had passed on a little further, I found him I sought".

"Paul rose from the ground and with open eyes saw nothing." I cannot see what is one. He saw nothing, that is: God. God is a nothing and God is a something.[6] What is something is also nothing. What God is, that He is entirely. Concerning this the illumined Dionysius, in writing about God, says: ' He is above being, above life, above light '. He attributes to Him neither this nor that, but makes Him out to be I know not what that far transcends these. Anything you see, or anything that comes within your ken, that is not God, just because God is neither this nor that. Whoever says God is here or there, do not believe him. The light that God is shines in the darkness. God is the true light: to see it, one must be blind and must strip from God all that is 'something'. A master says whoever speaks of God in any likeness, speaks impurely of Him. But to speak of God with nothing is to speak of Him correctly. When the soul is unified and there enters into total self-abnegation, then she finds God as in Nothing. It appeared to a man as in a dream — it was a waking dream — that he became pregnant with Nothing like a woman with child, and in that Nothing God was born, He was the fruit of nothing. God was born in the Nothing.[7] Therefore he says: "He arose from the ground with open eyes, see- ing nothing". He saw God, where all creatures are nothing. He saw all creatures as nothing, for He has the essence of all creatures within Him. He is an essence that contains all essence.

A second thing he means by saying "He saw nothing". Our masters say that whoever perceives external things, something must enter into him, at least an impression. If I want to get an image of anything, such as a stone, I draw the coarsest part of it into myself, stripping it off externally. But as it is in the ground of my soul, there it is at its highest and noblest, *there* it is nothing but an image. Whatever my soul perceives from without, an alien element enters in. But when I perceive creatures in God, nothing enters but God alone, for in God there is nothing but God. When I see all creatures in God, I see nothing. He saw God, in Whom all creatures are nothing.

The third reason why he saw nothing: the nothing was God. A master says, all creatures are in God as naught, for He has in Him the essence of all creatures. He is the essence that contains all essence. A master says there is nothing under God, however near it may be to Him, but has some alien taint. A master says an angel knows him- self and God without *means*. But into all else he knows, there comes an outside element — there is an impression, however slight. If we are to know God it must be with- out means, and then nothing alien can enter in. If we do see God in this light, it must be quite private and in- drawn, without the intrusion of anything created. *Then* we have an immediate knowledge of eternal life.

"Seeing nothing, he saw God". The light that is God flows out and darkens every light. The light in which Paul saw revealed God to him and nothing else. Therefore Job says: "He commands the sun not to shine and has sealed up the stars beneath Him as with a seal" (Job 9:7). Being enveloped in this light, he could see nothing else, for all pertaining to his soul was troubled and preoccupied with the light that is God, so that he could take in nothing else. And that is a good lesson for us, for when we concern ourselves with God we are little concerned with things from without.

Fourthly, why he saw nothing: the light that is God is unmingled, no admixture comes in. This was a sign that it was the true light he saw, which is Nothing. By the light he meant quite simply that with his eyes open he saw nothing. In seeing nothing, he saw the divine Nothing. St Augustine says: 'When he saw nothing, he saw God'. He who sees nothing else and is blind, sees God. Concerning this, St Augustine says: 'Since God is a true light and a support for the soul, and closer to her than the soul is to herself, when the soul turns from things become, it must needs be that God gleams and shines within her.'

The soul cannot experience love or fear without knowing their occasion. If the soul does not go out into external things, she has come home, and dwells in her simple, pure light. There she does not love, nor does she know anxiety or fear. Understanding is a foundation and support of all being. Love has no anchor except in understanding. When the soul is blind and sees nothing else, she sees God, and this must be so. A master says, 'The eye at its clearest, where it is colourless, *there* sees all colours.' Not only where it is in itself bare of all colours, but in its place in the body it must be without colour if we are to recognise colours. Whatever is without colour, with that we can see all colours, even if it were down in our feet. God is an essence that embraces all essence. For God to be perceived by the soul, she must be blind. Therefore he says, "He saw the Nothing", from whose light all lights come, from whose essence all essence comes. And so the bride says in the Book of Love: "When I had passed on a little further, I found Him that my soul loves". The *little* that she passed by was all creatures. Whoever does not put them behind him will not find God. She also means that however subtle, however pure a thing is that I know God by, yet it must go. Even the light that is truly God, if I take it where it touches my soul, that is still not right. I must take it there, where it wells forth. I could not properly see the light that shines on the wall unless I turned my gaze to where it comes from. And even then, if I take it where it wells forth, I must be free of this welling forth: I must take it where it rests in itself. And yet I say even that is wrong. I must take it neither where it touches nor where it wells forth nor where it rests in itself, for these are still all modes. We must take God as mode without mode, and essence without essence, for He has no modes. Therefore St Bernard says, 'He who would know thee, God, must measure thee without measure.'

Let us pray to our Lord that we may come to that understanding that is wholly without mode and without measure. May God help us to this. Amen.

Notes

1. St Luke. Like other writers of the period, Eckhart frequently leaves the reader to sort out the reference of personal pronouns.

2. E.g. Albertus Magnus.

3. Albertus Magnus again: the stars were not clearly distinguished from the planets. The ultimate source for this and the following remarks about fire is Aristotle.

4. Because angels do not have the lower 'soul powers'.

5. An imaginary, arbitrary name.

6. Quint supplies *iht* 'something' after *ein*. The sense requires it, as was perceived by Lasson in 1868.

7. Quint, while rightly denying any connection with the anecdote of the 'pregnant monk', thinks this story is an *ad hoc* illustrative invention of Eckhart's. I think it is the record of a personal experience. Eckhart probably uses the third person form just as St Paul does in 2 Cor. 12:2ff.

SERMON TWENTY

(Pf 20, Q 44)

POSTQUAM COMPLETI ERANT DIES. PUER JESUS
PORTABATUR IN TEMPLUM. ET ECCE, HOMO
ERAT IN JERUSALEM, CUI NOMEN SIMON ETC.

(Luke 2:22, 25)

St Luke writes in the gospel: "When the days were accomplished Christ was brought into the temple. And behold, there was a man called Simeon in Jerusalem. He was just and God-fearing, waiting for the consolation of the people of Israel, and the Holy Ghost was in him."

"And behold": this little word *et* in Latin denotes union, binding together and inclusion. Whatever is wholly bound together and included, that implies union. Here I mean that man should be bound together, included and united with God. Our masters say union presupposes likeness. Union cannot be without likeness. Whatever is bound together and included is what makes union. It does not constitute likeness that a thing is near me, as when I sit beside it or am in the same place. Accordingly St Augustine says, 'Lord, when I found myself far from thee, it was not due to remoteness of place, it came from the *unlikeness* in which I found myself.' A master says: 'He whose being and work is altogether in eternity, and he whose being and work is altogether in time, they are never in accord, they never come together.' Our masters say that between those things whose being and work is in eternity and those things whose being and work is in time, there must be a go-between. If God and the soul are to be united, this must come from likeness. Where there is no unlikeness, there must needs be unity; it is not merely united by inclusion, but it becomes one, not merely likeness but alike. Therefore we say the Son is not *like* the Father, but rather: he is the likeness, he is one with the Father.

Our best masters say, if an image in stone, or painted on a wall, had nothing added to it, then, taken as an image, that image would be one with him of whom it was an image. That is a fitting doctrine for when the soul enters the image, where there is nothing alien but just the image, with which it is one image. If a man is placed in that image where he is like God, then he receives God, then he finds God. Where there is a splitting-up, God cannot be found. When the soul enters her image and finds herself in the image alone, in that image she finds God; and the finding of herself and God is one and the same act, and is timeless — there she finds God. So far as she is therein, so far is she one with God. He means, as far as one is included there where the soul is God's image. As far as he is in there, so far is he divine — so far therein, so far in God, not included, not united, but *one.*

A master says all likeness means birth. He says further that like is not found in nature unless it is born. Our masters say that fire, however powerful it might be, would never burn unless it hoped for birth. However dry the wood placed in it, if it could not conceive (in) its likeness, it would never burn. What the fire wants is to be born in the wood, to become all one fire and to be maintained and last. If it went out and perished, it would no longer be fire, therefore it desires to be maintained. The nature of the soul would never give birth to her like if she did not desire God to be born in her. The soul would never have entered into her nature, would never have wanted to enter there, but that she expects this birth which God works; and God would not work it but that He wishes the soul to be born in Him. God works and the soul desires. God has the work and the soul has the desire and the power to have God born into her and herself into God. God performs this that the soul may become like Him. She must needs wait for God to be born in her, that her support may be in God, and she must desire union so that she may be supported in God. The divine nature flows into the light of the soul, and in that she is sustained. In this it is God's intention to be born in her, to be united with her and to be sustained in her. How can that be? For surely we say that God is His own support. When He draws the soul in there, she finds that God *is* His own support, and there she stays; otherwise she would not stay. Augustine says: 'As you love, so you are. If you love the earth, you will be earthly; if you love God, you will be divine. Then if I love God, shall I become God? I do not say that, I refer you to holy scripture. In the Prophets God said: "You are gods and the children of the Most High" (Ps. 81:6)'. And therefore I say it is in His *like* that God gives this birth. If the soul had no expectation of this, she would never desire to enter there. She wants to be sustained in Him — her life depends on Him. God has a support, an abiding-place, in His being. Therefore there is nothing for it but to peel off and shed all that belongs to the soul: her life, her powers, her nature — all must go, and she must stand in the pure light where she is one single image with God: *there* she will find God. It is characteristic of God that nothing alien enters Him, nothing is superimposed on Him or added to Him. Therefore the soul should have no alien impressions, nothing superimposed, nothing added. So much for the first word[1].

"And behold": *ecce. Ecce,* this little word contains within itself all that belongs to the Word, and nothing can be added to it. The Word, that is God, God is a Word, God's Son is a Word. He[2] means that all our life, our whole desire, should be altogether included in, dependent on and directed towards God. Therefore Paul says: "I am what I am by the grace of God" (1 Cor. 15:10), and he says further: "I live, yet not I but God lives in me altogether" (Gal. 2:20). What comes next?

"Homo erat". He says: "Behold, a man". We use the word *homo* for women as well as for men, but the Latins refuse it to woman because of her weakness.[3] *Homo* means as much as 'what is perfect', and 'lacking nothing'. *Homo* 'a man' means 'he who is of earth', and signifies humility[4]. The earth is the basest element and lies in the middle, and is entirely surrounded by heaven and is fully exposed to the influence of heaven. Whatever heaven performs and pours forth is received in the middle, in the ground of earth. *Homo* in yet another sense means 'moisture'[5], and signifies 'he who is watered with grace', meaning that the humble man receives at once the influx of grace. In this inflowing of grace the light of intellect climbs up straightway, and there God shines with unquenchable light. Anyone powerfully seized by this light would be as far superior to another man as a living man

is compared to one painted on a wall. This light is so potent that it is not merely in itself free of time and space, but whatever it falls on it robs of time and space and all corporeal images and whatever is alien to it. I have said before, if there were no time or place or anything else, all would be one being. If a man were one like this and would cast himself into the ground of humility, he would there be watered with grace.

Thirdly: this light takes away time and space. "There *was* a man". Who gave him this light? Purity. The word *erat* belongs most expressly to God[6]. In the Latin tongue there is no word so proper to God as *erat*. That is why John in his gospel comes to say so frequently *erat* 'there was', signifying naked essence. All things are additive, but it (*erat*) adds only in thought – a thought not of addition but of subtraction. Goodness and truth add, at least in thought, but naked essence with nothing added is the meaning of *erat*. Secondly, *erat* signifies birth, a perfect becoming. I have now come, today I was coming[7], and if time were eliminated from my coming and having-come, then the coming and having-come would be drawn into one and would be one. Where the coming and having-come coincide in one, there we are born and remade and re-formed into the primal image. I have also said before, as long as anything remains *of* a thing in its essence, it will not be re-created; it may be repainted or renewed like a seal that is old, which is renewed by re-stamping. A pagan master says what is *there*, no time can stale: there is blessed life in the evermore, where nothing is distorted, nothing is covered over, where there is pure being. Solomon says: "There is nothing new under the sun" (Eccl. 1:10). This is seldom understood in its proper sense. All that is under the sun grows old and declines, but *there* all is new. Time brings two things: age and decrescence. Whatever the sun shines on, is in time. All creatures are *now* and are from God. But there, where they are *in* God, they are as different from what they are here as the sun is from the moon, and far more so. Therefore he says: *erat in eo,* 'the Holy Ghost was in him', where being is and where coming-to-be is.

"There was a man". Where was he? "In Jerusalem". 'Jerusalem' denotes 'a vision of peace.' In short, it means that man should be at peace and well established. It may mean more. Paul says: "I wish you the peace that passes all understanding. May this guard your hearts and minds" (Phil. 4:7).

Let us pray to our Lord that we may be 'man' in this sense and established in this peace, which is himself. So help us God. Amen.

Notes

1. All this about the word *et!* In this sermon we see something of Eckhart the scholastic, arguing much as he does (though at even greater length) in his Latin works. But in so doing he never loses sight of the mystical goal.
2. St Luke. Pfeiffer has *et* instead of *er,* but as Quint points out, the discussion of *et* concluded with the previous paragraph.
3. Actually, *mensche* (modern *Mensch*) denotes a human being like Latin *homo,* whereas *man* (modern *Mann*) refers to the male only. French *homme,* like English *man,* can indeed have the wider sense in suitable contexts.
4. Latin *homo* is related by modern etymologists to *humus* 'earth', from which *humilis* 'humble' is derived.
5. Latin *humor* 'liquid' is not related to *humus,* but is by medieval

standards a reasonable guess. In any case, all such derivations are used for their symbolic meaning.

6. In explanation, Quint quotes from Eckhart's commentary on St. John's Gospel (*LW* III,9). According to Latin grammar, *erat* denotes 'substance' (being from the 'substantive verb' *esse!*), 'preterite', and 'imperfect'. The Word (*verbum*), as preterite (or past), is always 'born' (*natum est*); as imperfect, it is always 'being born' (*nascitur*). Grammar is here turned to symbolic account just as etymology above.

7. Eckhart's *was komende* is literally as in English 'was coming': impossible in modern German.

SERMON TWENTY ONE
(Pf 21, Q 17)

QUI ODIT ANIMAM SUAM IN HOC MUNDO ETC.

(John 12:25)

I have quoted a text in Latin which our Lord says in the gospel: "He that hates his soul in this world shall keep it in eternal life."

Now mark what our Lord means by these words, when he says a man should hate his soul. Whoever loves his soul in this mortal life and as she is in this world, shall lose her in eternal life; but whoever hates her as she is mortal and in this world will keep her in eternal life.

There are two reasons why he says 'soul' here. A master says the word 'soul' does not mean the 'ground' and does not apply to the nature of the soul.[1] Accordingly a master says, whoever writes of things in motion does not deal with the nature or the ground of the soul. Whoever would name the soul according to her simplicity, purity and nakedness, as she is in herself, he can find no name for her. They call her 'soul': that is like when we speak of a carpenter: we do not call him a man, or Henry, or truly according to his being, but according to his work. What our Lord means here is this: whoever loves his soul in the purity which is the soul's simple nature, hates her and is her foe in this dress; he hates her and is sad and distressed that she is so far from the pure light that she is in herself.

Our masters say the soul is called a fire because of the power and because of the heat and the radiance that is in her. Others say she is a spark of the celestial nature.

171

A third school calls her a light. A fourth says she is a spirit. A fifth says she is a number. We can find nothing so bare and pure as number. And so they wanted to name the soul after something that was bare and pure. There is number among the angels — we say one angel, two angels — and in light there is number as well. And so they called her after the barest and purest, but still this falls short of the ground of the soul. God, who has no name — He has no name — is ineffable, and the soul in her ground is also ineffable, as He is ineffable.

There is yet another reason why he says she hates.[2] The word that denotes the soul[3] means the soul as she is in the prison of the body, and therefore he means that whatever the soul is in herself, that she can think of, refers to her as she is in her prison. As long as she has any regard to these inferior things and draws them into herself at all through the senses, she is at once constricted; for words cannot give a name to any nature that is above her.

There are three reasons why the soul should hate herself. The first reason: as far as she is mine I should hate her, for as far as she is mine, she is not God's. The second: because my soul is not wholly set amd implanted and re-formed in God. Augustine says whoever wants God to be his own must first become God's own, and that must needs be so. The third reason is: if the soul savours herself as soul, and if she savours God with the soul, that is wrong. She should savour God in Himself, for He is entirely above her. This is what Christ meant by saying: "Whoever loves his soul shall lose it." Whatever of the soul is in this world or looks into this world, whatever is attached to her and

172

looks out, that she should hate. A master says that the soul at her highest and purest is above the world. Nothing brings the soul into this world but love alone. Sometimes she has a natural love which is for the body. Sometimes she has a voluntary love which is for creatures. A master says the soul in her own nature has as little to do with all that is in the world as the eye has to do with song, or the ear with colour. Accordingly, our natural philosophers say that the body is much more in the soul than the soul is in the body. As the vat contains the wine more than the wine the vat, so the soul keeps the body in her more than the body the soul.[4] Whatever the soul loves in this world she is bare of in her own nature. A master[5] says the nature and natural perfection of the soul is when she becomes in herself a rational world in which God has informed the images of all things. Whoever declares that he has 'attained to his nature' must find all things formed in him in the same purity as they are in God — not as they are in their own nature but as they are in God. Neither spirit nor angel touches the ground of the soul, or the soul's true nature. In it she comes into the first, into the beginning whence God bursts forth with goodness into all creatures. *There* she receives all things in God, not in that purity which is the purity of their own nature, but in the pure simplicity as they are in God. God has made all this world as if out of coal. An image made of gold is more solid than one made of coal. And so, all things in the soul are purer and more noble than they are in this world. The material which God has made all things from is baser than coal compared with gold. A man who wants to make a pot takes a little clay, that is the material he works with.

Then he gives it a form, which is in himself, and is finer in him than the material. By this I mean that all things are immeasurably nobler in the intellectual world, where the soul is, than they are in this world. Just like an image that is chased and engraved in gold, so the images of all things are simple in the soul. A master says the soul has the potentiality in herself for the images of all things to be impressed in her. Another says, never did the soul get to her bare nature without finding all things formed in her in the intellectual world, which is incomprehensible, for no thought can reach it. Gregory says whatever we say of things divine we must stammer, because we must use words.

One more word about the soul, and then no more. "You daughters of Jerusalem, pay no heed because I am brown! The sun has discoloured me, and the children of my mother have striven against me" (Cant. 1:4). Here she means the children of the world, to whom the soul says: Whatever of the sun, that is the joy of the world, shines on me and touches me, that makes me dark and brown. Brown is not a pure colour; it has something light and something of darkness. Whatever the soul thinks or does with her powers, however light that may be in her, is still mixed. And so she says: "The children of my mother have striven against me". The children are all the lower powers of the soul, they all strive against her and attack her. The heavenly Father is our father, and Christendom is our mother. However fair and however adorned she is, and however useful her works, yet all is imperfect. Therefore he says: "O thou fairest among women, go forth and depart!" (Cant. 1:7). This world is like a woman, for it is

174

weak. But why does he say 'fairest among women'? The angels are fairer, and are high above the soul. Therefore he says 'fairest' — in her natural light[6] — 'go forth and depart': go out of this world and leave everything your soul still inclines to. And wherever she is still attached to anything, let her hate it.

Pray to our dear Lord that we may hate our soul under the cloak in which she is our soul, that we may preserve her in eternal life. So help us God. Amen.

Notes

1. Miss Evans, misled by Pfeiffer's text, has got this badly wrong. The 'master' twice mentioned is Avicenna (Q).
2. There seems to be something wrong here: the text does not say the *soul* hates. Quint does not comment, but Clark translates freely 'the soul hates herself' (as stated in the next paragraph).
3. '*Anima* as opposed to *spiritus*' (Clark).
4. Cf. No. 14b.
5. Avicenna.
6. The intellect or higher reason.

SERMON TWENTY TWO
(Pf 22, Q 53)

MISIT DOMINUS MANUM SUAM ET TETIGIT OS MEUM ET DIXIT

MIHI ETC. . . ECCE CONSTITUI TE SUPER GENTES ET REGNA

(Jer. 1:9/10).

"The Lord put forth His hand and touched my mouth and said to me."

When I preach it is my wont to speak about detachment, and of how man should rid himself of self and all things. Secondly, that man should be in-formed back into the simple good which is God. Thirdly, that we should remember the great nobility God has put into the soul, so that man may come miraculously to God. Fourthly, of the purity of the divine nature, for the splendour of God's nature is unspeakable. God is a word, an unspoken word. Augustine says: 'All scripture is vain. If we say God is a word, He is spoken; if we say God is unspoken, He is ineffable.' Yet He is something, but who can utter this word? None can do so but He who is this Word. God is a word that utters itself. Where God is, He utters this Word — where He is not He does not speak. God is spoken and unspoken. The Father is a speaking work, and the Son is the speech at work. Whatever is in me has to come out: as soon as I think of it, my word makes it known but it remains within. Thus the Father speaks the Son unspoken, and he remains within. I have also said before, God's outgoing is His ingoing. In proportion to my nearness to God does He speak Himself in me. It is thus with all rational creatures, that, the more they go out of them-

selves with their work, the more they go into themselves.
This is not the case with physical things[1] ; the more they
work, the more they go out of themselves. All creatures
wish to speak God in all their works; they all speak as well
as they can but they cannot speak Him. Willy-nilly,
whether they like it or not, they all want to speak God,
and yet He remains unspoken.

David said: "The Lord is His name " (Ps 68:4). 'Lord'
means one set in authority: 'servant' is an underling.
Some names belong to God to the exclusion of all other
things, such as *God. God* as a name most proper to God, as
man is the name for man. A man is always a man,
whether he is foolish or wise. Seneca says: "That man is
contemptible who does not rise above man". Some names
are attached to God, such as *fatherhood* and *sonhood.*
When we speak of a father, we understand a son. A father
cannot be without having a son; a son cannot be without
having a father, but they bear within them, beyond time,
one eternal essence. As to the third, some names imply
a reference upwards to God as well as a pointing to
time.[2] Also, God is called by many names in scripture.
I say, if one knows anything in God and affixes any name
to it, that is not God. God is above names and above
nature. We read of a good man who was praying to God
and wanted to give Him names. Then a brother said,
'Be silent, you dishonour God!' We can find no name
that we could give to God, but we are permitted the names
the saints called Him by, whose hearts were consecrated
by God and flooded with His divine light. And here we
should learn, firstly, how to pray to God. We should
say: 'Lord, in the same names which thou hast thus

consecrated in the hearts of thy saints and flooded with thy light, we pray to thee and extol thee.' Secondly, we should learn not to give God any name with the idea that we had thereby sufficiently honoured and magnified Him: for God is above names and ineffable.

The Father speaks the Son out of the fullness of His power, and all things in him. All things speak God. What my mouth does in speaking and declaring God, is likewise done by the essence of a stone, and this is understood more by works than by words. The work wrought by the highest nature in its sovereign power cannot be grasped by the lower nature. If it did the same work then it would not be lower, but the same. All creatures would like to echo God in all their works. But it is precious little that they are able to reveal. Even when the highest angels climb up and touch God, they are as different from what is in God as black is from white. What all creatures have received is quite unequal, though they would all gladly speak the most they can. The prophet says: "Lord, thou speakest one, and I hear two" (Ps. 62:11)[3]. When God speaks into the soul, he and she are one; when this (one) falls away, it is divided. The higher we rise in our understanding, the more we are one in Him. Therefore the Father always speaks the Son in unity and pours forth all creatures in him. They all have a call to return whence they flowed forth. All their life and being is a calling and a hurrying back to what they came out of.

The prophet says: "The Lord put forth His hand", meaning the Holy Ghost. He says: "He touched my mouth", and adds immediately, "He spoke to me". The soul's mouth is the highest part of the soul, and she[4] means

179

this when she says: "He has put His word into my mouth"; that is the kiss of the soul, where mouth has come to mouth: there the Father bears His Son in the soul, and there He has "spoken to her". And now He says: "Behold, I have today chosen you and have set you over nations and kingdoms." In a 'today' God promises to choose us, where nothing is, where yet in eternity there is a 'today'. "And I have set you over nations", that is, over all the world, which you must be rid of, and "over kingdoms", that is: whatever is more than one is too much, for you must die to all things and be again informed in the height, where we dwell in the Holy Ghost. May God the Holy Ghost help us to this. Amen.

Notes

1. Quint has 'creatures' here again. I do not understand this, and follow Pfeiffer's text.
2. Not very clear. I think the 'third' refers to the 'eternal essence' just mentioned, whereas the 'pointing to time' refers to the normal everyday meanings of *father* and *son*.
3. Cf. No. 18.
4. The soul.

SERMON TWENTY THREE
(Pf 23, Q 47)

SPIRITUS DOMINI REPLEVIT ORBEM TERRARUM ETC.

(Sap. 1:7).

"The spirit of the Lord has filled the circle of the world".

A master says all creatures testify to the divine nature from which they pour forth by their will to work according to the divine nature they have flowed from. Creatures proceed forth in two ways. The first way of coming forth is at the roots, as the roots produce the tree. The second way of coming forth is by way of union. See, the emanation of divine nature is also in two ways. The first emanation is that of the Son from the Father, which occurs in the way of birth. The second emanation is that of the Holy Ghost by way of union: this emanation is by the love of the Father and the Son. This is the Holy Ghost, for they love one another in him. Observe that all creatures prove that they have emanated and flowed forth from the divine nature, and they testify to this in their works. Concerning this a Greek master[1] says that God keeps all creatures on a leash, to work in His likeness. Hence nature continually works the highest that she can. Nature would fain make not only the Son, but if she could, she would make the Father. Accordingly, if nature worked timelessly, she would not have any accidental deficiencies. Concerning this, a Greek master says, 'Because nature works in time and space, the Son and the Father are different'. A master[2] says: 'A carpenter who builds a house has already formed it in himself, and if the timber were

181

sufficiently subject to his will, then as soon as he willed it, it would come to be, and, but for the material, there would be no other difference than between the bearing and the suddenly born, observe that with God it is not so, for in Him there is no time or place: therefore they are one in God and the only difference is that between outpouring and outpoured.

"The spirit of the Lord". Why is He called 'Lord'? That He may fill us. Why is He called 'spirit'? That He may unite with us. Lordship is known by three things. The first, that He is rich. Rich is whatever has all things without lack. I am a man and am rich, but I am not therefore another man. If I were all men, I still would not be an angel. Even if I were an angel *and* a man, I still would not be all angels. And so none is really rich but God alone, who embraces in simplicity all things in Himself. Therefore He can always give, and this is the second point about riches. A master says God hawks Himself to all creatures and each takes as much as it wants. I say, God offers Himself to me as He does to the highest angel, and if I were as ready as he, I should receive as he does. I have also said before that God has always behaved just as if He were at pains to be pleasing to the soul. The third point about riches is, that one gives without expecting any return, for he who gives in exchange for anything is not really rich. Therefore God's richness is shown in this, that He gives all His gifts for nothing. Hence the prophet says: "I said to my Lord, thou art my God, for thou needest not my possessions" (Ps. 16:2). This alone is 'lord' and 'spirit'. I say that He is spirit for our bliss lies in His union with us[3].

The noblest thing that God works in all creatures is being. My father can give me my nature, but he does not
give me my being: God alone does that. That is why
all things that exist take rational delight in their being.
See, that is why, as I said once before and was not properly understood, Judas in hell would not want to be
another in heaven. Why? Because if he were to become
another, he would have to become nothing in his own
being. But that cannot be, for being does not deny itself.
The being of the soul is receptive to the influence of the
divine light, though not as limpid and pure as God can
send it, but rather obscured. We can see the sun's light well
enough when it falls on a tree or any other object, but in
the sun itself we cannot apprehend it. See, thus it is with
divine gifts: they must be measured according to him who
is to receive them, not according to him who gives them.

A master says God is the measure of all things, and in so
far as a man has more of God in him than another, to that
extent he is wiser, nobler and better than the other. To
have more of God simply means being more like Him: the
more likeness to God there is in us, the more spiritual
we are. A master says where the lowest spirits end, the
highest material things begin. The meaning of all this is
that since God is a spirit, so the least thing that is spirit
is nobler than the highest that is material. Therefore a soul
is nobler than all material things, however noble they may
be. The soul is created as if at a point between time and
eternity, which touches both. With the higher powers she
touches eternity, but with the lower powers she touches
time. Thus, observe, she works in time not according to
time but according to eternity. This she has in common

with the angels. A master says the spirit is a sledge[4] which bears life into all the members by virtue of the close union of soul and body. But although the spirit is rational and does the entire work that is wrought in the body, yet we should not say, my *soul* knows or does this or that, but rather we should say, I do or know this or that, on account of the close union between the two: for both together make up a man. If a stone were to absorb fire into itself, it would work by the power of the fire; but when the air takes up the sun's light, there is nothing radiant but the air. This comes from the air's great receptivity to light, though there is more air in a mile than in half. So I make bold to state, for it is true: because of the close union that the soul has with the body, the soul is in the least member as perfectly as in the entire body. Concerning this, St Augustine says, if the union is close between body and soul, that union is much closer that links spirit to spirit. See, that is why He is 'lord' and 'spirit', that he may beatify us by uniting with us.

It is a question difficult to answer, how the soul can endure it without perishing when God presses her into Himself. I say that whatever God gives her, He gives her in Himself for two reasons. Firstly, if He gave her anything outside of Himself, that would be intolerable to her. Secondly, since He gives to her within Himself, she is able to receive and endure in His own and not in her own, for what is His is hers. As He has brought her out of her own, therefore His must be hers, and hers is truly His. In this way she is enabled to endure the union with God. This is 'the spirit of the Lord that has filled the circle of the world'.

Why the soul should be called a "circle of the world", and how the soul should be that is to be chosen, I have not said, but just note this much about that: just as He is 'Lord' and 'spirit', so we should be a spiritual 'earth' and 'a circle' which is to be "filled with the spirit of the Lord"[5].

We pray to our beloved Lord that we may be thus filled with this spirit that is 'Lord' and 'spirit'. Amen.

Notes

1. Not identified.
2. Avicenna.
3. Our salvation lies in the recognition that God is pure spirit, pure intelligence, thus making it possible for us, as spiritual beings, to be united with Him (Q).
4. A strange metaphor! Pfeiffer, following one MS, has *slibte*, which means 'level or slippery place'. All other MSS have *slite* 'sledge' (Q). Miss Evans dodges the issue with her rendering 'a subtle thing'. The master quoted is unknown. The passage may be corrupt.
5. Here, as in some other places, Eckhart seems to have run out of time before making all the points he intended.

SERMON TWENTY FOUR (a)
(Q 13)

VIDI SUPRA MONTEM AGNUM STANTEM ETC.

(Rev. 14:1 – 4).

St John saw a lamb standing on Mount Sion, and he had written on his forehead his name and his Father's name, and he had standing with him a hundred and forty-four thousand. He says they were all virgins and sang a new song, which none but they could sing, and they followed the lamb wherever he went.

Pagan masters say that God has so ordered all creatures that one is always above the others, and that the highest touch the lowest and the lowest the highest. What these masters have declared in obscure words, another[1] states openly, saying that the golden chain is pure and bare nature, which is raised up to God and which relishes nothing that is outside of Him, and which touches God. Each creature affects the other, and the foot of the highest is set on the crown of the lowest. No creatures can reach God in their capacity of created things, and what is created must be broken for the good to come out. The shell must be broken for the kernel to come out. All this implies a growing out. For outside of this pure nature an angel knows no more than this piece of wood, in fact without this nature an angel has no more than a midge has without God.

He says: "On the mountain". How is it possible to attain to this purity? They were virgins and were upon the mountain, they were affianced to the lamb and estranged

187

from all creatures, and they followed the lamb where-
ever he went. Some people follow the lamb as long as it
suits them; but when it does not suit them, they turn
away. This is not what it means when it says: "They
followed the lamb wherever he went". If you are a virgin
and affianced to the lamb and estranged from all creatures,
then you will follow the lamb wherever he goes: thus,
if suffering comes to you through your friends or from
yourself because of some temptation, you are not
disturbed.

He says: "They were above". What is above does not
suffer on account of what is below it, unless there is
something above it which is higher than it is. A pagan
master[2] says as long as a man is with God, it is impossible for him to suffer. A man who is high above,
estranged from all creatures, and wedded to God, does not
suffer: if he should, it would strike God to the heart.

They were on Mount Sion. '*Sion*' means 'vision'.
Jerusalem means 'peace'. As I said recently at St
Margaret's,[3] these two compel God, and if you have them
in you, He *must* be born in you. I will tell you half a
story. Our Lord was once walking in a large crowd. Then
a woman came and said, 'If only I could touch the hem of
his robe, I would be cured!' Then our Lord said, 'I have
been touched'. 'God bless us!' said St Peter, 'What makes
you say, Lord, that you have been touched? There is a
great crowd surrounding you and pressing on you.'

A master[4] says we live on death. If I am to eat a chicken
or an ox, it must be dead first. We must take suffering
upon ourselves and follow the lamb in sorrow as in joy.
The apostles took joy and sorrow upon themselves equally,

and so whatever they suffered was sweet to them: death was as dear to them as life.

A pagan master likens creatures to God[5]. Scripture says we shall become like God. 'Like' is bad and deceitful. If I am like a man, or if I find a man who is like me, that man acts as if he were myself, but he is not and that is a deception. Many a thing is like gold, but it lies and is not gold. So too, all things liken themselves to God, but they lie, for they are not like at all. Now a pagan master[6], who arrived at this by his natural understanding, says God can no more endure likeness than He can endure not to be God. Likeness is something that does not exist in God. There is oneness in the Godhead and in eternity, but likeness is not oneness. If I were one, I should not be *like*. In unity there is nothing alien: it gives me oneness in eternity, not *like*ness[7].

He says: "They had their name and their Father's name written on their foreheads". What is our name and what is our Father's name? Our name denotes that we are to be born, and the Father's name means giving birth, there where the Godhead flashes forth out of the primal brightness, which is the plenitude of brightness, as I said at St Margaret's. Philip said: "Lord, show us the Father, and it will suffice us" (John 14:8). He means, first, that we should be a father, secondly, that we should be grace[8], for the Father's name is 'giving birth': He bears His like in me. If I see some food that is like me, I am attracted; if I see a man who is like me, I am attracted. Thus it is: the heavenly Father bears His like in me, and from the likeness arises love, which is the Holy Ghost. He who is the father begets the child naturally; he who lifts the child out of the font is not its father.

Boethius says God is an unmoving good that moves all things[9]. The fact that God is steadfast makes all things move. Something is so joyous that it moves and pursues and sets all things in motion, so that they return to the source whence they flowed, and yet it remains motionless in itself. And the nobler anything is, the more steadily it moves. The ground sets them all moving. Wisdom and goodness and truth add something; oneness adds nothing but the ground of being.

Now he says: "In their mouth no lie was found". As long as I have a creature and as long as a creature has me, that is a lie, and *that* was not found in their mouths. It is the sign of a good man that he praises good people. So if a good man praises me, then I am truly praised, but if a bad man praises me, then in truth I am blamed. But if a bad man blames me, then in truth I am praised. "Of that which fills the heart, the mouth speaks" (Matt. 12:34). It is always the sign of a good man that he likes to speak of God, for people like to speak of what they are concerned with. Those who are concerned with tools like to talk about tools, those who are concerned with sermons like to talk about sermons. A good man likes to speak of nothing so much as God.

There is a power in the soul, of which I have spoken before. If the whole soul were like it, she would be uncreated and uncreatable, but this is not so[10]. In its other part it has a regard and a dependence on time, and there it touches on creation and is created. To this power, the intellect, nothing is distant or external. What is beyond the sea or a thousand miles away is as truly known and present to it as this place where I am standing. This power is a virgin, and follows the lamb wherever he goes. This power seizes God naked in His essential being. It is one in unity, not like in likeness.

May God help us to come to this experience. Amen.

Notes

1. Macrobius.

2. Aulus Gellius, according to Eckhart's Genesis commentary.

3. The Dominican nunnery in Strassburg? But it may be St.Maccabaeorum In Cologne (Q).

4. Seneca.

5. Not traced by Quint. Clark refers to Cicero's *De natura deorum*.

6. Avicenna, quoting the Koran (Sura 112) (Clark).

7. Cf. the discussion of this theme in No.7.

8. One MS has *name* 'name' instead of *gnâde* 'grace'. Quint finds 'name' unintelligible, and 'grace' difficult. He hazards the guess that it may be a reference to the name John (*Johannes* 'grace of God'), as in the parellel passage in No.24b.

9. Boethius, *De consolatione philosophiae* III, m.9 (Q).

10. This statement was denounced in article 27 of the papal bull of 1329.

SERMON TWENTY FOUR (b)
(Pf 24, Q 13a)[1]

St John saw in a vision a lamb standing, and with him were forty-four[2] who were not of this world and had not the name of wife. They were all virgins and stood as close as possible to the lamb. And wherever the lamb turned, they followed, and they sang a special song with the lamb, and had their names and the name of their father written on their foreheads.

Now John says he saw a lamb standing on the mountain. I say John was himself the mountain on which he saw the lamb. And whoever wants to see the lamb of God must himself be the mountain, and ascend into his highest and purest part. Secondly, when he says he saw the lamb standing on the mountain: whatever stands on anything else, its lowest part touches the highest part of that which is below. God touches all things and remains untouched[3]. God is above all things an instanding in Himself, and this standing in Himself sustains all creatures[4]. All creatures have an upper and a lower part, but God has not. God is above all things and is touched by none. All creatures seek outside of themselves: each seeks in the other what it lacks. God does not do this. God seeks nothing outside of Himself. What all creatures have God has entire within Him. He is the ground and the encirclement of all creatures. It is true that one is before the other, or at least that one is born of[5] the other. But she does not give it her being: it retains something of its own[6]. God is a simple instanding, an insitting, in Himself. With every creature,

193

according to the nobility of its nature, the more it in-
dwells in itself, the more it gives itself out. A simple stone,
such as limestone, points to nothing more than that it is
a stone. But a precious stone, which has great power[7],
because it has an instanding, an indwelling in itself, thereby raises its head and looks abroad. The masters say no
creature has such close indwelling in itself as body and
soul, yet nothing has such a great sallying-forth as the soul
in her highest part.

Now he says: "I saw the lamb standing". From this
we can draw four good lessons. First: the lamb gives food
and clothing, and does this most readily. That should be
a spur to our understanding that we have received so much
from God and He provides it so kindly. This should cause
us to seek nothing in all our works but His honour and
glory. Second: "The lamb stood". It is very good when
friend stands by friend. God stands by us, and remains
standing by us, constant and unmoved.

Now he says: "By him stood a great multitude, and each
of them had written on his forehead his name and his
father's name". Let at least God's name be written in us.
We must bear God's image in us, and His light must shine
in us, if we would be John[8].

Notes

1. This fragmentary sermon is a parallel to No.24a. Pfeiffer printed
it from a Basle MS, and Quint has not discovered any other copies.
It may have originally ended similarly to 24a.
2. This is a scribal mistake for the biblical 144,000, as in 24a.
3. Or 'God *moves* all things'. The verb *rüeren* can mean both 'touch'
and 'stir into activity'. Cf. No.24a, note 9.
4. God is both transcendent and immanent.
5. Quint accepts Lasson's conjecture (1868) of *von* instead of
vor, which makes the best sense. Miss Evans has gone hopelessly

wrong here.

6. The child does not derive all its being from the mother (or the parents).

7. See No.14b, note 6.

8. *John* means 'grace of God'. See 24a, note 8.

SERMON TWENTY FIVE
(Pf 25, Q 3)

NUNC SCIO VERE QUIA MISIT DOMINUS ANGELUM SUUM
(Acts 12:11)[1]

When Peter was released by the power of the supreme God from the bonds of his imprisonment, he said: "Now I know truly that God has sent me His angel and has freed me from the power of Herod and from the hands of the enemy".

Now let us turn this phrase round and say: 'Because God has sent me His angel, therefore I know truly.' *Peter* is as much as to say 'knowledge'[2]. I have said before, knowledge and intellect unite the soul with God. Intellect penetrates into the pure essence; knowledge runs ahead, preceding and blazing a trail so that God's only-begotten Son may be born. Our Lord says in Matthew that none knows the Father but the Son (Matt. 11:27). The masters say knowledge resides in likeness. Some masters say the soul is made of all things, because she has the potentiality of understanding all things. It sounds stupid, but it is true. The masters say that for me to know anything, it must be fully present to me and like my understanding. The saints say potentiality is in the Father, likeness in the Son, and unity in the Holy Ghost. Therefore, since the Father is wholly present in the Son and the Son is wholly like Him, none knows the Father save the Son.

Now Peter says: "Now I know truly". How does one know truly here? it is because it is a divine light which deceives nobody. Secondly, because there one knows

197

barely and purely with nothing veiling it. Therefore Paul says: "God dwells in a light which is inaccessible" (1Tim. 6:16). The masters say the wisdom which we acquire here will remain with us yonder, though Paul says it will fall away[3]. One master says pure knowledge, even in this life, takes such great delight in itself that the joy of all created things is a mere nothing compared to the joy that pure knowledge brings[4]. And yet, however noble it may be, it is but contingent, and just as one little word is insignificant compared to all the world, so insignificant is all the wisdom we can acquire here, compared to the naked, pure truth. That is why Paul says it must fall away. Even if it remained, it would be like a foolish virgin and as nothing to the naked truth we shall know there. The third reason why we shall truly know there is this: the things we see here as mutable we shall know there as unchanging; we shall apprehend them there in undivided form and close together: for that which here is distant, there is near, for *there* all things are present. That which happened on the first day and that which is to happen on the last day, *is* there all in the present.

"Now I know truly that God has sent me His angel". When God sends His angel to the soul, she becomes truly knowing. It was not for nothing that God entrusted the key to Peter, for Peter denotes knowing, and knowledge has the key and opens up and breaks through and finds God naked, and then she says to her companion, will, what she has obtained, though she had the will already: for what I will, I seek. Knowledge goes before. She is a princess, seeking her dominion in the highest and purest realms, and she conveys it to the soul and the soul to nature and nature to all the bodily senses. The soul is so noble at her highest and purest that the masters cannot find any name for her. They call her 'soul' as giving essence to the body. Now the masters declare that, after the first emanation of the Godhead, where the Son breaks out of the Father, the angel is formed most like God. This is true: the soul is made in God's image in her highest part, but the angel is a closer copy of God. All that belongs to the angel is modelled on God. That is why the angel is sent to the soul, so that he may bring her back to the same image after which he was formed, for knowledge comes from likeness. And since the soul has the potentiality of knowing all things, therefore she never rests till she gains the primal image where all things are one; and there she rests, there she is in God. In God, no creature is nobler than another.

The masters say being and knowing are all one, for what does not exist is not known; whatever has most being is best known. And since God has transcendent being, therefore He transcends all knowledge, as I said the day before yesterday in my last sermon, that the soul is in-formed in the highest purity, in the impress of pure essence, where she tastes God before He assumes truth or cognisability, where all naming has been dropped: *there* she knows Him most purely — there she receives being on an equal footing. Therefore Paul says: "God dwells in a light which is inaccessible". He is an indwelling in His own pure essence, where there is nothing that is contingent. Whatever is accidental must drop away. He is a pure presence in Himself, where there is neither this nor that, for whatever is in God, is God.[5] A pagan master says the powers that hover below God have a dependence on God, and though they have a pure subsistence in themselves, yet they have a dependence on Him who has neither beginning nor end: for nothing alien can enter God. Heaven illustrates this, for it can never receive an alien impression in alien wise.

Thus it happens that whatever comes to God is transformed: however base it may be, if we bring it to God, it sheds itself. Here is an example: if I have wisdom, I am not wisdom myself. I can gain wisdom, and I can also lose it. But whatever is in God, is God: it cannot drop away from Him. It is implanted in the divine nature, for the divine nature is so powerful that whatever is proferred to it is either firmly implanted in it, or else it remains wholly outside. Now observe a wondrous thing! Seeing that God transforms such base things into Himself, what do you think He does with the soul, which He has dignified with His own image?

That we may attain to this, may God help us.[6] Amen.

Notes

1. Preached on the feast of St Peter's Chains (in English: Lammas Day), 1 August.
2. According to St Jerome (Clark). The real meaning, of course, is "rock". The association with Peter is through the 'key' of knowledge (see below).
3. 1 Cor. 13:8.
4. Aristotle.
5. Clark notes: 'This is Scholastic doctrine'. True, but the censors misread this passage as 'whatever is, is God', which would be pantheism.
6. The conventional conclusion is found only in the Basel print. This text is a poor witness, but Quint does not think it likely that anything has been lost at the end.

VIDI CIVITATEM SANCTAM JERUSALEM DESCENDENTEM DE

CAELO ETC.

(Rev. 21:2)

St John saw a city. A city denotes two things: firstly, it is fortified so that none can harm it, and secondly, the concord of the people. "This city had no prayer-house: God Himself was the temple. There is no need of light, whether of sun or of moon: the glory of our Lord illumines it". This city denotes each spiritual soul; as St Paul says: "The soul is a temple of God" (1 Cor. 3:16), and is so strong, as St Augustine says, that none can harm it unless by its own wilfulness.

First we should note the peace there should be in the soul. Therefore she is called 'Jerusalem'. St Dionysius[1] says divine peace pervades and orders and ends all things; if peace did not do this, all things would be dissipated and there would be no order. Secondly, peace causes creatures to pour themselves out and flow in love and without harm. Thirdly, it makes creatures serviceable to one another, so that they have a support in one another. What one of them cannot have of itself, it gets from another. Thus one creature derives from another. Fourthly, it makes them turn back to their original source, which is God.

In the second place, he says that the city is 'Holy'. St Dionysius says that holiness is complete purity, liberty and perfection. Purity means that a man is separated from sin, and this makes the soul free. Likeness is the chief

delight and joy there is in heaven; if God were to enter
the soul and she were not like Him, she would suffer torments, for St John says: "Whoever commits a sin is the
slave of sin" (John 8:34). Of the angels and the saints
we may say that they are perfect, but the saints not
wholly so, for they still feel affection for their bodies
which now lie in ashes.[2] In God alone is complete perfection. I marvel that St John ever dared to say, if he had not
seen it in the spirit, that there are three Persons, how the
Father empties Himself completely into the birth, into the
Son, and pours Himself with goodness in a flow of love
into the Holy Ghost.[3] Again, 'holiness' denotes 'what is
withdrawn from the world'. God is something and is pure
being, and sin is nothing and draws us away from God.
God made the angels and the soul after something, that is:
God. The soul is created, so to speak, under the shadow
of the angels, yet they have a common nature, but all
material things are created after nothing, far from God.
By being poured into the body, the soul is darkened,
and must together with the body be raised up again to
God. When she is free from earthly things the soul is
holy. Zacheus, while he was on the ground, could not
see our Lord.[4] St Augustine says, 'If a man would be
holy let him forsake mundane things'. I have often said
that the soul cannot be pure unless she is reduced to her
original purity, as God made her, just as gold cannot be
made from copper by two or three roastings: it must be
reduced to its primary nature. For all things which melt
on heating or solidify on cooling are altogether of a
watery nature.[5] They must therefore be wholly reduced
to water and get quite rid of their present nature, then

heaven and science combine to transmute it all into gold. Iron can be compared to silver, and copper to gold: but the more we equate it without subtraction, the more false it is.[6] It is the same with the soul. It is easy to make show of virtues, or to talk of them: but to have them in reality is extremely rare.

In the third place, he calls the city 'new'. *New* denotes what is unused or near to its beginning. God is our beginning. When we are united with Him we shall be new. Some folk foolishly think that God has for ever been making or keeping the things we now see, and gives them forth in time. But we must understand that divine acts are effortless,[7] as I shall tell you. I am standing here and suppose I had been standing here for thirty years with my face showing, though nobody had seen it, I should have stood here all the same. Now if there were a mirror handy, if it were held before my face my face would cast an image in it with no effort on my part; and if that happened yesterday then it would be new, and again today, it would be newer still, and so on for thirty years or for all time, it would be ever new; and if there were a thousand mirrors, that would cost me no effort. Thus, God has eternally in Him all images, not as the soul and other creatures, but as God. With Him there is nothing new, no image, but as I was saying of the mirror, so with us there is new and eternal as well.

When the body is ready God pours a soul therein, formed like the body and having a likeness with it, and because of the likeness a liking. Hence there is no one free from self-love: they deceive themselves who think they have no love of self. They would have to hate them-

selves, and could not stay. We must love those things
that further our progress to God: that alone is love with
God's love. If I desire to cross the sea and want a ship,
that is solely from wishing to be across: having crossed
over, I have no more need of the ship. Plato says, 'What
God *is*, I do not know' (he meant that as long as the soul
is wrapped up in the body she cannot see God), 'but what
He is not I know well enough', as we can see by the sun,
whose radiance none can endure unless it is first en-
wrapped in the air, and thus shines on the earth. St
Dionysius says: 'If the divine light shines in me, it must
be shrouded, as my soul is shrouded'.[8] He further says
the divine light appears to five kinds of people. The first
are not alive to it. They are like cattle, not capable of
receiving it, as a simile will show: if I am crossing the
water and if it were rough amd muddy, I would not be
able to see my face in it on account of its roughness.
To the second group a little light appears, like the flash
of a sword being forged. The third get more of it, like a
great flash of lightning, which is bright, and then immediately dark again. They are all those who fall away from
the divine light again into sin. The fourth group receive
more of it, but sometimes He withdraws Himself for no
other purpose but to spur her[9] on and increase her desire.
It is certain that if someone were ready to fill all our laps,
then everyone would make his lap wide to receive a great
deal. St Augustine says to receive a great deal, a man
must enlarge his capacity. The fifth are aware of a great
light as bright as day, but still as it were through a chink.
As the soul says in the Book of Love: "My beloved looked at me through a chink. His face was comely" (Cant.

2:9,14). About this St Augustine says, 'Lord, thou givest me sometimes such great sweetness that, if it were perfected in me, if this is not heaven I know not what heaven can be'. A master says, 'He who would see God, unless he is adorned with godly works, will be cast back among evil things.' Is there then no way of seeing God quite clearly? Yes. In the Book of Love the soul says: "My love looked at me through the window" — that is, without hindrances — "and I knew him, he stood by the wall" — that is, by the body, which is perishable — and said: "Open up to me, my beloved" — that is because she is altogether mine in love, for "he is mine and I am his alone"; "my dove" — that is, simple in longing — "my beautiful" — that is, in act. "Arise, make haste and come to me. The cold is past", of which everything dies: all things live in the warmth. "The rain is over" — that is delight in temporal things. "The flowers are coming up in our land" — these are the fruit of eternal life. "Begone, o north wind, which withers up" — here God is forbidding temptation to hinder the soul any more. "Come, wind from the south, blow through my garden and make my spices to flow" — here God bids all perfections to enter the soul.[10]

Notes

1. 'Dionysius the Areopagite', *De divinis nominibus XI, 1*.
2. i.e. have not yet been resurrected.
3. Cf. No.23.
4. Luke 19:2-3.
5. In terms of the four elements: earth, water, fire and air.
6. Without abstraction of its true nature, i.e. unless it has been (alchemically) changed.
7. Or 'timeless' (Q).
8. i.e. in the flesh.

9. The soul.
10. The usual concluding prayer is missing. Quint has slight doubts about the authenticity of this sermon, but concludes that it is probably genuine.

GAUDETE IN DOMINO, ITERUM GAUDETE
(Phil. 4:4)

St Paul says: "Rejoice in the Lord always and have no more care: the Lord is here. Your thoughts are known to God in gratitude or prayer."

Now he says: "Rejoice!" Jerome says no man can receive skill, wisdom or joy from God unless he is a virtuous man.[1] He is not a virtuous man who has not changed his old ways: he cannot receive from God skill, wisdom or joy. Now he says: "Rejoice in the Lord". He did not say 'in our Lord' but 'in the Lord'. I have said before that God's lordship does not consist merely in His being lord of all creatures, but His lordship consists in this, that He could create a thousand worlds and transcend them all in His pure essence: therein lies His lordship.

Now he says: "Rejoice in the Lord". Let us note two things here. The first is that we should remain all within the Lord, not seeking outside Him in knowledge or in joy but merely rejoicing *in* the Lord. The second thing: "Rejoice in the *Lord*", in His inmost and first, from which all things receive though He receives from none. Now he says: "Rejoice in the Lord *always*". The masters say that two hours cannot exist at the same time, nor two days. St Augustine[2] says he rejoices *all the time* who rejoices *above* time. He[3] says: "Rejoice all the time". that is, above time, and "have no care: the Lord is at hand and is near". The soul that is going to rejoice in the Lord must of

207

necessity cast off all care, at least during the time when she yields herself to God. That is why he says: "Have no care: the Lord is at hand and is near". That means in our inmost part, if He finds us at home and the soul has not gone out for a walk with the five senses. The soul must be at home in her inmost and in the highest and purest, staying within and not looking out, and *then* "God is at hand and is near."

Another sense is: "The Lord is *by*" — He is *by* Himself and does not go far out. Now David says: "Lord, make my soul rejoice, for I have raised her up to thee!" (Ps. 86:4). The soul must rise with all her might above herself and be translated beyond time and place into the expanse and breadth where God is by Himself and near, not going far out and not touching anything alien. Jerome[4] says: 'It is as possible for a stone to have angelic wisdom as it is for God ever to give Himself in time or in temporal things.' Therefore he says: "The Lord is near by". David says: "God is near by to all who praise Him and speak Him and name Him, and that in truth" (Ps. 145:18). How one praises, speaks and names Him, that I will leave on one side. But he says: "in truth". What is truth? The Son alone is truth, not the Father or the Holy Ghost, except as they are one truth in their essence. That is truth, if I declare what I have in my heart, and say it with my mouth as I have it in my heart, without hypocrisy or concealment. The revealing of this is truth. And so the Son alone is truth. All that the Father has and can perform, He speaks fully in His Son. The revealing and the performance is the truth. Therefore he says, 'in truth'.

Now St Paul says: "Rejoice in the Lord", and adds:

"Your thoughts shall be known by the Lord", that is, in *this* truth by the Father. Faith inheres in the light of intellect, hope inheres in the aspiring power which is ever striving upwards into the highest and purest — into truth.[5] I have sometimes said — note my words — that this power is so free and so aspiring that it will endure no restraint. The fire of love inheres in the will.

Now he says, "Your thoughts" — and all the powers — "shall be known by the Lord, thoughts of gratitude and prayer". If a man had no more to do with God than to be thankful, that would suffice.

That we may rejoice eternally in the Lord and by the Lord in the truth, and that our thoughts may be known to Him, and that we may be thankful to Him for all goodness and be blessed in Him, so help us God. Amen.

Notes

1. Quotation untraced (Q).
2. Quotation untraced (Q).
3. Paul.
4. Quotation untraced (Q).
5. The three highest powers of the soul.

SERMON TWENTY EIGHT
(Pf 28, Q 78)

MISSUS EST GABRIEL ANGELUS ETC.
(Luke 1:26)

St Luke says in his gospel: "An angel was sent from God into a land called Galilee, into a town called Nazareth, to a virgin called Mary, who was betrothed to Joseph, who was of the house of David". Bede, a master, says this was the beginning of our salvation. I have said before and say again that everything our Lord has ever done he did simply to the end that God might be with us and that we might be one with Him, and that is why God became man. The masters say that God was born spiritually in our Lady before he was born of her in the flesh, and from the overflow of that begetting whereby the Heavenly Father begot his only-begotten Son in her soul, the eternal Word received its human nature in her, and she became physically pregnant.

Now he says: "An angel was sent from God". I say it had to be, that he was sent from God. The soul would have been demeaned by receiving the angelic light had it not been sent to her from God, and had the divine light not inhered concealed in it, which made the angel's light delectable; otherwise she would have had none of it.

Now he says: "An angel". What is an angel? Three teachers give three different explanations of what an angel is. Dionysius[1] says, An angel is a mirror without flaw, surpassing clear, receiving in itself the reflection of the divine light. Augustine[2] says, An angel is close to God,

211

and matter is close to nothing. John Damascene[3] says, An angel is an image of God and through all that is his there shines the image of God. The soul has this image in her summit, in her topmost branch, whereon the divine light for ever shines. This is his first definition of an angel. Later on he calls him a sharp sword, aflame with divine desire, and adds the angel is free of matter — so free that he is inimical to matter. See, that is an angel.

Now he says: "An angel was sent from God". What for? Dionysius says an angel has three functions. First, he purifies, secondly, he enlightens, and thirdly he perfects. He purifies the soul in three ways: first, he purifies her from stains that have accrued to her; secondly, he purges her from matter and makes her collected, and thirdly, he purifies her from ignorance, as one angel does another. In the second case, he enlightens the soul in twofold fashion. The divine light is so overwhelming that the soul is unable to bear it unless it is tempered and shaded in the angel's light, and so conveyed into the soul. Then he illumines her by likeness. The angel conveys his own understanding to the soul and so strengthens her to receive and endure the divine light. If I were in a wilderness alone and was afraid, the presence of a child would dissipate my dread and give me courage, so noble, so joyous and so mighty a thing is life itself. And failing a child, even a beast would comfort me. That is why those who practise magic by necromancy keep an animal, such as a dog, the animal's vitality invigorating them.[4] Likeness gives strength in all things. That is why the angel brings it to the soul, for he resembles her, and so strengthens and prepares her to receive the divine light.

Now he says: "An angel was sent from God". The soul must be like the angel in the ways I have named, if the Son is to be sent to her and born in her. But we cannot here go into the question of how the angel perfects her.[5]

May God send His angel to us to purify, illumine and perfect us so that we may be eternally blessed with God. So help us God. Amen.

Notes

1. *De divinis nominibus* ch.4 (Q).
2. *Confessions*, ch.12 (Q).
3. *De fide orthodoxa II*, ch.3 (Q).
4. A remarkable comparison!
5. As elsewhere, Eckhart does not expatiate on the final point. Since this is a very short sermon, the reason is not clear. Pahncke (quoted by Quint) may be right in thinking that the note-taker gave up at this point.

SERMON TWENTY NINE

(Pf/Evans 29 (part), Q 38)[1]

IN ILLO TEMPORE MISSUS EST ANGELUS GABRIEL A DEO:

AVE GRATIA PLENA, DOMINUS TECUM

(Luke 1:26, 28)

These words are written by St Luke: "At that time the angel Gabriel was sent by God". At what time? "In the sixth month"[2] that John the Baptist was in his mother's womb. If anyone were to ask me, Why do we pray, why do we fast, why do we do all our works, why are we baptised, why (most important of all) did God become man? — I would answer, in order that God may be born in the soul and the soul be born in God.[3] For that reason all the scriptures were written, for that reason God created the world and all angelic natures: so that God may be born in the soul and the soul be born in God. All cereal nature means wheat, all treasure nature means gold, and all generation means man. Therefore one master says no animal exists but has some likeness to man.

"In time". When the word is first conceived in my intellect, it is so pure and subtle that it is a true word, before taking shape in my thought. In the third place, it is spoken out loud by my mouth, and then it is nothing but a manifestation of the interior word. Thus the eternal Word is spoken inwardly, in the heart of the soul, in the inmost and purest, in the head of the soul of which I just spoke, in the intellect, and *therein* the birth takes place. He who has nothing but a firm conviction and hope of this would be glad to know how this birth occurs and

215

what conduces to it.

St Paul says: "In the fullness of time God sent His Son" (Gal. 4:4). St Augustine says what this fullness of time is: 'Where there is no more time, that is the "fullness of time"'. The day is full, when there is no more day. That is a necessary truth: all time must be gone when this birth begins, for there is nothing that hinders this birth so much as time and creatures. It is an assured truth that time cannot affect God or the soul by her nature. If the soul could be touched by time, she would not be the soul, and if God could be touched by time, He would not be God. But if it were possible for the soul to be touched by time, then God could never be born in her, and she could never be born in God. For God to be born in the soul, all time must have dropped away from her, or she must have dropped away from time with will or desire.

Another meaning of "fullness of time": if anyone had the skill and the power to gather up time and all that has happened in six thousand years or that will happen till the end of time, into one present Now, *that* would be the "fullness of time". That is the Now of eternity, in which the soul knows all things in God new and fresh and present and as joyous as I have them now present. I was reading recently in a book[4] — who can fully understand it? — that God is now making the world just as on the first day, when He created the world. Here God is rich, and this is the kingdom of God. The soul in which God is to be born must drop away from time and time from her, she must soar aloft and stand gazing into this richness of God's: there there is breadth without breadth, expanseless expanse, and there the soul knows all things, and knows

216

them perfectly. As for what the masters say of the expanse
of heaven, it would be unbelievable to say it. Yet the least
of the powers of my soul is wider than the expanse of
heaven. I do not speak of the intellect, which is expanseless expanse. In the soul's head, in the intellect, I am as
near to a place a thousand miles away across the sea as to
the spot where I am standing now. In this expanse and in
this richness of God's the soul is aware, there she misses
nothing and expects nothing.

"The angel was sent". The masters declare that the
multitude of angels is beyond all numbering. They are too
numerous for number to contain; their number cannot
even be conceived. But for anyone who could grasp
distinctions without number and quantity, a hundred
would be as one. Even if there were a hundred Persons in
the Godhead, a man who could distinguish without number and quantity would perceive them only as one God.
Unbelievers and some untutored Christian people wonder
at this, and even some priests know as little about it as
a stone: they think of three like three cows or three
stones. But he who can make distinction in God without
number or quantity knows that three Persons are one
God.[5]

Also, an angel is so exalted, that the best teachers declare each angel has a complete nature.[6] It is just the same
as if there were a man who had everything that all men
have ever had, have now or ever will have of power and
wisdom and everything; that would be a miracle, and yet
he would be no more than a man: for even though he had
all things that all men have, yet he would be far from the
angels. Thus every angel has a complete nature and is

distinct from the other angels as one animal is from another that has a different nature.[7] In this multitude of
angels God is rich, and whoever is aware of this is aware of
the kingdom of God.[8] It proclaims God's kingdom just
as a lord is proclaimed by the number of his knights.
Therefore He is known as the "Lord God of Hosts". All
this multitude of angels, however lofty they are, co-
operate and help when God is born in the soul. That is to
say, they have pleasure and joy and delight in the birth,
but they do not act. No work is done there by creatures,
for God performs the birth alone, but the angels minister
to this. Whatever ministers thereto is a work of service.

The angel was called Gabriel. He did what he was
called.[9] He was no more called Gabriel than Conrad. No
one can know an angel's name. No master and no understanding ever got to where an angel received his name:
perhaps he is nameless. The soul, too, has no name. Just as
no one can find a true name for God, so none can find the
soul's true name, although mighty tomes have been written
about this. But she is given a name according as she has a
regard to her activity. 'Carpenter' is not a man's name,
but the name is taken from the work of which he is a
master. He took the name 'Gabriel' from the work of
which he was a messenger, for *Gabriel* means 'power'. In
this birth God works powerfully or exerts power. What
is the object of all the power of nature? To effect herself. What does all nature intend in generation? To effect
herself. The nature of my father wanted to produce a
father in his nature. When that could not be, she wanted
to produce one who was in all respects like him. When
the strength for this was lacking, she produced one that

218

was as like as possible — a son. But when the power is
still less strong, or some other accident occurs, then she
produces a human being still less alike.[10] But in God there
is plenitude of power, therefore in *His* birth He produces
His like. All that God is in power, truth and wisdom, He
bears altogether in the soul.

St Augustine says: 'What the soul loves she grows to be
like. If she loves earthly things she becomes earthly. If
she loves God (one might ask), does she then become
God?' If I said that, it would sound heretical to those
whose intelligence is weak and who cannot understand it.
But St Augustine says: 'I do not say it, but I refer you to
scripture, which says: "I have said that you are gods"
(Ps. 82:6)'. Anyone possessing anything of the riches I
have spoken of, a glimpse, a hope or an inkling, would
quite understand this. Never was there born anything so
akin, so like, so one with God as the soul becomes at
this birth. If it so happens that there is any hindrance, so
that she does not become like in all respects, that is not
God's fault: just as far as all her failings drop away from
her, just so far does God make her like Himself. That a
carpenter is unable to build a fine house out of worm-
eaten wood is not his fault; the trouble lies in the wood.
And thus it is with God's work in the soul. If the least of
the angels were able to take shape or be born in the soul —
the whole world would be as nothing to that, for in a
single spark of the angel there grows, flourishes and shines
forth everything that is in the world. But God performs
this birth Himself: the angel can do no work here except
ministering.

"Ave": that means 'without woe'.[11] Whoever is without

219

creaturehood is without woe and without hell, and he who is least creature and has least of it, has the least woe. I once declared that he who has the world least, has it most. No one possesses the world so truly as he who has abandoned all the world. Do you know why God is God? He is God because He is without creature. He did not name Himself in time. In time are creatures and sin and death. These are in a certain sense akin, and inasmuch as the soul has dropped away from time, there is there no woe or pain; even distress is turned for her to joy. All that could ever be conceived of delight and joy, of happiness and pleasure, is no joy at all when set against the bliss which is in this birth.

"Full of grace". The least work of grace is loftier than all angels in their nature. St Augustine says that a work of grace performed by God, such as that He converts a sinner and makes a good man of him, is greater than if God created a new world. It is as easy for God to turn round heaven and earth as it is for me to turn round an apple in my hand. Where grace is in the soul, that is so pure and so like and akin to God, and grace is without works just as in the birth of which I spoke before there is no work. Grace performs no works. St John "performed no sign" (John 10:41). The work that an angel has in God is so lofty that no master and no intelligence ever came to an understanding of it. But from that work there falls a chip, just as a chip might fall from a plank that is being cut — a lightning-flash, which is where the angel touches heaven with his lowest part — and from that there shoots and blossoms and springs into life everything that is in the world.

I sometimes mention two springs. Though this may sound strange, we must speak according to out understanding. One spring, from which grace gushes forth, is where the Father bears forth His only-begotten Son. From that source grace arises, and there grace flows forth from that same spring. Another spring is where creatures flow out of God. This one is as far from the spring whence grace flows as heaven is from earth. Grace does not perform works. Where fire is in its own nature, it does no harm and burns nothing. The heat of the fire burns here below. But where the heat is in the nature of fire, it does not burn and is harmless. Yet when the heat is in the fire it is as far from the fire's true nature as heaven is from earth. Grace performs no works, it is too delicate for this, work is as far from grace as heaven is from earth. An indwelling, an attachment and a union with God, — *that* is grace, and God is 'with' that, for there immediately follows:

"God be with you" — and there the birth occurs. Let no one think this is beyond him. What matters the hardship to me, if He does the work? All His commandments are easy for me to keep. Let Him bid me do what He will, I care not at all, it is all a trifle to me, if He gives me His grace with it. Some people say they have not got it. I say, 'I am sorry. Do you want it?' — No. — 'Then I am sorrier still'. If you cannot have it, you should at least have a desire for it. If you can't have a desire for it, you should at least desire to desire it. David says: "I have desired a desire, Lord, for thy justice" (Ps. 119:20).[12]

That we may so desire God that He may be willing to be born in us, so help us God. Amen.

Notes

1. Pfeiffer's No.29 is from a fragmentary text. Miss Evans translates this in vol.I as No.29, but gives the full text as No.27 in vol.II, following Sievers.

2. This is what the gospel actually says, but Eckhart has quoted it differently because he wants to talk about time.

3. See No.2, note 8.

4. Probably St Augustine's *Confessions* XI, ch.13 (Q).

5. The Trinity.

6. According to St Thomas, each angel is a species in himself (Q).

7. Or belongs to a different species.

8. A play on *rîche* 'rich' and *rîche* 'kingdom' (modern *reich* and *Reich*).

9. *Gabriel* 'the power of God'.

10. A daughter (Q).

11. Eckhart explains this pseudo-etymology in *LW* II, 267: *'Ave,' sine vae* (Q).

12. A literal rendering of the Vulgate *Concupivit anima mea desiderare justificationes tuas.*

SERMON THIRTY
(Pf 30, Q 45)

BEATUS ES, SIMON BAR JONA, QUIA CARO ET SANGUIS ETC.

(Matt. 16:17)

Our Lord says: "Simon Peter, thou art blessed; flesh and blood have not revealed that to thee, but my Father who is in heaven". St Peter has four names: he is called Peter, and is called Bar-Jona, and is called Simon, and is called Cephas.

Now our Lord says: "Thou art blessed". All people desire blessedness. And a master[1] says all people desire to be praised. But St Augustine says a good man desires no praise, he desires to be worthy of praise. Now our masters say virtue is so pure, so wholly abstract and detached from all corporeal things in its ground and true nature that nothing whatever can enter into it without defiling the virtue and making it a vice. A single thought or any seeking of one's own advantage, and it is not a true virtue, it is turned to vice. Such is virtue by nature.

Now a pagan master[2] says if a man practises virtue for the sake of anything else but virtue, then it never was a virtue. If he seeks praise or anything else, he is selling virtue. One should never give up a virtue by nature for anything in the world. Therefore a good man desires no praise, but he desires to be worthy of praise. A man should not be sorry if people are angry with him, he should be sorry to deserve the anger.

Now our Lord says: "Blessed art thou". Blessedness lies in four things: in having everything that has essence, that is delightful to desire and brings appetite; to have it all undivided with one's whole soul; further, received in God in the purest and highest, bare, unconcealed, in the primal breaking forth and in the ground of being; and all taken whence God Himself takes it — that is blessedness.[3]

Now he says: "Peter", which is to say 'he who sees God'.[4] The masters ask whether the kernel of eternal[5] life lies more in the intellect or in the will. Will has two operations: desire and love. The intellect's work is one-fold, and therefore it is better.[6] Its work is knowing, and it never rests till it touches nakedly that which it knows. And thus it goes ahead of will and declares to it what to love. As long as one desires things, one has not got them. When we have them, we love them, then desire falls away.

How should a man be who is to see God? He must be dead. Our Lord says: "No man can see me and live" (Ex. 33:20).[7] Now St Gregory says he is dead who is dead to the world. Now judge for yourselves what a dead man is like and how little he is touched by anything in the world. If we die to the world we do not die to God. St Augustine prayed a variety of prayers. He said: 'Lord, grant me to know thee and me'; 'Lord, have mercy on me and show me thy face and grant me that I may die, and grant me that I may not die, so that I may eternally behold thee.' This is the first point: that one must be dead if one would see God. This is the first name, Peter.

One master[8] says if there were no 'means', we could see an ant in heaven. But another master[9] says if there were no means, we could see nothing. They are both right. The colour that is on the wall, if it is to be transmitted to my eye, must be filtered and refined in the air and in the light and thus spiritually conveyed to my eye. Thus too the soul must be strained by light and by grace, in order to see God. Therefore that master was right who said if there were no means we should see nothing. But the other master is also right who said if there were no means we could see an ant in heaven. If the soul were without means, she would see God naked.

The second name, Bar-Jona, means as much as 'son of grace',[10] in which the soul is purified and borne aloft and prepared for the divine vision.

The third name is Simon, which means as much as 'that which is obedient', or 'that which is submissive.' He who would hear God must be far removed from people. Accordingly David says: "I will be silent and hear what God speaks in me. He speaks peace to His people and over all His saints and to all those who have turned again towards their hearts" (Ps. 85:9). Blessed is that man who diligently listens to what God is saying in him, and he will be directly exposed to the ray of divine light. The soul that is turned with all her powers under the light of God becomes fired and inflamed with the love of God. The divine light shines directly above him. If the sun were to shine directly above our heads, few could survive it. Thus the highest part of the soul, which is the head, should be raised up directly under the ray of divine light, so that the divine light can shine into that place I have often spoken of: this is so pure and transcendent and lofty that all lights are darkness and nothing compared with this light. All creatures, as such, are as nothing; but when they are illumined from above with the light from which they receive their being, they are something.[11]

Therefore the natural mind can never be so noble as to be able to touch or seize God without means, unless the soul has these six things of which I have spoken: — First, to be dead to all that is unlike; second, to be well purified in light and in grace; third, to be without means; fourth, to be obedient to God's word in the inmost part; fifth, to be subject to the divine light; the sixth is what a pagan master says: blessedness is when one lives according to the the highest power of the soul, which should be always striving upwards and receiving her blessedness from God. Where the Son himself receives it in the primal source, there too we should receive it from God's highest part, and so we too must keep our highest part erect towards this.

Cephas means the same as 'head'.[12] The intellect is the head of the soul. Those who put the matter roughly say that love has precedence, but those who speak most precisely say expressly — and it is true — that the kernel of eternal life lies in understanding more than in love. You should know why. Our finest masters — and there are not many of them — say that understanding and intellect go straight up to God. But love turns to the loved object and takes there what is good, whereas intellect takes hold of what makes it good. Honey is sweeter in itself than anything made from it. Love takes God as He is good, but intellect presses upwards and takes God as He is being. Therefore God said: "Simon Peter, thou art blessed". God gives the righteous man divine being and calls him by the same name that belongs to that being. And so he says after that: "My Father, who is in heaven". Of all names there is none more proper than 'He who is'.

226

For if a man should seek to indicate something by saying 'it is', that would seem silly, but if he said 'it is a piece of wood or a stone', then we should know what he meant. And so we say that when everything is removed, abstracted and peeled off so that nothing at all remains but a simple 'is' — *that* is the proper characteristic of His name. Therefore God said to Moses: "Say 'He that is has sent me'" (Ex. 3:14).[13] Therefore our Lord calls his own with his own name. Our Lord said to his disciples: "Those who are my followers shall sit at my table in my Father's kingdom and eat my food and drink my drink which my Father has prepared for me; thus I have also prepared it for you".[14] Blessed is the man who has attained to this, that he shall receive with the Son just where the Son receives. Right there we too shall find our bliss, there whereon *his* bliss depends, and whence he receives his being, in that same ground, there all his friends shall find their bliss and draw it from there. That is the "table in God's kingdom".

That we may come to this table, may God help us. Amen.

<hr />

Notes

1. Ennius, quoted by St Augustine (Q).
2. Seneca (Q).
3. The reference is not to material, sensual pleasures. These for Eckhart have no 'essence'.
4. Cf. No.25, note 2. Eckhart stretches the alleged meaning a little further here!
5. Miss Evan's 'external' is obviously a misprint.
6. The Dominican view. The Franciscans gave priority to the will (see No.8, note 5). But Eckhart is not merely scoring a debating point.

7. Note that Eckhart says 'our Lord' though the words are attributed to the God of the Old Testament.

8. Democritus (Q). Miss Evans has 'the beloved' instead of 'an ant'. She was thinking of amîs 'lover', from French ami.

9. Aristotle (Q).

10. St Jerome says it means either 'son of the dove' or 'son of grace' (Q).

11. This modifies the more extreme position, 'all creatures are nothing', condemned in art 26 of the bull of 1329.

12. Isidore of Seville derived this from Greek *kephale* 'head'; but as Albertus Magnus knew, Bede was aware of the true meaning: 'rock' (Q).

13. This text is dealt with at length in Eckhart's Exodus commentar (*LW* II, 20ff.).

14. A combination of Matt. 19:28 and Luke 22:29f.(Q).

SERMON THIRTY ONE
(Pf 31, Q 37)

VIR MEUS SERVUS TUUS MORTUUS EST

(2 Kings 4:1ff.)

"A woman said to the prophet, 'Sir, my husband your servant is dead. And now the creditors have come and taken my two sons and made them bondsmen for the debt, and I have nothing but a little oil.' The prophet said, 'Just borrow some empty vessels and pour a little into each, that will grow and increase; sell it and pay off your debt and release your sons. With what is left over, keep yourself and your two sons.'"

The spark of intellect, which is the head of the soul, is called the husband[1] of the soul, and is none other than a tiny spark of the divine nature, a divine light, a ray and an imprint of the divine nature. We read of a woman who requested this gift from God.[2] The first gift that God gives is the Holy Ghost. Therein God gives all His gifts: that is the "living water; to whom I give that, he shall never thirst again." This water is grace and light, and it wells up in the soul, surging up within and thrusting upwards, "leaping into eternity". "Then the woman said, 'Sir, give me of the water'. Then our Lord said, 'Bring me your husband', and she said, 'Sir, I have none.' Then our Lord said, 'You are right, you have none. But you have had five, and the one you have now is not yours'." St Augustine says, 'Why does our Lord say, "You are right"? He means to say "the five husbands are the five senses: they had you in your youth according to all their will and

229

desire. Now you have one in your old age and he is not yours: that is the intellect, that you do not obey".' When this 'husband' is dead, it bodes ill. When the soul departs from the body, that is very painful, but when God departs from the soul, the pain is immeasurable. As the soul gives life to the body, so God gives life to the soul. As the soul flows into all members, so God flows into all the powers of the soul and suffuses them so that they overflow with goodness and love over all about them, so that all things become aware of Him. Thus He flows all the time, that is, above all time, in eternity and in that life in which all things live. Therefore our Lord said to the woman: "I give the living water. Whoever drinks of it will never thirst again and he will live in eternal life".

Now the woman says, "Sir, my husband, your servant, is dead". 'Servant' means one who receives and keeps things for his lord. If he kept them for himself, he would be a thief. Intellect is more truly the 'servant' than will or love. Will and love fall on God as being good, and if He were not good, they would ignore Him. Intellect penetrates right up into the essence without heeding goodness or power or wisdom, or whatever is accidental. It does not care what is added to God, it takes Him in Himself, sinks into the essence and takes God as He is pure essence. Even if He were not wise nor good nor just, it would still take Him as pure being. Here intellect is like the highest rank of angels, of which there are three choirs. The Thrones receive God into them and keep God among themselves, and God rests among them; the Cherubim know God and persist therein; Seraphim means 'burning fire'.[3] Intellect is like these and keeps God in itself. With

230

these angels the intellect receives God in His robing-room, naked, as He is One without distinction. Now the woman says, "Sir, my husband your servant is dead. The creditors have come and taken my two sons". What are the 'two sons' of the soul? St Augustine speaks — and with him another, pagan master[4] — of the two faces of the soul. The one is turned towards this world and the body; in this she works virtue, knowledge and holy living. The other face is turned directly to God. There the divine light is without interruption, working within, even though she does not know it, because she is not at home. When the spark of intellect is taken barely in God, then the 'husband' is alive. *Then* the birth takes place, then the Son is born. This birth does not take place once a year or once a month or once a day, but all the time, that is, above time in the expanse where there is no here or now, nor nature nor thought. Accordingly we say 'son' and not 'daughter'.[5]

Now we will speak of the 'two sons' in another sense, that is: understanding and will. Understanding bursts forth first out of intellect, and will then proceeds from them both. But no more of this.

Now we will speak in another sense of the 'two sons' of intellect. One is potentiality, the other is actuality.[6] A pagan master[7] says, 'The soul has in this power the potentiality to become all things spiritually'. In her active power she is like the Father, making all things into a new being. God would gladly have impressed the nature of all creatures on her, but before the world was she did not exist. God had created all this world spiritually in every angel, before the world was made in itself. An angel has

231

two understandings. The one is morning light, the other is evening light. The morning light means that he sees all things in God. The evening light means that he sees all things in his natural light. If he went out among things, it would be night. But he stays within, and therefore it is called evening light. We say the angels rejoice when a man does a good deed.[8] Our masters ask whether the angels are sad when a man commits sin. We say No: for they see into God's justice and accept all things therein, as they are in God. Therefore they cannot be sad. Now, intellect in its *potential* power is like the natural light of the angels, which is the evening light. With the *active* power it bears all things aloft into God, and is all things in the morning light.

Now the woman says, "The creditors have come to take my two sons into their service". The prophet says, "Borrow some empty vessels from your neighbours". These neighbours are the five senses and all the powers of the soul — the soul contains many powers which work in great secrecy — and also the angels. From all these "neighbours" you should "borrow empty vessels".

That we may "borrow many empty vessels", and that they may all be filled with divine wisdom, that we may "pay our debts" with this and live eternally from "what is left over", so help us God. Amen.

Notes

1. *Man* can mean either 'husband' or 'man'.
2. The woman of Samaria (John 4:7ff.).
3. The enumeration of the nine choirs of angels, of which these are the first three, goes back to 'Dionysius the Areopagite'. Quint gives references in Isidore, Peter Lombard, etc.

4. Avicenna (Q).
5. See No.17, note 5.
6. See No.3.
7. Avicenna.
8. See No.7.

St Luke writes for us in his gospel: "A man had made a great supper or evening feast". Who made it? A man. What does he mean by calling it a supper? One master[2] says that it means great love, for God admits none to it but him who is intimate with God. Secondly, he means to say how pure they must be who enjoy this supper. Now it never becomes evening but a full day has gone before. If there were no sun, there would never be any day. When the sun rises that is morning light, then it shines more and more until midday arrives. In the same way the divine light breaks forth in the soul to illuminate the soul's powers more and more, until it becomes midday. It never becomes spiritually day in the soul, unless she has received a divine light. Thirdly, he means that whoever would worthily receive this meal must come in the evening. When the light of this world fades away, it it evening. Now David says: "He climbs up in the evening, and His name is the Lord" (Ps. 68:4). Just as Jacob, when it was evening, lay down and slept (Gen. 28:11). This denotes the repose of the soul. Fourthly, he means it as St Gregory says, that after the evening meal there is no more food. He to whom God gives this food finds it so sweet and delicious that thereafter he hankers after no other food. St Augustine[3] says God is of such nature that he who understands it can never repose on anything else. St Augustine says, 'Lord, if thou takest thyself from us, give us another thee, or we shall never rest: we want nothing but thee'. Now one saint[4] says that a God-loving

235

soul forces God to do whatever she wants, making Him completely infatuated so that He can deny her nothing that He is. He withdrew Himself in one way and gave Himself in another way: He took Himself away as God and man and gave Himself as God and man, as another self in a secret vessel. A very precious relic is not willingly allowed to be touched or seen. Therefore He clothed Himself in the cloak of the likeness of bread, just as my bodily food is transformed by my soul, so that no corner of my nature is not united with it. For there is a power in nature that separates the basest part and throws it out, and it carries up the noblest part, so that there is not so much as a needle's point that is not united with it. What I ate a fortnight ago is as much one with my soul as what I received in my mother's womb. So it is that whoever receives this food purely becomes as truly one with it as my flesh and blood are one with my soul.

There was a man. That man had no name, for that man is God. Now a master[5] says of the first cause, that it is beyond words. The deficiency lies in language. This comes of the surpassing purity of its essence. We can only speak of things in three ways: first, of what is above things; second, of the likeness of things; and third, of the operation of things. I will give you a simile. When the power of the sun draws the noblest sap from the root up into the branches and turns it into blossom, the power of the sun yet remains above it. This, I say, is how the divine light works in the soul. When the soul pronounces God, this utterance does not comprise the real truth about His essence: no one can truly say of God what He is. Sometimes we say one thing is like another. Now since all creatures contain next to nothing of God, they cannot declare Him. We can judge the skill of a painter who has made a perfect picture. And yet we cannot fully judge it from that. All creatures cannot fully express God, for they are not receptive to what He really is.

That God and man has prepared the supper, that inexpressible man for whom there are no words. St Augustine says whatever we say of God is not true, and what we do not say of Him is true. Whatever we say God is, He is not; what we do not say of Him He is more truly than what we say He is.[6]

Who prepared this feast? A man: the man who is God. Now King David says: "O Lord, how great and how manifold is thy feast, and the taste of the sweetness that thou hast prepared for those that love thee, not those that fear thee" (Ps. 31:19). St Augustine thought of this food and felt revulsion and he had no taste for it. Then he heard a voice near him, from above: 'I am the food of great people. Grow and become great and eat me. But you should not suppose that I shall be turned into you. You will be turned into me'.[7] When God works in the soul, whatever is unlike in the soul is purified and cast out by the burning heat. By the pure truth, the soul enters more into God than any food into us – in fact it turns the soul into God. And there is one power in the soul that splits off the coarser part and becomes united with God: that is the spark in the soul. The soul becomes more one with God than the food with my body.

Who prepared this feast? A man. Do you know what his name is? The man who is unuttered. This man sent out his servant. Now St Gregory says this servant means the preachers. In another sense this servant means the angels. Thirdly, it seems to me, this servant means the spark in the soul which is created by God and is a light, imprinted from above, and an image of the divine nature, which is always striving against whatever is ungodly, and it is not a power of the soul, as some masters would have it,[8] and it is always inclined to the good — even in hell it is inclined to the good. The masters say this light is so natural that it is always striving, it is called *synteresis*,[9] which means to say a binding and a turning away from. It has two functions. One is to bite against that which is impure. Its other task is that it ever attracts to the good — and that is directly impressed in the soul — even those who are in hell. Therefore it is a splendid feast.

Now he said to the servant: "Go out and bid those come who are invited; everything is now ready". The soul receives everything that He is. Whatever the soul desires is now ready. Whatever God gives has been eternally becoming: its becoming is now new and fresh and altogether in one eternal Now. A great master[10] says, 'Something that I see is purified and made spiritual in my eyes, and the light that enters my eye would never enter my soul but for the power which is above it.' St Augustine says that the spark is more akin to the truth than anything man can learn. A light burns. People say one is lit from the other. If that is to happen, then that which burns must necessarily be above the other. Just as if one were to take a candle which had gone out but was still glowing and smoking, and hold it up to the other, then the light would flash down and kindle the other. People say one fire kindles another. I deny this. A fire kindles itself. But that which kindles the other must be above it. Just so heaven does not burn and is cold, nevertheless it kindles the fire, and that takes place by the touch of the angel. Likewise the soul prepares herself by exercises. Then she is kindled from above. This comes from the light of the angel.

Now he says to the servant: "Go out and bid them come who are invited; everything is now ready". Then one said, "I have bought a village, I cannot come". These are the people who are still somewhat bound by worldly cares. They will never taste this supper. Another says, "I have bought five yoke of oxen". The five yokes, it seems to me, really refer to the five senses, for each sense is double, and the tongue is twofold in itself. And so, as I said the day before yesterday, when God said to the woman, 'Bring me your husband', she said, 'I have none'. Then he said to her, 'You are right. But you have had five, and the one you have now is not your husband'.[11] That means in truth that those who live according to the five senses will never taste this supper. The third one said, "I have taken a wife, I cannot come". The soul is wholly male when she turns to God. When the soul faces downwards, she is called 'woman', but when one knows God in Himself and seeks Him at home, the soul is a man. It was forbidden in the old law for any man to put on women's dress, or a woman man's dress. She is a man when she penetrates simply into God without means. But when she looks out here at all, then she is a woman.

Then the Lord said, 'In truth, they shall never taste my supper!', and he said to the servant, 'Go out into the narrow and broad streets and by the hedges and the main roads'. The narrower, the wider. "By the hedges": some

239

powers are hedged in at one place. I do not hear with the power by which I see, and I do not see with the power by which I hear. And so, too, it is with the others. Nevertheless the soul is entire in every member, and some powers are in no way bounded.

Now, what is the 'servant'? The angels and the preachers. But as it seems to me, the servant is the spark. Now he said to the servant, 'Go out into the hedgerows and drive in these four kinds of people: the blind and the lame, the sick and the feeble'. Of a surety, no one else shall taste my supper'.

That we may cast off these three things, and thus become man, so help us God. Amen.

Notes

1. This and No.32b are closely related, so much so that some have held them to be different versions of one and the same sermon. Miss Evans translates the first of these with the incorporation (marked by asterisks) of some doubtful additions from Spamer which Quint rejects. They are omitted here.

2. Unidentified.

3. *Confessions* I, 1 (Q).

4. Unidentified, but Eckhart himself says something very similar in No.91. Cf. also No.10.

5. Proclus, *De causis,* known to Eckhart in the Latin version now ascribed to Gilbert de la Porrée (Clark).

6. The so-called apophatic (or negative) theology.

7. *Confessions* VII, 10 (Q).

8. In No.80 Eckhart explains that it is more than a 'power of the soul'.

9. See Introduction, Note A: *Synteresis.*

10. Aristotle (Q).

11. See No.31.

HOMO QUIDAM FECIT CENAM MAGNAM ETC.

(Luke 14:16)

"A man had made a great supper or evening feast". Whoever makes a feast in the morning invites all sorts of
people, but to an evening feast one invites great people,
people one likes, and especially intimate friends. Here in
Christendom we celebrate today the evening feast that our
Lord prepared for his disciples, his intimate friends, when
he gave them his blessed body for food. That is the first
point. The supper has another meaning. Before it comes to
evening there must be a morning and a midday. The divine
light rises in the soul and makes morning, and the soul
ascends in the light into an expanse and height to midday;
after that comes the evening. Now let us speak in a different sense about the evening. When the light fades it is
evening; when the whole world fades away from the
soul, it is evening, and the soul attains to repose. St
Gregory says of supper: when one eats in the morning,
another meal follows, but after supper there is no other
meal. When the soul tastes the food at the evening feast,
and the spark of the soul comprehends the divine light,
then it needs no more food, it does not seek outside things
and cleaves entirely to the divine light. Now St Augustine
says, Lord, if thou takest thyself from us, give us another
thee, nothing else satisfies us but thou, for we want
nothing but thee. Our Lord withdrew from his disciples as
God and man, and gave himself to them again as God and

241

man, but in another guise and another form. Just as we do not let a precious relic be handled or seen bare, but we enclose it in crystal or something else, so did our Lord when he gave himself as another self. God gives Himself, all that He is, in the supper as food to His dear friends. St Augustine felt revulsion at this food, and so a voice spoke to him in spirit: 'I am the food of great people, wax and grow and eat me. You will not transform me into you, but you will be transformed into me'. Of the food and drink I consumed a fortnight ago, one power of my soul took the purest and subtlest part and carried that into my body and united it with everything that is in me, so that there is not the least part of me, not so much as one could put on a needle's point, that is not united with it. It is as much one with me as what I received in my mother's womb when my life was first poured into me. Just as truly does the power of the Holy Ghost take the purest and the subtlest and the highest, the spark of the soul, and bear it all aloft in the brand of love, in the same way as I now say of a tree: the power of the sun seizes on the purest and subtlest in the root of the tree and draws it right up into the branch, where it becomes a blossom. Thus in every way the spark in the soul is borne up in the light and in the Holy Ghost and carried right up into the primal source, and it becomes so wholly one with God, and seeks so wholly the One, and is more truly one with God than the food is with my body — indeed far more, inasmuch as it is much more pure and noble. And so he said: "A great evening feast". Now David says: "Lord, how great and how manifold is the sweetness and the food which thou hast hidden from all those that fear thee" (Ps. 31:19).

242

And he who receives this food with fear, he never gets the true taste of it, for one must receive it with love. Therefore a God-loving soul conquers God, so that He must give Himself wholly to her.

Now St Luke says: "A man made a great evening feast". That man had no name, that man had no equal, that man is God. God has no name. A pagan master[2] says that no tongue can produce a true word to speak of God, on account of the loftiness and purity of His being. As we say of the tree, so we say concerning the things which are superior to the tree, like the sun, which works in the tree. Therefore it is impossible to speak truly of God, for nothing is superior to God, and God has no cause. Secondly, we speak of things in terms of equality, and therefore we cannot truly speak of God, for God has no equal. Thirdly, we speak of things in regard to their works: as we speak of the skill of the master, so we speak of the picture he has made: the picture reveals the master's skill. All creatures are too base to be able to reveal God, they are all nothing compared with God. Therefore no creature can utter a single word about God in His works. Accordingly Dionysius says all who wish to declare God are wrong, for they do not declare Him. Those who do not try to declare Him are right, for no word can declare God; yet He declares Himself in Himself. Therefore David says: "We shall see this light in thy light" (Ps. 36:9). Luke says: "A man". He is one and is a man, like none, transcending all.

The Lord sent forth His servants. St Gregory says these servants are the order of preachers.[3] I speak of another servant, who is the angel. But we will speak of yet another

243

servant of whom I have spoken before: That is the intellect in the circuit of the soul,[4] where it touches the angelic nature and is an image of God. In this light the soul has community with the angels — even with those angels who sank into hell and have yet retained the nobility of their nature. There, this spark stands bare, untouched by any pain, directed to God's essence. She is also like the good angels who continually work in God and bear all their works back to God and receive God from God in God. The spark of intellect resembles these good angels, being created without distinction by God, a transcending light and an image of the divine nature and created by God. The soul bears this light within her. The masters say this is a power in the soul called *synteresis*,[5] but this is not so. It means that which always hangs on God, and it never wills any evil. Even in hell it inclines to the good; it always strives within the soul against whatever is not pure and divine, and continually invites to the feast.

Therefore he says: "He sent forth his servants that they should come, for all was ready." Nobody need ask what he is to receive in our Lord's body. The spark, that stands ready to receive our Lord's body, stands evermore in God's essence. God gives Himself to the soul ever anew in one becoming. He does not say 'it has become' or 'it will become', but it is all new and fresh as in one becoming without cessation.

Therefore he said: "It is now all ready".

Now a master says that one power in the soul lies above the eye, which is wider than all the world and wider than the heavens. This power takes in everything that is presented to the eyes, and bears it all up into the soul.

Another master contradicts this, saying, 'No, brother, it is not so. Whatever is brought by the senses into that power does not enter the soul, but rather it purifies and prepares and overcomes the soul, so that she may receive barely the light of the angel and the divine light.' Therefore he says: "It is now all ready".

And those who are invited do not come. The first says, 'I have bought a village, I cannot come'. By the village is to be understood all that is earthly. As long as the soul has anything earthly about her she does not come to the feast. The second said, 'I have bought five yoke of oxen, I cannot come, I must see to them'. The five yoke of oxen are the five senses. Each sense has two aspects, that is five yoke. As long as the soul follows the five senses, she will not come to the feast. The third said, 'I have taken a wife, I cannot come'. I have said before, the man in the soul is the intellect. When the soul is directly pointed up towards God, the soul is a man and is one and not two, but when the soul turns down here below, she is a woman. With a single thought and a single downward glance she puts on woman's dress. These too do not come to the feast.

Now our Lord says a hard thing: "I tell you truly, none of these will ever taste my supper". Then the Lord said, "Go forth into the narrow and wide roads". The more the soul is collected, the narrower she is, and the narrower, the wider. "Now go out into the hedges and the main roads". Part of the soul's powers are hedged in, in the eyes and the other senses. The other powers are free, they are unbounded and unhindered by the body. All these he invites in, and he invites the poor and the blind and the lame and the feeble. These come to the feast and no one else.

Therefore St Luke says: "A man had made a great feast".
That man is God and has no name.

That we may come to this feast, so help us God. Amen.

Notes

1. See No.32a, note 1. Miss Evans prints extracts from this version, under the heading *Synderesis,* together with parallel passages which were incorporated into a sermon by Nikolaus von Landau.
2. See No.32a, note 5.
3. Eckhart's hearers will doubtless have thought, anachronistically, of the Dominicans.
4. See No.31.
5. See No.32a, note 9.

SI CONSURREXISTIS CUM CHRISTO, QUE SURSUM SUNT ETC.

(Col. 3:1)

St Paul says: "If you are then raised up with Christ, then seek those things which are above, where Christ is seated at the right hand of his Father, and do not savour the things that are on earth". He then says further: "You have died, and your life is hidden with Christ in God", in heaven. The third thing is that the women sought our Lord at the sepulchre. There they found an angel, "whose countenance was like lightning and his raiment white as snow". "And he said to the women: 'whom do you seek? If you seek Jesus who was crucified, he is not here'" (Matt. 28:1ff.). For God is nowhere. Of God's lowest all creatures are full, and His greatest is nowhere. They did not reply, for they were disappointed at finding the angel and not God. God is not here or there, not in time or place.

Now St Paul says: "If you are then raised up with Christ, then seek those things which are above". His first word expresses two things. Some people are half raised up: they practise one virtue but not another. Some, ignoble by nature, covet riches. Others of a nobler nature care nothing for possessions but are bent on honour. One master says all the virtues are necessarily interdependent. Though a person may incline to the practice of one virtue rather than the others, yet they are all interconnected. Some people are fully raised up,[1] but are not raised up with Christ. Therefore, that which is his must rise up fully.

247

Again, we find some people who rise with Christ for good and all; but he must be very wise who experiences a true resurrection with Christ. The masters say that alone is a true resurrection, when there is no more death. Now there was never any virtue so great but some might be found to have acquired it by their natural powers, for natural powers work many signs and wonders; and all the outward works which have ever been found in the saints have also been found in the heathen. That is why he says: you shall be "raised up with Christ", for he is on high, where nature cannot reach. All that pertains to us must make the ascent.

There are three signs of our having fully risen. The first is if we "seek the things that are above". The second is, if we savour the things above. The third is, if we have distaste for the "things that are on earth". St Paul says: "Seek those things that are above". But where, and in what way? King David says: "Seek the face of God" (Ps. 105:4). What is common to many things must needs come from above. The cause of fire must be above it, like heaven and the sun. Our best teachers hold that heaven is the locus of all things, and though it has itself no place, no natural place, yet it makes room for all things. My soul is undivided, yet it is entire in each member. Where my eye sees my ear does not hear; where my ear hears my eye does not see. What I see and hear physically, comes into me by spirit. My eye perceives colour through light, but it is not present to the soul by reason of defect. All that the outward senses perceive, if the spirit is to take it in, must come from above, from the angel, who imprints it in the upper part of the soul. Now our masters say the above orders and places the

248

below. On this St James says: "Every good and perfect gift comes from above" (James 1:17). One who is fully risen with Christ is known by his seeking for God above time. He seeks God above time who seeks Him timelessly.

Now he says: "Seek those things that are above". Where are we to look? "Where Christ is sitting on the right hand of his Father". Where is Christ sitting? He is sitting nowhere. Whoever seeks him anywhere will not find him. His least part is everywhere, his highest nowhere. A master says that whoever knows anything does not know God. *Christ* means the anointed, he who is anointed by the Holy Ghost. The masters say sitting denotes rest and implies timelessness. What turns and changes has no rest, and also, resting adds nothing. Our Lord says: "I am God and do not change" (Mal. 3:6).

"Christ is sitting on the right hand of his Father". The greatest good that God can give is His right hand. Christ says: "I am a door" (John 10:9). The first outburst and the first effusion God runs out into is His fusion into His Son, who flows back into the Father. I said one day that the door was the Holy Ghost: there He is poured out in goodness into all creatures. Where there is a natural man, that is the beginning of His work with the right hand. One master says the heavens receive from God direct. Another denies this, for God is a spirit and pure light, therefore anything receiving direct from God must needs be spirit and pure light. A master says it is impossible that in the first eruption, when God bursts forth, any corporeal thing should receive it: it must be either light or pure spirit. Heaven is above time and the cause of time. One master says heaven is by nature too lofty to stoop to be the cause of time. In its nature it is not the cause of time, but in its revolution it is — being timeless — the cause of time, which is a product of heaven. My complexion is not my nature, but it is a product of my nature: our souls are far above, "hidden in God". And so I say not only above time, but hidden in God. Is that the meaning of heaven? Everything corporeal is a product, an accident and a descent. King David says: "A thousand years are in God's sight as a day that is past" (Ps. 90:4), for all the future and the past are there in one Now.

That we may attain to this Now, so help us God. Amen.

Notes

1. i.e. not 'half' like those just mentioned.

SERMON THIRTY FOUR
(Pf 34, Q 55)

MARIA MAGDALENA VENIT AD MONUMENTUM ETC.
(John 20:1)

"Mary Magdalene went to the grave" seeking our Lord Jesus Christ, and she "bent forward and looked in. She saw two angels by the grave, and they said, 'Woman, whom do you seek?' — 'Jesus of Nazareth' — 'He has arisen, he is not here'". And she was silent and did not answer them, "and she looked back and forth and over her shoulder and saw Jesus, and he said, 'Woman, whom do you seek?' — 'Oh sir, if you have lifted him up, show me where you have placed him, I will carry him away'. And he said, 'Mary!'" And because she had often heard this word tenderly from him, she recognised him and fell at his feet and wanted to seize hold of him. And he moved away, saying: "Do not touch me. I have not yet gone to my Father!"

Why did he say: "I have not yet gone to my Father"? For he had never left the Father! He meant, 'I have not yet truly arisen in you'. Why did she say: "Show me where you have carried him, for I want to take him"? If he had carried him to the judge's house, would she have taken him? 'Yes', declared one master,[1] 'she would even have taken him from the judge's palace.'

Now you might ask why she ventured so close though she was a woman and those who were men — one who loved God and another whom God loved[2] — were afraid. To this the master says, 'It was because she had nothing to lose, for she had given herself to him, and because she

251

was his, she had no fear'. As if I had given my cloak to
someone, if another wanted to take it from him, it would
not be my duty to prevent him, because it would be his,[3]
as I have said before. She was not afraid for three reasons.
First, because she was his. Second, because she was so far
from the gate of the senses, and within. Third, because her
heart was with him. Where he was, her heart was. Therefore she was not afraid. The second reason the master
gives,[4] why she stood so near, was because she desired that
they should come and kill her, since she could nowhere
find God alive, so that her soul might find God somewhere. The third reason why she stood so near was because
of this: if they had come and killed her — for she well
knew that none could get to heaven before Christ himself had gone there,[5] and her soul must have a resting-
place somewhere — so she desired that her soul should
dwell in the grave and her body by the grave: her soul
in it and her body beside it — because she had a hope
that God had broken forth out of man, and something of
God had remained in the grave. As if I had held an apple
for some time in my hand, if I put it down, something
would remain such as a slight odour. Thus she hoped
that something of God had remained in the grave. The
fourth reason why she stood so close to the grave was
because she had lost God twice, living on the cross and
dead in the grave, and so she was afraid that if she went
away from the grave, she would lose the grave as well.
For if she had lost the grave, she would have nothing
left at all.

Now you might ask why she stood and did not sit. For
she would have been as close to him sitting down as stand-

ing up. Some people think that if they are far out in a level, broad field where there is nothing to obscure their vision, they can see as far sitting down as standing up; but though they may think so, it is not so. Mary stood up so that she could see further round about, in case there were a bush anywhere under which God was hidden, so that she could seek him there. Secondly, she was inwardly so wholly upturned towards God with all her powers, that she stood up outwardly. Thirdly, she was so entirely penetrated with grief. Now there are some who, when their beloved superior dies, are so penetrated with grief that they cannot stand on their own and have to sit down. But since her grief was for God and was based on steadfastness, she had no need to sit. The fourth reason why she remained standing was, if she saw God anywhere she could catch him more quickly. I have sometimes said that a man standing up is more receptive to God. But now I say something different: that when seated one can receive with more true humility than standing, just as I said the day before yesterday that heaven can only work in the ground of the earth. Thus God cannot work except in the ground of humility, for the deeper we are in humility, the more receptive to God. Our masters say if a man took a cup and put it under the ground, it could hold more than if it stood on the ground: even if it were so little that one could scarely notice it, yet it would be something. The more a man is sunk in the ground of true humility, the more he is sunk in the ground of divine being.

One master says: 'Lord, what didst thou mean by withdrawing for so long from this woman? How had she deserved it, or what had she done? Since thou forgavest her

her sins she had done nothing except love thee. If she did anything, forgive that in thy goodness. If she loved thy body, yet she well knew that thy Godhead was in it. Lord, I appeal to thy divine truth, thou hast said thou wilt never be taken from her. And that is true, for thou hast never left her heart and thou hast said that whoever loves thee thou wilt love in return, and to him who rises early thou wilt appear.' And St Gregory says, if God had been mortal and had hidden from her for so long, it would have broken his heart.

Now the question is, why she did not see our Lord, since he was so near her. It may be that her eyes were so blinded with tears that she could not see him quickly. Secondly, perhaps love had blinded her, so that she did not believe he was so near her. Thirdly, she kept looking away further than he was, so that she did not see him. She was looking for a dead body, and found two[6] living angels. An angel means the same as a messenger, and a messenger means one who is sent. We find indeed that the Son is sent and the Holy Ghost is sent — but they are *like*. But it is a characteristic of God, as a master says, that nothing is like Him.[7] For she sought what was like and found what was unlike: "one at the head, the other at the feet". And the master[8] says again that it is characteristic of God that He is one, Because she sought *one* and found *two* she was disconsolate, as I have said before. Our Lord says: "That is eternal life, that they know thee, the one true God" (John 17:3).

That we may thus seek Him and also find Him, so help us God. Amen.

Notes

1. Eckhart is here largely following a homily ascribed to Origen (Q).
2. Peter and John.
3. To whom I had given it.
4. Somewhat confusingly, after giving his own three reasons, Eckhart now reverts to quoting 'Origen's' reasons.
5. It was held that no one went to heaven before Christ.
6. 'Two' supplied by Quint to complete the sense.
7. See especially No.7.
8. Moses Maimonides.

SERMON THIRTY FIVE
(Pf 35, Q 19)

STA IN PORTA DOMUS DOMINI ET LOQUERE VERBUM

(Jer. 7:2)

Our Lord says: "Stand in the gate of God's house and preach the word, declare the word!" The heavenly Father speaks one Word and speaks it eternally, and in the Word He expends all His might and utters His entire divine nature and all creatures in the Word. The Word lies hidden in the soul, unnoticed and unheard unless room is made for it in the ground of hearing, otherwise it is not heard; but all voices and all sounds must cease and perfect stillness must reign there, a still silence. But I shall not speak further about this sense.

Now: "Stand in the gate". Whoever stands there, his limbs are ordered. He means that the highest part of the soul should always stand erect. Whatever is ordered must be subordinated to that which is above it. All creatures are displeasing to God unless the natural light of the soul, from which they get their being, illumines them from above, and the angel's light illumines from above the light of the soul, preparing and fitting her so that the divine light may work within; for God does not work in corporeal things, He works in the eternal. Therefore the soul must be collected and drawn up straight and must be a spirit. There God works and there all works are pleasing to God. No work ever pleases God unless it is wrought there.

Now: "Stand in the gate of God's house". God's house is the unity of His being. What is one is best all alone. There-

257

fore unity stands by God and keeps God together, adding nothing. There He sits in His best part, His *esse*,[1] all within Himself, nowhere outside. But where He melts, He melts outside. His melting-out is His goodness, just as I have now said of knowledge and love. Knowledge detaches, for knowledge is better than love. But two are better than one, for knowledge includes love. Love infatuates and entangles us in goodness, and in love I remain caught up in the gate, and love would be blind if knowledge were not there. A stone also possesses love, and its love seeks the ground. If I am caught up in goodness, in the first effusion, taking Him where He is good, then I seize the gate, but I shall not seize God. Therefore knowledge is better, for it leads love. But love seeks desire, intention. Knowledge does not add a single thought, but rather detaches and strips off and runs ahead, touches God naked and grasps Him in His essence.

"Lord, it is meet that thy house be holy, in which we praise thee, and that it should be a house of prayer in the length of days" (Ps. 93:5). I do not mean the days here: when I say length without length, *that* is length; when I say breadth without breadth, *that* is breadth. When I say all time, I mean above time, more than this, altogether above *here*, where there is neither here nor now.

A woman[2] asked our Lord how we should pray. Then our Lord said: "The time shall come and is now, when true worshippers will worship in the spirit and in truth. For God is a spirit, therefore you should pray in the spirit and in truth" (John 4:23f.). That which is truth in itself, we are not; rather, we are true, but something of falsehood is mixed in us too. With God it is not so. But in the primal eruption where truth breaks forth and originates, there, in the doorway of God's house, the soul should stand and pronounce and declare the Word. Everything that is in the soul should speak His praise, yet none shall hear its voice. In the silence and peace — as I just said concerning the angels who sit beside God in the choirs of wisdom and fire[3] — *there* God speaks in the soul and utters Himself completely in the soul. There the Father begets His Son and has such joy in the Word and is so fond of it, that He never ceases to utter the Word all the time, that is to say timelessly. This fits well with our words when we say: "It is meet that thy house be holy", and that there should be praise therein and nothing there but what praises thee.

Our teachers ask, '*What* praises God?' Likeness does. Thus everything in the soul that is like God, praises God. Whatever is unlike God does not praise God; just as a picture praises the artist who has lavished on it all the art that he has in his heart, making it entirely like himself. The likeness of the picture praises the artist without words. That which one can praise with words is a paltry thing, and so is prayer with the lips. For our Lord said once: "You worship you know not what, but true worshippers will come who will worship my Father in the spirit and in truth" (John 4:22f.). What is prayer? Dionysius[4] says a true ascent into God is prayer. A pagan says where spirit is, and unity and eternity, there God will work. Where flesh strives against spirit, where disruption opposes unity, where time opposes eternity, God does not work: He can do nothing with it. Further, all joy and satisfaction and pleasure and comfort that we have *here* must go. He who would praise God must be holy and collected and be one spirit and not be anywhere 'outside', but rather all equally borne aloft into the everlasting eternity transcending all things. I mean not only all creatures that have been created, but all the things he could do if he wished — the soul must rise above them all. As long as anything remains above the soul and as long as anything stands before God that is not God, she can never enter the ground "in the length of days".

Now St Augustine says when the light of the soul, in which they receive their being, shines over all creatures, it is morning. When the light of the angel shines over the light of the soul and embraces it, that he calls 'mid-morning'. David says: "The path of the just man waxes and grows to a full midday" (Prov. 4:18). The path is fair and easy and delightful and familiar. But when the divine light shines over the angel's light, and the light of the soul and the angel's light are embraced in the divine light, that he calls midday. Then the day is at its highest and longest and most perfect, when the sun stands at its zenith and pours its light into the stars and the stars pour their light into the moon, so that it is ordered under the moon. Thus the divine light has embraced the angel's light and the soul's light, so that it stands orderly and erect, and there it does nothing but praise God. Then there is nothing more that does not praise God, and everything is like God — the more like, the fuller of God — and everything praises God. Our Lord said: "I will dwell with you in your house" (Jer. 7:3/7).

We pray to our dear Lord that he may dwell with us here, that we may eternally dwell with him. So help us God. Amen.

Notes

1. This is the Latin *esse* 'being'; it could also be a play on *esse* 'furnace', which leads to the 'melting'.

2. The woman of Samaria.

3. The Cherubim and Seraphim: cf. No.31, note 3.

4. Actually St John Damascene, *De fide orthodoxa* III, 24 (Q).

SERMON THIRTY SIX

(Pf 36, Q 18)

ADOLESCENS, TIBI DICO: SURGE

(Luke 7: 11ff.)

Our Lord went to a city called Naim, and with him went many people as well as his disciples. And when they came under the gate they were carrying out a dead youth, the only son of a widow. Our Lord went up and touched the bier on which the dead man lay, saying: "Young man, I tell you, stand up!" The young man arose and at once began to speak — this was on account of his *likeness* whereby he had arisen through the eternal Word.

Now I say: "He went into the city". This city is the soul, which is well ordered and fortified and protected from harm and which has excluded all multiplicity and is united, well established in Christ's salvation and walled round and embraced by the divine light. Therefore the prophet says: "God is a wall round Zion" (cf. Is. 26:1). The eternal wisdom says: "In the holy and sanctified city I shall have like repose" (Eccl. 24:15). Nothing gives rest and unity so much as likeness: therefore everything like is within and near by. That soul is sanctified in which God alone is and in which no creature finds a resting-place. Therefore he says: "In the holy and sanctified city I shall have like repose". All holiness comes from the Holy Ghost. Nature passes over nothing: it always begins to work in the lowest, thus working upwards into the highest. The masters say that air never becomes fire unless it is first rarefied and hot. The Holy Ghost takes the soul and purifies her in the

263

light and in grace and draws her up to the highest. Therefore he says: "In the holy and sanctified city I shall have
like repose". God rests in the soul as much as the soul rests
in God. If she partly rests in Him, He partly rests in her;
if she rests wholly in Him, He rests wholly in her. Therefore the eternal wisdom says: "I shall have *like* repose."

The masters say that the yellow and the green in the
rainbow merge into one another so equally that no eye is
so sharp-sighted as to distinguish them; so equally does
nature work, being so like the first effusion, and this is so
like the angels that Moses did not dare to write about this
for fear of the weakness of men's hearts, lest they should
pray to them, because they are so like the first effusion.
A very great master[1] says that the highest angel is so close
to the first effusion and has within him so much of divine
likeness and divine power that he created all this world and
also all the angels who are beneath him.[2] There is good
doctrine in this, in that God is so lofty and so pure and so
simple that He causes His highest creature to work by His
power, just as a steward works by the king's power and
rules his land. He says: "In the holy and sanctified city I
find like repose."

I spoke recently[3] of the gate through which God melts
outwards, which is goodness. But essence is that which
keeps to itself and does not melt outwards — rather it
melts inwards. But that is unity, which remains one in itself, apart from all things, and does not communicate itself, while goodness is where God melts outwards and com-
municates Himself to all creatures. Essence is the Father,
unity is the Son with the Father, goodness is the Holy
Ghost. Now the Holy Ghost takes the soul (the sanctified

city) in her purest and highest and bears her into her source which is the Son, and the Son bears her further into his source which is the Father, into the ground, into the beginning, where the Son has his being, where the eternal wisdom is in like repose 'in the holy and sanctified city', in the innermost.

Now he says: "Our Lord went to the city of Naim". *Naim* means 'son of a dove',[4] and denotes simplicity. The soul should never rest in her potential power, but become one with God. It also signifies a flood of water, and means that man should be immovable towards sin and imperfection. The 'disciples' are the divine light which should flow in and flood the soul. The 'many people' are the virtues I spoke of recently. The soul must ascend with fiery aspiration and surpass the great merits of the angels in the highest virtues. Then we shall pass under the 'gate', that is, into love and unity: the gate through which they carried out the young man, a widow's son. Our Lord went up and touched that on which the dead man was lying. How he went up and how he touched, I will not dwell on, except for his words: "Stand up, young man!"

He was the son of a widow. Her husband was dead, and therefore her son was also dead. The only son of the soul is will and all the powers of the soul, which are all one in the inmost part of the intellect. Intellect is the man in the soul. Now that the man is dead, the son is also dead. To this dead son our Lord said: "I tell you, young man, stand up!" The eternal Word and the living Word in which all things live and which supports all things, spoke life into the dead, and "he arose and began to speak". When the Word speaks in the soul and the soul replies in the living

Word, then the Son is alive in the soul. The masters discuss which is better: the power of herbs or the power of words or the power of stones.[5] Let us consider which to choose. Herbs have great power. I heard how a snake and a weasel were fighting. Then the weasel ran away and fetched a herb and wrapped something round it and threw the herb at the snake, and it burst asunder and fell dead. What gave the weasel this wisdom to know the power of the herb? Great wisdom resides in this. Words too have great power: we could work wonders with words. All words have their power from the first Word. Stones too have great power through the likeness wrought in them by the stars and the might of heaven. For like works in like so strongly, and therefore the soul should arise in her natural light into the highest and purest, and thus enter the angelic light, and with the angelic light come into the divine light, and thus stand between the three lights at the crossroads, at the peak, where the lights come together. There the eternal Word speaks life into her, there the soul becomes living and replies in the Word.

That we may thus reply in the Word, so help us God. Amen.

Notes

1. Avicenna.
2. Two MSS insert here: 'But this is not so'. However, the censors did not object to the passage, unorthodox though it is.
3. Cf. No.35, n. 1.
4. This is actually the meaning of *Bar-Jona,* Peter's patronymic. The second meaning, 'flood of water' (or 'commotion') is appropriate to *Naim.* But Quint thinks the confusion goes back to Eckhart.
5. Precious stones were held to possess magic power.

ADOLESCENS, TIBI DICO: SURGE

(Luke 7:14)

We read in the gospel that a woman came to our Lord Jesus Christ. She said: "Sir, I am a widow and had an only son who is dead." Our Lord said: "Young man, stand up!"

We should understand it like this. The woman who was a widow, whose husband and only child were dead: by the woman we should understand the understanding, by the husband the man in the soul, and by the youth the highest intellect, for that is the young man. This is how we should take it. When a man is dead in imperfection, the highest intellect arises in the understanding and cries to God for grace. Then God gives it a divine light, so that it becomes self-knowing. Therein it knows God. I say the intellect alone can receive the divine light. The other powers of the soul are tools and instruments to bring the intellect to its maximum lucidity.

It is a question among the masters, which ranks higher: understanding or love? Some say understanding, some say love, and there is great debate about this. Understanding says: 'How could you love what you do not understand?' Love says: 'What use is much understanding, if you do not love?' If you have no love, you will never attain to eternal bliss.' Understanding says: 'I am born in the clear light in which I can understand myself.' Love says: 'Though you understand much and have no love, your understanding is of no avail.' Understanding says: 'You must give place, you

are only my servant: you help me up and remain below.'
Love says: 'I am the goodness that God is Himself'. Understanding says: 'You make yourself too high and mighty:
when I am not there you can do nothing.' Love says:
'You should learn to know me better.' Understanding
says: 'I have risen higher when not fettered by you. Clear
awareness shines in me: I do not need you. I have what I
want as long as I know what I have known hitherto, into
which I have now flowed in a perfect union in which I
shall abide for ever. Here I stand above love and all works.
As long as I now have knowledge and true cognisance of all
things, whatever I believed before I now find to be true.
Faith and hope, and all the powers of the soul must stay
behind, they can go no further.' True love says: 'I must
stay with you, for I am eternal. That our sisters should
stay without is meet, for they are our servants and have
accompanied you to the actual true knowledge of eternal
bliss.' Now comes the highest intellect, that which receives
all things barely from God, and says: 'I have apprehended
the highest good wherein naught can stand but unity.'
Understanding says: 'I shall remain, you must let me stay
with you.' Intellect says: 'Understanding and love, you
must remain behind.' Understanding says: 'I claim the reward for having known.' Love says: 'I claim the reward for
having loved.' The highest intellect says: 'He to whom you
have led me, and whom I have hitherto known, He knows
Himself now in me, and He whom I have loved, He loves
Himself in me. Thus I realise that I need no one any more.
All created things must remain behind and all that was
ever made. I stand before my source.'

By these words you must understand what our Lord

said, "Young man, stand up!", thus: whatever is close to its birth we call 'young'. Thus it happens to the intellect when, in face of its source, it forgets all that helped it in its ascent, for it deems it was always there and always will be there. That cannot be.

Now you are to understand the woman as understanding, the son as intellect, the husband as the man in the soul. You must also understand, when the man in the soul begins to rise up, the masters say it is another man. You should not take this as being another soul: it is another being of the soul, for the old habits are all gone and dead. The soul has assumed her true being and stands in her primal innocence. The man in the soul, transcending angelic being and guided by intellect, pierces to the source whence the soul flowed. There, intellect must remain outside, with all named things. There the soul is merged in pure unity. *This* we call the man in the soul, and you should understand it thus: the man in the soul is he who has accomplished all this, so that he needs no further help. What he did hitherto, God now works in him. God knows him as he knew Him, God loves him as he loved Him. Thus God performs all works, and the man in the soul is bare and empty of all things.

You should know what a man is like who has come to this: we can well say he is God and man. Observe, he has gained by grace all that Christ had by nature, and that his body is so fully suffused with the noble essence of the soul, which she has received from God and the divine light, that we may well declare: That is a man divine! Alas, my children, you should pity these people, for they are strangers, unknown to anybody. All who ever hope to come to God may well be mistaken in these folk, for they are hard for strangers to perceive: none can truly recognise them but those in whom the same light shines. This is the light of truth. It may well be that those who are on the way to the same good but have not yet attained it, can recognise these perfected ones of whom we have spoken, at least in part. Indeed, if I knew one such man, I would give a minster full of gold and precious stones, if I had it, for a single fowl for that man to eat. I say further: if I owned everything God ever created, I would give it all for that man to consume all at once, and rightly so, for it all belongs to him. I say yet further: God is his with all His power, and if all sinners stood starving before me, I would not take away one wing from that man's fowl to feed all the people. For you should know that if a man is in sin, whatever he eats or drinks, that draws him down to sin and his sin becomes greater. But if the man remains in sin, whatever he has eaten remains in him in his sin. But it is not thus with the good man: whatever he eats or drinks bears him up in Christ to the Father. Therefore you should look well to yourselves.

Note Christ's words: "Where two are gathered together in my name I will be with them" (Matt. 18:20). You should understand it thus: Christ means the soul and the body in a true unity, so that the body wants nothing but what the soul wants. Know that God would be with these, for they are the people we have just spoken about. When the man of the soul is in true possession of his eternal bliss, when the powers[2] are cut off, then that man meets with no opposition from anything. But note, you must pay good heed, for such people are very hard to recognise. When others fast, they eat, when others watch, they sleep, when others pray, they are silent — in short, all their words and acts are unknown to other people; because whatever good people practise while on their way to eternal bliss, all that is quite foreign to such perfected ones. They need absolutely nothing, for they are in possession of the city of their true birthright. I can call that my own which will eternally remain to me, and which none can take from me. You should know that these people perform the most valuable work. You should understand it thus: they practise inwardly in the man of the soul. Indeed that kingdom is blessed in which one such person dwells! They do more eternal good in an instant than all outward works that were ever performed externally. See to it that you withhold nothing that is theirs.

That we may come to recognise such people and, loving God in them, may enter into possession of the city they have won, so help us God. Amen.

Notes

1. On the same text as No.36. Not included in Quint.
2. Of the soul.

STETIT JESUS IN MEDIO DISCIPULORUM ET

DIXIT: PAX ETC.

(John 20: 19ff.)

St John writes in his gospel: 'On the first day of the week, when it was evening, our Lord came when the doors were shut, among his disciples and said: "Peace be with you!", and again: "Peace be with you!", and at the third time: "Receive the Holy Ghost!"'

Now it is never evening unless a morning and a midday have gone before. We say that midday is hotter than evening. But in so far as evening takes in midday and stores up its heat, it is hotter, for the evening is preceded by a perfect, pure day. But late in the year, as after the solstice when the sun approaches near to the earth, the evening grows warm. It can never be midday till morning is past, nor can it ever be evening till midday is past. The meaning of that is this: when the divine light breaks forth in the soul, more and more until a pure and perfect day comes, then morning does not give place to midday, or midday to evening, but all close up in one. That is why the evening is hot. There is a perfect and pure day in the soul when everything the soul is is filled with divine light. But it is evening in the soul, as I said before, when the light of this world fades and a man is indrawn and rests.[1] Then God said: "Peace", and again: "Peace" and: "Receive the Holy Ghost."

"Jacob the patriarch came to a place, when it was evening, and he took some stones that lay in that place, put them under his head, and rested. As he slept, he saw a ladder ascending into heaven and the angels climbing up and down, and God was leaning down over the top of the ladder," (Gen. 28: 11-13). The place where Jacob slept had no name. That means that the Godhead alone is the place of the soul, and is nameless. Now our masters say that which is another's place must be above it, as heaven is the place of all things and fire is the place of air and air is the place of water and of earth, and water is, though not fully, the place of earth, and earth is not a place.[2] An angel is the place of heaven, and any angel who has got a drop more of God than another is the place, the position of the other, and the highest angel is the place, position and measure of all the others, and is himself without measure. But though he is without measure, yet God is his measure.

"Jacob rested in that place", which is nameless. By not being named, it is named. When the soul comes to the nameless place, she takes her rest. There, where all things have been God in God, she rests. That place of the soul which is God, is nameless. I say God is unspoken. But St Augustine[3] says that God is not unspoken, for if He were unspoken that would be speech, and He is more silence than speech. One of our most ancient masters,[4] who discovered the truth long, long before God's birth, ere ever there was a Christian faith as there is now, considered that whatever he could say about things contained in itself something alien and untrue, and therefore he wanted to keep silent. He did not want to say 'Give me bread' or 'Give me a drink'. He would not speak of things because he could not express them as purely as they were when they sprang from the first cause. He therefore preferred to be silent, and made known his wants by pointing with his finger. If he could not speak of things, it beseems us all the more to preserve total silence about Him Who is the source of all things.

Now we say God is a spirit. That is not so. If God were really a spirit, He would be spoken. St Gregory says we cannot truly speak of God. What we say of Him, we can but stammer. In that place which is nameless, all creatures bud and blossom in due order, and the location of all creatures is altogether taken from the ground of this place of due ordering, and the location of the soul proceeds from this ground.

"Jacob wanted to rest". Observe, he *wanted* to rest. Whoever rests in God, his rest is without his volition. Now we say the will is unpractised. The will is free, taking nothing from matter. In that one point it is freer than knowledge, and some foolish people, stumbling over this, would place it above knowledge. That is not so. Knowledge is also free, but knowledge takes from matter and from corporeal things in one point of the soul, as I said at Easter Eve,[5] that some powers of the soul are bound to the five senses, such as sight and hearing, which bring in what we have to learn. Now one master says: 'God forbid that anything should be conveyed within by eye or ear which could fill the noblest part of the soul, instead of by the 'nameless place' which is the place of all things.' It is a good preparation and is indeed useful in that way, being involved with colour and sound and corporeal things. It is merely an exercising of the senses, and the soul

275

is thereby awakened, and the image of knowledge[6] is imprinted by nature into her. Plato says,[7] and following him St Augustine,[8] that the soul has within her all knowledge, and whatever we practise outwardly serves only to awaken that knowledge.

'Jacob rested in the evening'. We prayed before for the Now.[9] Now let us pray for a little thing — just for an 'evening'.

That it may be granted us, so help us God. Amen.

Notes

1. See No.35.
2. The four elements: cf. *In Gen.* 49f. (*LW* I, 221f.).
3. Sermon 117.
4. Heraclitus, according to Albertus Magnus.
5. See No.33.
6. Of the Platonic ideas (Q).
7. *Meno*, esp. 15, 81C (Q).
8. *De civitate Dei* VIII,7 (Q).
9. See No.33, conclusion.

SERMON THIRTY NINE

(Q 36b, Jostes 69,2)[1]

VENIT JESUS ET STETIT IN MEDIO

(John 20:19)

"It was the evening of the day. Then our Lord came to his disciples and stood in the middle and said: 'Peace be with you!'"

Now he says: "It was the evening of the day". When the heat of midday penetrates the air and makes it hot, then the heat of the evening is added to it and it becomes hotter still: then it is hottest in the evening owing to the additional heat. In the same way the year has its evening, which is August, when it is the hottest time of the year. Thus in a God-loving soul it is evening. There there is nothing but repose, where a man is thoroughly penetrated and made incandescent with divine love. That is why he says: "It was the evening of the day". In that day morning, midday and evening stay together and do not pass away, but in this temporal day morning and midday pass and evening follows. It is not thus in the day of the soul: there it remains one. The natural light of the soul is morning. When the soul breaks forth into the highest and purest part of that light, and thus enters the light of the angel, in that light it is midmorning; and then the soul rises up with the angelic light into the divine light, and then it is midday; and the soul remains in the light of God and in the silence of pure repose, and that is evening: then it is hottest in the divine love. Now he says: "It was the evening of the day". That is, the day in the soul.

277

"Jacob the patriarch came to a certain place and wanted to rest in the evening, when the sun had gone down" (Gen. 28:10). He says: "To a place"; he does not name it. The place is God. God has no name of His own, and is the place and position of all things and is the natural place of all creatures. Heaven has no place in its highest and purest part, but in its descent, in its operation, it is the place and position of all corporeal things which are under it. And the fire is the place of the air, and the air is the place of water and the earth. That is a place, that surrounds me, in which I stand. Thus the air surrounds the earth and water. The subtler a thing is, the more powerful: therefore it can operate in things which are coarser and are beneath it. The earth cannot truly be a place, because it is too coarse and is the lowest of the elements. Water is in part a place, for it is subtler and hence more powerful. The more powerful an element is, and the subtler, the more it is the position and place of another. Thus the sky is the place of all corporeal things, and it has no corporeal place, but rather, the least of the angels is its place, its ordering and its position, and so on, up and up: each angel who is more noble is the place and position and measure of the other, and the highest angel is place, position and measure of all the other angels who are beneath him, and he himself has no place or measure. But God has his measure and is his place, and He is pure spirit. But God is not a spirit according to the words of St Gregory, who declares that all the words we speak about God are just a stammering about God. Therefore he says: "He came to a place". The place is God, Who gives position and order to all things. I have said before that all creatures are full of the least of God,

and grow and flourish therein, and His greatest is nowhere. As long as the soul is anywhere, she is not in the
greatest of God, which is nowhere.

Now he says: "He wanted to rest at that place". All
wealth and poverty and bliss depends on the will. The will
is so free and so noble that it takes nothing from corporeal
things, but performs its work of its own liberty. Intellect
takes from corporeal things: in that respect the will is
nobler. But it is in a *part* of the intellect, in a downward-
glancing and a descent, that this understanding receives
images from corporeal things: but in its highest the intellect works without adducing any corporeal things. A
great master says that whatever is carried in by the senses
does not enter the soul or the highest power of the soul.
St Augustine says, and Plato, a pagan master, says too, that
the soul has in herself by nature all knowledge, therefore
she has no need to draw knowledge into herself from
without, but by the practice of outward knowledge that
knowledge is revealed which is by nature concealed in the
soul, just as a physician cleans my eye and removes the ob-
struction which hindered vision, but he does not give sight
to the eye. The power of the soul which works naturally
in the eye, this alone gives sight to the eye when the
obstacle is removed. Thus whatever is conveyed inwards
by the senses of images and forms does not give light to
the soul, but merely prepares and purifies the soul so that
in her highest part she may receive unveiled the angel's
light and, with it, God's light.

Now he says: "Jacob wanted to rest at that place". The
place is God and the divine essence, which gives a place,
and life and being and order to all things. In that place the

soul will rest, in the highest and inmost part of that place. And in the same ground, where He has His own rest, we too shall have our rest and possess it with Him. The place has no name, and no one can utter a word concerning it that is appropriate. Every word that we can say of it is more a denial of what God is *not* than a declaration of what He *is*[2]. A great master saw that and it seemed to him that, whatever he could say in words about God, he could not really say anything which did not contain some falsehood. And so he was silent and would not say another word, though he was greatly mocked by other masters. Therefore it is a much greater thing to be silent about God than to speak.

Now he says too: "It was the evening of the day; then our Lord stood in the midst of his disciples and said, 'Peace be with you!'" That we may come to eternal peace and to the nameless place that is the divine essence, so help us the Holy Ghost. Amen.

Notes

1. A variant of No.38.
2. A succinct definition of 'apophatic' or negative theology.

SERMON FORTY
(Pf 40, Q 4, QT 4)

OMNE DATUM OPTIMUM ET OMNE DONUM PERFECTUM

DESURSUM EST

(James 1:17)

St James says in his epistle: "Every good gift and every perfection comes from above, from the Father of lights". Now you must know that people who resign themselves to God and diligently seek to do His will alone, whatever God sends them will be the best. As God lives, be sure that it must be the very best, and there could never be any better way. Though some other way may seem better to you, yet it would not be so good for you; God wills this way and no other, and so this way is bound to be best for you. Sickness or poverty, hunger or thirst, whatever God sends you or does not send you, what He grants you or witholds, that is best for you. Even should you lack fervour and inwardness — whatever you have or lack, be minded to honour God in all things, and then, whatever He sends you will be for the best.

Now you might say, 'How do I know whether it is God's will or not?' Be sure, if it were not God's will it would not be. You have neither sickness nor anything else unless God wills it. And so, knowing it is God's will, you should so rejoice in it and be content that pain would be no pain to you: even in the extremity of pain, to feel any pain or affliction would be altogether wrong, for you should accept it from God as the best of all, for it is bound to be best for you. For God's being depends on His willing the

281

best. Let me then will it too, and nothing should please me better. If there were someone I tried hard to please and who I knew for certain liked me better in a grey coat than in any other, however good — assuredly that coat would delight and please me too more than any other, however good. If I wanted to please anybody, whatever I knew that he liked, of words and deeds, I would do and that alone. So now, judge for yourselves of your love! If you loved God, you could rejoice in nothing more than in that which pleases Him best and that His will is done in us. However great may seem the pain or distress, unless you have an equal delight in it, it is wrong.

One thing I am wont to say and it is a fact, that we daily cry in our *pater noster,* 'Lord thy will be done!', and when His will is done, we are angry and discontented with it. But whatever He did should please us best. Those who do take it as best ever remain in perfect peace. But sometimes you think and say, 'Oh, it would be better if it had turned out differently', or, 'If it had not been so, things might have been better.' As long as you think this way you will never find peace. You should accept it all for the best. This is the first meaning of our text.

There is another meaning, mark it well! He says: "Every gift". Only the very best and the very highest are true gifts in the truest sense. God gives nothing so gladly as great gifts. Once in this very place I said God likes forgiving big sins more than small ones. The bigger they are, the more gladly and quickly He forgives them. It is the same with graces, gifts and virtues: the greater they are, the more gladly He bestows them, for His nature depends on giving great gifts. And so, the better the things, the more of them. The noblest creatures are the angels, who are purely spiritual and have nothing corporeal; their number is greatest and there are more of them than of all corporeal things. Great things are truly called gifts, and belong to Him most truly and inwardly.

I once said whatever can be truly put into words must come from within, moved by its inner form: it must not come in from without, but out from within. It truly lives in the inmost part of the soul. *There* all things are present to you, living within and seeking, and are at their best and highest. Why are you unaware of this? Because you are not at home there. The nobler a thing is, the more general it is. Feeling I have in common with beasts and life even with trees. Being is still more innate in me, and that I share with all creatures. Heaven is greater than everything that is under it, and so it is the nobler. The nobler things are, the greater and the more universal. Love is noble because it is universal. It seems hard to do as our Lord commands, and love our fellow-Christians as ourselves. The common run of men generally say we should love them for the good for which we love ourselves. Not so. We should love them exactly the same as ourselves, and that is not difficult. Properly considered, love is more a reward than a behest. The command seems hard, but the reward is desirable. Whoever loves God as he ought and must (whether he would or not), and as all creatures love Him, he *must* love his fellow-man as himself, rejoicing in his joys as his own joys, and desiring his honour as much as his own honour, and loving a stranger as one of his own. This way a man is always joyful, honoured and advantaged, just as if he were in heaven, and so he has more joy than if he rejoiced only in his own good. And you should know in truth that if you take more pleasure in your own honour than in that of another, that is wrong.

Remember, if you seek anything of your own, you will never find God, for you are not seeking God alone. You are looking for something *with* God, treating God like a candle with which to look for something; and when you have found what you were looking for, you throw the candle away. That is what you are doing: whatever you look for *with* God is nothing, whatever it might be, whether profit or reward or inwardness or anything at all: you are looking for nothing, and so you will find nothing. The reason why you find nothing is simply because you seek nothing. All creatures are pure nothing. I do not say they are a trifle or they are anything: they are pure nothing.[1] What has no being, is not. All creatures have no being, for their being consists in the presence of God. If God turned away for an instant from all creatures, they would perish. I have sometimes said, and it is true, that he who possessed the whole world with God would have no more than if he had God by Himself. All creatures have nothing more without God than a midge would have without God — just the same, neither more nor less.

Now listen to a true saying! If a man gave a thousand marks of gold for building churches and convents, that would be a great thing. Yet that man would give far more who could regard a thousand marks as nothing; he would have done far more than the other. When God created all creatures, they were so poor and narrow that He could not move in them. But the soul He made so like Himself and so much in His own image, on purpose to give Himself to her; for whatever else He gave her she had no care for. God must give me Himself for my own as He is His own, or I shall get nothing and nothing will be to my taste. Whoever shall thus receive Him outright must have wholly renounced himself and gone out of himself: he gets straight from God all that He has, as his own just as much as it is His, and our Lady's and all theirs who are in heaven. It belongs equally and as much to them. Those who have gone out of themselves and renounced themselves in equal measure will receive equally, and no less.

Thirdly the words: "From the Father of lights". The word 'father' implies a filial relationship. The word 'father' implies pure begetting and means the life of all things. The Father begets His Son in the eternal intellect, and thus the Father begets His Son in the soul just as He does in His own nature, and begets him in the soul as her own, and His being depends on His bringing His Son to birth in the soul, whether He would or no. I was once asked what the Father is doing in heaven. I said, He is begetting His Son, an act He so delights in and which pleases Him so well that He does nothing else but beget His Son, and the two burgeon forth the Holy Ghost. When the Father bears His Son in me, I am the same Son and not another: true, we are different in humanity, but *there* I am the same Son and none other.[2] "Being sons, we are heirs" (Rom. 8:17). He who understands the truth knows well that the word 'father' connotes pure generation and the having of sons. Therefore, in this we are sons and are the same Son.

Now consider the words: "They come from above". As I have clearly stated before: Whoever would receive from above must needs be below in true humility. Know this truly: he who is not fully below obtains and receives nothing, however small. If you have an eye to yourself or to any thing or person, you are not right under and will get nothing, but if you are right under, you will receive fully and perfectly. It is God's nature to give, and His being depends on His giving to us when we are under. If we are not, and receive nothing, we do Him violence and kill Him. If we cannot do this to Him, then we do it to ourselves, as far as in us lies. If you would truly give Him all, see to it that you put yourself in true humility under God, raising up God in your heart and your understanding. "Our Lord God sent His Son into the world" (Gal. 4:4). I once said here, God sent His Son into the world in the soul's fullness of time, when she had finished with time.[3] When the soul is free from time and place, then the Father sends His Son into the soul. This is the meaning of the words: "The best gift and perfection come from above, from the Father of lights".

That we may be made ready to receive this best gift, may God help us, the Father of lights. Amen.

Notes

1. This sentence was condemned in art. 26 of the Bull of 1329: *Omnes creature sunt unum purum nichil: non dico quod sint modicum vel aliquid, sed quod sint unum purum nichil.*
2. Cf. No.8.
3. Cf. No.29.

SERMON FORTY ONE
(Pf 41, Q 70, QT 53)[1]

MODICUM ET NON VIDEBITIS ME, ETC.

(John 16:16)

Our Lord said to his disciples: "A little, a tiny bit, a wee while, and you will not see me; again a little, and you shall see me". The disciples said: "We do not know what he is saying". This is written by St John, who was there. When our Lord saw their hearts, he said: "A little while, and you shall see me, and your hearts will rejoice, and that joy shall never be taken from you." Now our Lord says: "A little, and you will not see me". The finest masters say that the kernel of salvation lies in understanding. A prominent theologian[2] recently came to Paris and opposed this with loud fulminations. Then another master[3] spoke up better than all those of Paris who held to the better doctrine: 'Master, you cry out and fulminate very positively. If it were not God's word in the holy gospel, you would be making a great fuss'. Knowledge seizes on that barely which it knows. Our Lord says: "That is the eternal life, that we know thee alone as true God" (John 17:3). The perfection of blessedness lies in both, knowledge and love.

Now he says: "A little, and you will not see me". This has four meanings which sound much alike, but are very different. "A little, and you will not see me". All things must be little in you, and as nothing. I have said before that St Augustine says, 'When St Paul saw nothing, he saw God'.[4] Now I will turn the phrase round (which is better), and say, 'when he saw naught,[5] he saw God'. That is the

287

first meaning.

The second meaning is: Unless all the world and all time become little in you, you will not see God. St John says in the Apocalypse: "The angel swore by the eternal life that time should be no more" (Rev. 10:5). St John says openly:[6] "The world was made by Him, and it did not know Him" (John 1:10). Also a pagan master says that world and time are small things. Unless you transcend world and time, you will not see God. "A little, and you will not see me".

The third meaning is: As long as anything adheres to the soul, however little, of sin or akin to sin, you will not see God. The masters declare that heaven receives no alien impressions.[7] There are many heavens: each one has its spirit and its angel who is allotted to it.[8] If he were to operate in another heaven to which he was not allotted, he could do nothing with it. One priest said, 'I wish your soul were in my body'. Then I said, 'Truly, she would be foolish in there, for she could do nothing with it, nor could your soul in my body'. No soul can do anything except in the body to which she is allotted. The eye does not tolerate anything alien in itself. A master says, 'If there were no means, we could see nothing'. If I am to see the colour on the wall, it must be made small in the light and and in the air and its image must be conveyed to my eye. St Bernard says the eye is like heaven, it receives heaven in itself. The ear does not do that: it does not hear it, nor does the tongue taste it. Secondly, the eye is shaped round like heaven. Thirdly, it stands high like heaven. Therefore the eye receives the impression of light, because it has the property of heaven.[9] Heaven receives no alien impressions.

The body does receive alien impressions, and the soul also receives alien impressions, as long as she works in the body. If the soul is to know anything outside of herself, such as an angel, or anything, however pure, she must do this with a subtle glimpse without any image.[10] So too an angel, if he is to recognise another angel or anything that is under God, must do it with a subtle glimpse without any image such as the images here. But he knows himself without this subtle glimpse, without image and without likeness. So too the soul knows herself without glimpse, without image and without likeness, im-mediately. If I am to know God, that must occur without images and immediately. The greatest masters say that one knows God without means. That is how the angels know God, just as He knows Himself without image and without 'a little'.[11] If I am to know God without 'means' and without image or likeness, then God must become practically 'I', and I practically God, so wholly one that when I work with Him it is not that I work and He incites me, but that I work wholly with what is mine. I work as truly with Him as my soul works with my body. That is a great comfort for us, and if we had nothing else, that should be spur enough for us to love God.

The fourth sense is entirely opposite to these three. We must be great and lofty if we are to see God. The light of the sun is little compared to the light of the intellect, and the intellect is little compared to the light of grace. Grace is a light that transcends and soars above everything that God ever created or could create. Yet the light of grace, great as it is, is little indeed compared with the divine light. Our Lord rebuked his disciples and said: "In you is

289

yet but a little light" (John 12:35). They were not without light, but it was small. We must ascend and grow great in grace. As long as we are growing in grace, it is grace and it is little, and in it we see God from afar. But when grace is perfected in the highest, it is not grace: it is a divine light in which one sees God. St Paul says: "God lives and dwells in a light to which there is no access" (1 Tim. 6:15). There is no access, there is only an attainment. Moses says: "No man has seen God" (cf. Exodus 33:20). As long as we are men and as long as anything human attaches to us and we are approaching, we cannot see God; we must be raised up and set in pure rest, and thus see God. St John says: "We shall know God as God knows Himself" (cf. 1 John 3:2). God's nature is that He knows Himself without 'a little' and without this or that. That is how the angels know God, as He knows Himself. St Paul says: "We shall know God as we are known" (cf. 1 Cor. 13:12). And I say we shall know Him just as He knows Himself, in the reflection which is solely the image of God and the Godhead, but the Godhead only in as far as it is the Father.[12] In so far as we are like *this* image, from which all images have flowed out and fled, and as we are reflected in this image and equally entered into the image of the Father — as far as He knows that in us, so far do we know Him as He knows Himself.

Now he says: "A little, and you will not see me; a little again, and you shall see me". Our Lord said: "That is the eternal life, that we know thee alone as true God".

That we may come to this knowledge, may God help us. Amen.[13]

Notes

1. This, according to Quint, is a better version of Pfeiffer's No. 41, which he reprints as an appendix to his No.70, with variants from the Basle Tauler edition of 1521.

2. Probably the Franciscan Gonsalvus, with whom Eckhart debated in Paris in 1302 or 1303 (see Introduction).

3. The master who thus opposed Gonsalvus can scarcely be Eckhart himself. Quint thinks it may have been the distinguished Dominican Jean Quidort.

4. See No.19.

5. The inversion is hard to bring out in English. At the first place Eckhart has *Dô Sant Paulus niht ensach,* and at the second place *dô er sach niht,* which is more emphatic and in which *niht* clearly means 'nothing'. For the meanings of *niht,* see No.6, n.5, and No.13b, n.2.

6. 'Openly' in the gospel, not in the 'secret' revelation of the Apocalypse.

7. This is Aristotelian doctrine, as taught by Albertus Magnus (Q).

8. Cf. John 14:2, "In my Father's house are many mansions". As regards the spirits, Quint refers to the *substantiae separatae* of Neoplatonism, who are often identified with the angels.

9. Cf. St Bernard of Clairvaux, *In Cant. sermo 31 no. 2* (Q). As in modern German, *himel* means both 'heaven' and 'sky'.

10. *Mit einem kleinen bildelín âne bilde,* lit. 'with a little (or subtle) imagelet without an image', i.e. abstractly.

11. *'Kleine'* (in quotes) in Quint's edition. This is the same word as is used in the scriptural text for the sermon, where it renders *modicum.* It means not only 'little' as in modern German, but 'fine, subtle', &c. (etymologically cognate with English *clean*). Here it means without the least, or subtlest thing intervening, without 'means'. Another example of the difficulty of translating this sermon.

12. The Son as image of the Father (Q).

13. I have not thought it necessary to translate the second version of this sermon which Quint appends (see n. 1), as it is on the whole inferior and adds little of interest or importance. But attention may be drawn to an example of Eckhart's free use of scripture to express his meaning. In the last paragraph he says (Miss Evan's translation): 'As our Lord said to St Mary Magdalene, "Touch me not, I am not yet ascended *in thee* to my Father" (John 20:17), rendering the Vulgate

Noli me tangere, nondum enim ascendi ad Patrem meum. The words 'in thee' have no equivalent in the Latin, being inserted to give Eckhart's mystical interpretation of the passage. We may compare his treatment of the text to No.8. Medieval exegesis was often pretty free, but Eckhart seems to go further than most. None of his inquisitors objected to these additions, and Quint too, more surprisingly, does not comment on them.

SERMON FORTY TWO
(Pf 42, Q 69)

MODICUM ET IAM NON VIDEBITIS ME
(John 16:16)

I have quoted a text in Latin which is written in St John's Gospel which we read on Sunday. It is what our Lord said to his disciples: "A little, a short while, and suddenly you will not see me".

Anything, however small, adhering to the soul, prevents us from seeing God. St Augustine asked what eternal life was, and said by way of answer: 'If you ask what eternal life is, ask and listen to eternal life itself'. No one knows better what heat is than he who is hot; no one knows better what wisdom is than he who is wise; no one knows better what eternal life is than eternal life itself. Now the Eternal Life, our Lord Jesus Christ, says: "That is eternal life, that we know thee alone as true God" (John 17:3). If a man espied God from afar as by some medium or in a cloud, he would not depart from God for an instant for all the world. What do you think, then, how tremendous that is if one sees God without medium? Now our Lord says: "A little, a short while, and suddenly you will not see me". All creatures God ever created or might yet create, if He wished, are little or nothing compared with God. Heaven is so vast and so wide that if I told you, you would not believe it. If you were to take a needle and prick the heavens with it, then that part of heaven that the needle-point pricked would be greater in comparison to heaven and the whole world, than heaven and the world are compared with God. Therefore it is well said: "A little or a short while, and you will not see me". As long as anything of creaturehood shines in you, however small, you cannot see God. Therefore the soul says in the Book of Love: "I have run around and sought him that my soul loves, and have not found him" (Cant. 3:2). She found angels and many things, but she did not find him her soul loved. She goes on: "After that, when I had leapt over a little or a small space, I found him that my soul loved" (Cant. 3:4). It is as if she were to say, 'When I had leapt over all creatures (which are a little or a small thing), *then* I found him that my soul loved.' The soul that is to find God must leap over and pass beyond all creatures.

Know then that God loves the soul so mightily, it is a wonder. If anyone were to rob God of loving the soul, he would rob Him of His life and being, or he would kill God, if one may say so; for the self-same love with which God loves the soul is His life, and in that same love the Holy Ghost blossoms forth, and that same love *is* the Holy Ghost. Since God loves the soul so mightily, the soul must be a very important thing.

A master says in the book *On the Soul,* 'If there were no medium, the eye could see an ant or a midge in the sky', and he was right, for he meant the fire and the air and other things that are between the sky and the eye. A second master says, 'If there were no medium, my eye could see nothing'. They are both right.[1] The first says, 'If there were no medium, the eye could see an ant in the sky', and he is right. If there were no medium between God and the soul, she would at once see God, for God has no medium and brooks no intervention. If the soul were wholly stripped and denuded of all means, God would appear stripped and bare before her and would give Himself wholly to her. All the while that the soul is not entirely stripped and denuded of all means, however slight, she cannot see God; and if there were anything intervening, even of a hair's breadth, between body and soul, there would never be a proper union between them. Since this is so with corporeal things, how much more is it with spiritual things! Boethius[2] says, 'If you would know truth clearly, cast off joy, and fear, expectation and hope and pain'. Joy is a means, fear is a means, expectation and hope and pain are all means.[3] As long as you regard them and they regard you, you cannot see God.

The second master says, 'If there were no means, my eye would see nothing'.[4] If I put my hand over my eye, I cannot see the hand. If I hold it out before me, I see it at once. This is due to the dense nature of the hand; accordingly it must be clarified and rendered subtle in the air and light, and conveyed to my eye as an image. You can observe this with a mirror: if you hold it before you, your image appears in the mirror. The eye and the soul are such a mirror, in that whatever is held before them appears therein. Hence I do not see my hand, or a stone, but rather I see an image of the stone. But I do not see that image in another image or in a medium. Rather, I see it without means and without image, for the image *is* the means and not another means. That is because an image is without image as motion[5] is without motion, though the cause of motion, and magnitude is without size, though the cause of size. Thus too an image is imageless, in that it is not seen in another image. The eternal Word is the medium and the image itself (which is without means or image), so that the soul may grasp God in the eternal Word, and know Him im-mediately and without any image.

There is a power in the soul, which is the intellect. From the moment that it becomes aware of God and tastes Him, it has five properties. The first is that it becomes detached from here and now. The second is that it is like nothing. The third is that it is pure and uncompounded. The fourth is that it is active and seeking in itself. The fifth is that it is an image.

The first point: it becomes detached from here and now. 'Here and now' means the same as place and time. *Now* is the minimum of time; it is not a portion of time or a part of time. It is just a taste of time, a tip of time, and end of time. Yet, small though it be, it must go: everything that touches or smacks of time must go. Again, it is detached from *here*. 'Here' means the same thing as place. The place where I am standing is small, but however small, it must still go before I can see God.

The second point: it is like nothing. A master says God is a being that nothing is like and nothing can become like.[6] Now St John says: "We shall be called children of God" (John 3:1), and if we are God's children we must resemble God. How is it then that the master says God is a being whom *nothing* is like? This is how you must understand it: By virtue of being like nothing, this power is like God. Just as God is like nothing, so too this power is like nothing. You must know that all creatures strive and work naturally to become like God. The heavens would not revolve if they did not pursue or seek for God, or a likeness to God. If God were not in all things, nature would cease operation and not strive for anything; for, whether you like it or not, and whether you know it or not, nature secretly and in her inmost parts seeks and aims at God. No man was ever so thirsty that, when offered a drink, he would not refuse it unless there were something of God in it. Nature seeks neither eating nor drinking, nor clothes nor comfort, nor anything whatsoever, unless God were in it; she seeks privily, struggling and striving ever more to find God in it.

The third point: it is pure and uncompounded. By nature God can tolerate no mingling or admixture. Thus too, this power has no mingling or admixture; there is nothing alien in it, nor can anything alien invade it. If I were to tell a handsome man that he was pale and black, I should do him an injustice. The soul should be entirely without admixture. If someone fixed anything to my hood or stuck anything on it, whoever pulled at the hood would pull all that with it. If I go away from here, all that is attached to me will go with me. Whatever the spirit rests on or is fastened to, whoever pulls that, pulls the spirit with it. If a man were to rest on nothing, and cling to nothing, then, if heaven and earth were overturned, he would remain unmoved, since he would cling to nothing, and nothing would cling to him.

The fourth point: it is ever inwardly seeking. God is a being such that He ever abides in the innermost. Therefore the intellect goes ever seeking within. But the will goes *out* to seek what it loves. So, when my friend comes to me, my will pours itself out over him with *its* love and he is gladdened. Now St Paul says: "We shall know God as we are known by God" (1 Cor. 13:12). St John says: "We

297

shall know God as He is". If I am to have a colour, I must
have in me what pertains to colour. I shall never have any
colour, unless I have the essence of colour in me. I can
never see God except in that in which God sees Himself.
Speaking of this, St Paul says: "God dwells in a light which
is inaccessible". Let none despair on that account! One can
dwell on the way or in the approaches, and that is good,
and yet it is far from the truth, for it is not God.

The fifth point: that it is an image. Well now! Mark this
well and remember it: here you have the whole sermon in
a nutshell. Image and image are so fully one and joined,
that no difference can be discerned. We can well understand fire without heat, and heat without fire. We can
understand the sun without light and light without the
sun. But we can understand no difference between image
and image. I say further: God in His omnipotence can
understand no difference between them, for they are born
together and die together. Because my father dies, I do not
die too. When he dies, you can no longer say, 'He *is* his
son', but you have to say, 'He *was* his son'. If you whiten
the wall, then, in so far as it is white, it is like all whiteness. But if you blacken it, it is dead to all whiteness. Now
see, it is the same here: if the image should perish that is
formed after God, then God's image would also disappear.
I will say one word — or two or three! Now mark me well!
Intellect peeps in and ransacks every corner of the Godhead, and seizes on the Son in the Father's heart and in the
ground, and sets him in its own ground. Intellect forces its
way in, dissatisfied with goodness or wisdom or truth or
God Himself. In very truth, it is as little satisfied with God
as with a stone or a tree. It never rests; it bursts into the

ground whence goodness and truth proceed, and seizes it *in principio*, in the beginning where goodness and truth are just coming out, before it has any name, before it burgeons forth, in a much higher ground than goodness and wisdom. But its sister, the will, is well satisfied with God as He is good. But intellect strips all this off and enters in and breaks through to the roots, where the Son wells up and the Holy Ghost blossoms forth.

That we may understand this and attain eternal bliss, may the Father and the Son and the Holy Spirit help us. Amen.

Notes

1. See No.30. There are difficulties of translation here: *mitel* is 'medium' or 'means', i.e. anything intervening; *himel* is both 'sky' and 'heaven'. There is confusion between the 'masters' here: Aristotle, *De Anima* B 7,419, says that if there were no medium we should see nothing. The other master is said to be Democritus. Eckhart refers to these two in his commentary on the *Book of Wisdom*, n. 285 (*LW* II, p. 619).

2. Clark (1957, p. 178) says, 'No such passage can be found in the works of Boethius, but Quint refers to *De Consolatione Philosophiae* I, *metrum* vii: *Tu quoque si vis/ lumine claro/ cernere verum/... gaudia pelle,/ pelle timorem/ spemque fugato/ nec dolor adsit.*

3. I have followed Pfeiffer's text here against Quint, since this agrees with the order 'joy, fear, hope, pain' in Boethius. Eckhart inserts *zuoversiht* 'expectation'. Clark renders this 'confidence', and Evans 'trust' and 'faith', all of which would do for the modern German *Zuversicht*, but in Eckhart's day the word could mean expectation of anything, good or bad.

4. Aristotle this time!

5. The *principle* of motion.

6. See No.24a.